ISRAEL—
AMERICA'S KEY
TO SURVIVAL

by Mike Evans

Logos International
Plainfield, New Jersey

First edition: August, 1981

ISRAEL—AMERICA'S KEY TO SURVIVAL
Copyright © 1981 by Lovers of Israel, Inc.
All Rights Reserved
Printed in the United States of America
Library of Congress Catalog Card Number: 81-80866
International Standard Book Number: 0-88270-518-0
Logos International, Plainfield, New Jersey 07060

To Carolyn, whose constant love
and encouragement have been a
source of immeasurable strength.

Contents

Acknowledgments

I owe a deep debt of gratitude to the many who cooperated with me as I did the research for this book. It would be impossible to list all of those, but I would like to express special thanks to Major General James E. Freeze, Assistant Deputy Director for Plans and Policy, National Security; General Robert Huyser, commander in chief of U.S. military airlift command; General Jerry Curry, department of defense in the Pentagon; General George Keegan (retired), chief of Air Force intelligence from 1972 to 1977; Lt. General Richard F. Schaeffer (retired) Deputy Chairman of NATO Military Committee from January '74 to June '75; Prime Minister Menachem Begin; Dr. Reuben Hecht, personal advisor to the Prime Minister; Dr. Benjamin Natanyahu, president of the Jonathan Institute on world terrorism, and the father of Jonathan Natanyahu, the deceased leader of the Uganda raid on Entebbe; Mr. Isser Harel, former head of Israeli intelligence and security. Mr. Harel is probably most famous for his capture of Adolph Eichmann; Major Saad Haddad from Lebanon; and dozens of others reaching into the offices of the White House, the State Department and so many more throughout our land and Israel.

It is important for you to understand that this book does not necessarily reflect the viewpoints of any single individual interviewed.

Introduction

"Mike, Russia's desire to dominate the Persian Gulf is long-standing and well documented." I sat listening to Maj. Gen. George J. Keegan, who had been chief of Air Force intelligence between 1972 and 1977. He continued, "In 1945 our boys managed to capture the records of the German Foreign Office. They're stored today in our own National Archives and they make fascinating reading. One of the files deals with the Soviet-Nazi Non-Aggression Pact that Stalin and Hitler signed in the late 1930s. Right there, in black and white, is the Soviets' clear statement of their desire to be the dominant force in the Persian Gulf.

"The Soviets have duped us with all their talk of détente. Now that we've let down our guard by cuts in military spending, they can afford to be more aggressive without much to fear from us. Twenty years of appeasement diplomacy from our side has left us pretty neutralized in the face of Russian moves. We could not have come to the help of Poland during the strikes, we were unable to do anything to intercede on behalf of Afghanistan, and the hostage crisis in Iran found us powerless to protect our diplomatic representatives abroad.

"And now that we're seeking to build up our power in the Persian Gulf and the Indian Ocean, we're finding the going hard. Our navy has been sorely neglected for twenty years—virtually cut in half under the last four administrations. What with that and the lack of our airlift capacity, we really couldn't deploy and seriously sustain a significant number of troops or ships around the Persian Gulf or the Arabian Sea if we wanted to. So, we've made do with a shoehorn exercise in hopes of dissuading the Soviets from further adventures."

"Then," I asked, "what role does Israel play in this game in the Middle East?"

"By pursuing her own national interests," he answered, "to

guarantee her survival against the Arabs, who are supported by the Soviets, she defends American interests. And, ironically, the existence of Israel has kept the radical Arab powers from gobbling up Saudi Arabia. Nasser and the Soviets tried to move into Saudi Arabia by way of Yemen, but Israel stood in their way. Jordan and Syria have attempted to capture Arabia, but Israel thwarted them. Israeli intelligence has prevented the assassination of President Sadat of Egypt on three occasions.

"The United States needs stability in the Middle East, and now, with the Shah gone, Israel is almost the only stabilizing force in the area. The Israeli Air Force keeps Soviet troops from being permanently stationed in Iraq, Syria, Libya, or wherever. And, of course, Israeli intelligence gathers the information about Soviet submarines that makes it possible for the U.S. Sixth Fleet to remain in the eastern Mediterranean.

"Israel is the only parliamentary democracy from Morocco to Iraq. Whatever its internal problems, it has remained the only stable government in the entire Middle East. The Carter Administration failed to recognize this record of history and let itself be blackmailed by Arab oil interests so that it sold advanced weapons to Egypt and Saudi Arabia. That served only to further destabilize the area."

"What do you think, then, of the claims that instability in the Middle East is entirely the result of Israel's existence and her occupation of the West Bank, Gaza, and East Jerusalem?" I asked.

"That is a myth of Palestinian propaganda. The war between Iraq and Iran, for example, had nothing to do with Israel. And the Arabs would be at each others' throats as usual, whether or not Israel existed. The cause of unrest in the Middle East is not Israel, but the character of the Arab states themselves and the revolutionary efforts of the Soviets which work to keep things as chaotic as possible in the region. That's why the Soviets quietly support both sides of the conflict between Iran and Iraq. It puzzles our State Department, but it shouldn't. Anything that disturbs the stability of the area works to their advantage and our disadvantage."

As I listened to General Keegan I began to see Israel in a new light. She might eventually turn out to be the only serious obstacle to Soviet control of the entire Middle East. The fulfillment of the biblical prophecies seemed quite possible in our generation, especially the ones in Ezekiel about a vast alliance of nations descending, out of the North mostly, to attack Israel (Ezek. 38-39).

Evangelist Billy Graham expressed the fact that every president he has been privileged to know was amazed to discover how limited his power was when he got to the White House. The president may believe something, he may want to do something, but he finds that he has the bureaucracy to deal with, he has the courts to deal with, he has the Congress to deal with. And of course those who directly influence the president must not be taken lightly.

It is important to consider the other people who strategically affect American foreign policy. Henry Kissinger is not thought of as a good friend by the Israelis. In fact, many of them look upon him as an arch-betrayer. And then there's Sen. Charles Percy, chairman of the powerful Senate Foreign Relations Committee. It was reported in the newspapers that he told Soviet leaders in 1980, during his visit to Moscow, that he favored a Palestinian state with Yasir Arafat as its ruler. President Reagan, meanwhile, is on record as having agreed that the PLO, of which Yasir Arafat is the head, is a wholly-owned subsidiary of the Soviet KGB. Will Reagan's views prevail easily? Not likely. Especially not in the face of the extreme pressures which the PLO, and behind them, the Soviets, may be able to exert on the Reagan Administration. When Reagan labeled the PLO a terrorist organization—contrary to the PLO's desire to be regarded as a legitimate political entity—a PLO spokesman responded with a bald threat. He said Reagan's attitude could seriously undermine American interests in Third World countries. This sort of thing did not come to the attention of most of the American public, but we can be sure that President Reagan heard it. And we can be reasonably certain that he is aware of how much influence the PLO exerts in the Third World.

A recent article in *Time* magazine discusses Israel's enormous internal problems—many of which are obviously a direct result of their bold stand against the PLO. In the same issue of *Time* there is an article about the revolutionary-front guerrillas of El Salvador who killed over 10,000 people last year and promise to murder many others in 1981. There is evidence that a link exists between Palestinian guerrillas and leftist guerrillas in El Salvador, as reported by the daily newspaper *Al-Liwa* on

January 28, 1981.

Many of the revolutionary guerrillas working in South and Central America, and in Mexico, have been trained and equipped through PLO and Soviet agencies. It's a fact that Arafat and Castro are spending quite a bit of time together. The Soviet Union, with the help of the PLO, is literally orchestrating revolutions throughout the entire world, as we will demonstrate later on in this book.

America is in danger of failing to seek its own best interests. We've become so entangled in the immediate problems of oil supplies and inflation that we're misreading the situation. I believe the course we have taken in the Middle East, because of Soviet and Arab manipulation, can only be likened to dancing with a gorilla. Obviously the dance isn't over until the gorilla says so. As a consequence, we're steadily losing our ability to make a serious impact on the outcome of events that vitally affect us. It is as Mordechai Abir wrote in the May, 1980, issue of *Middle East Focus*, "The Iranian revolution, America's humiliation in Teheran, subversion in Saudi Arabia and anti-American demonstrations throughout the Muslim world signal the bankruptcy of U.S. policy in the Middle East. These events, moreover, could signal the decline of America as a world power and of the West as a whole."

Meanwhile, alarming developments have occurred which threaten to undo radically the fabric of life to which we have grown accustomed. Our nation is being blackmailed by Arab oil, and Arab money has even begun to influence the outcome of American political races. Our wavering foreign policy contributed directly and deliberately to the overthrow of the Shah of Iran. Increasingly, we are becoming aware of the enormous acceleration of Soviet involvement in the Middle East, and the enormous economic problems within our own nation that are encouraged greatly through Arab blackmail. At least seventy-five universities and colleges in America have received gifts from various Arab states, with definite strings attached. Many of America's industrial and commercial giants, including Ford, Westinghouse, IBM, Bank of America, and the Chase Manhattan Bank, are dues-paying members of the Arab-American Association for Commerce and Industry, which represents the member nations of the Arab League, the same organization that founded the PLO. All of these factors represent the growing influence of Arab interests within our borders—influence that has already produced a significant shift of opinion among important American leaders.

This same shift in opinion is being strongly fostered at the United Nations. Its new constituency of Third World nations has aligned itself with the Arabs and against Israel. Consequently, the General Assembly has labeled Zionism as a form of racism, and, in general, the United Nations has become a forum for and has lent respectability to a resurgence of anti-Semitism throughout the West. The U.N. Conference on Women held in Copenhagen in 1980, for example, was turned into an anti-Zionist and anti-Jewish demonstration.

Nor are the Arab states content to rely solely on the PLO or the United Nations. In addition they have created an enormous war machine. They boast, for example, of 500,000 more men under arms than has NATO and three times the artillery of the combined NATO forces. Their tank force exceeds NATO's by 3,000, their combat aircraft by several hundred. In fact, Arab airpower equals that of the Warsaw Pact countries and exceeds Communist China's by a factor of three. Put in another setting, Arab ground forces are equipped with as many tanks and more artillery than the United States Army.

The existence of these enormous forces threatens Israel not only militarily but also economically. By the end of 1980 her inflation rate had reached almost 130 percent, the world's greatest. A big contributor to this intolerable rate is the fact that Israel is compelled to spend 31 percent of its gross national product on defense. That compares with 5.2 percent in the United States and 1.7 percent in Canada. In addition, the Arabs have become increasingly effective in the implementation of their boycott. American exporters, for example, are frequently asked by Arab customers to state that they do not sell to Israel. Manufacturers must certify that none of their goods contain components made in Israel. In general, companies that want Arab business learn that their chances are better if they do not deal with Jewish-owned or Jewish-managed companies. And Saudi Arabia and some other Arab states usually will not grant entry visas to Jews assigned to work with teams of American companies.

As a matter of fact, the world became enraged when the United

States expressed kindness to the Shah of Iran during his illness. Surprisingly, however, no one came out against the fact that Saudi Arabia has been giving sanctuary for several years to Idi Amin, former "president for life" of Uganda. This seems incongruous in light of the fact that Amin was responsible for the massacre of tens of thousands of people. This figure includes many Israelis, who were killed during the PLO-coordinated terror at Entebbe Airport.

Perhaps the most haunting specter of this nightmare is that of nuclear weapons in the hands of irresponsible leaders. Two Islamic nations, Pakistan and Iraq, are well on their way toward building atom bombs. Pakistan received much of its funds for their nuclear project from Libya. Libya is headed by Muammar al Qadaffi, whose links with the PLO, as well as with Idi Amin and other sinister figures, are strong. Under Qadaffi, Libya has become a storehouse of Soviet arms which are used by terrorist organizations throughout the world. What will happen if he gains access to nuclear weaponry?

A recent report from the *Washington Star* News Service reveals that Soviet forces are being strengthened in the Middle East region. Russian troops near the borders of Turkey, Iran and Afghanistan are seen as being capable of an all-out thrust toward the Persian Gulf, according to a warning from the chairman of the Joint Chiefs of Staff, Gen. David C. Jones.

General Jones said that any "direct intervention by the Soviets or their proxies in Southwest Asia has the potential for bringing the industrial world to its knees without a single Soviet soldier having to cross a Western border."

The Middle East is a cauldron of change and trouble. It is on fire. And the Soviet Union is stoking that fire in its quest for world domination. According to a recent CIA report, the Soviet Union military expenditures for Third World countries was in excess of fourteen billion in 1980. Ninety percent of these were allocated to Arab countries. If the Soviet Union gains control of the Persian Gulf, it will gain a stronghold on the West and Japan. Surely it is truer than it sounds to declare that Israel is the key to our survival.

In the coming pages, then, we're going to explore U.S. foreign policy in the Middle East. We will see how Israel is our only totally reliable ally against Soviet expansion there; how our government's attitude toward Israel has seriously shifted since 1948;

how the Palestine Liberation Organization (PLO), supported by
the USSR, is maneuvering toward their stated goal of destroying
Israel; how our government has failed to take this goal seriously;
how, if Israel falls, the United States can no longer remain a
democracy; how our foreign policy has changed from one based
on good versus bad to one of global interdependence with no
moral absolutes; how Arab money is being used to control and
influence major U.S. corporations, making it economically more
and more difficult for the United States to stand against world
terrorism. I believe the problems are enormous, but in spite of
this dismal news, there is great hope if we are willing to stand for
what is right.

chapter 1

America and Israel

Tuesday morning, January 20, 1981. I just finished talking on the phone with Dr. Reuben Hecht, personal advisor to the prime minister of Israel. I could sense great anxiety in his voice. I knew he was struggling with the economic problems within the country, which were being precipitated by an enormous buildup of arms throughout the Arab world, paving the way for a potential PLO state and Soviet satellite in the heart of the Middle East. As I hung up, meditating on my conversation with Dr. Hecht, I quickly stepped into the next room where the television was on and I heard those very famous words, "I, Ronald Reagan, do solemnly swear. . . ." As I sat and watched this time-honored rite of transfer of power, I pondered the future. The next forty-eight months would be critical for our nation. And much of what would happen depended largely on events in the Middle East. What would Reagan do? Israeli experts calculated it would take a year for Reagan to become sufficiently familiar with the complexities of the Middle East to act effectively with regard to it. In the meantime, would he push the Camp David accords, with their potential for creating a Palestinian state, or would he let them fall by the way now that things were more or less settled between Israel and Egypt?

Meanwhile, Anwar Sadat has not been idle. With the Camp David accords on hold as Reagan formulates his foreign policy, Sadat has been gathering support for the Arab cause in Europe. He recently addressed the European Common Market in Luxembourg, which has issued declarations to the effect that the PLO should be recognized in the negotiations with Israel, and that the Palestinians' right to self-determination is as valid as Israel's right to exist. From Luxembourg, Sadat moved to France, which agreed in principle to sell Egypt its first nuclear power reactors.

During the time of Sadat's European tour, the Reagan

Administration was not completely silent concerning the Middle East. The administration criticized Israel's expansion of settlements on the West Bank as "unhelpful to the peace process and ill-advised."

During the 1980 presidential campaign, Reagan made statements about recognizing Jerusalem as the capital of Israel. Since 1948 the American embassy has been located in Tel Aviv in deference to a United Nations resolution calling for the internationalization of Jerusalem. The Arabs had been furious in 1980 when the Israeli Knesset (parliament) claimed sovereignty over Jerusalem. Of course there was no discussion on the very secret resolution coming out of the Egyptian cabinet, previous to that Jerusalem resolution, to make Jerusalem yet another capital of Islam. Enough of a fuss was raised at the United Nations to cause most of their oil customers who maintained embassies in Jerusalem—like the Netherlands—to withdraw them. What if Reagan decided to move our embassy there? How vehemently would the Arabs vent their spleen against us? It seems there was little to worry about though. Enough signs had already surfaced to indicate that a serious change in foreign policy under Reagan was less likely than might have seemed to be the case at first.

A very important factor influencing U.S. foreign policy should be mentioned at this point. We need to understand the extent to which the practice of international banking by men like David Rockefeller has made it seem imperative to them that they control U.S. foreign policy in order to assure that our nation does nothing to endanger their financial interests abroad. These international bankers seek to exert their influence through such associations as the Trilateral Commission, the Council on Foreign Relations, and the Rockefeller-Kissinger team.

It all began shortly after World War II and, since then, under Democratic and Republican administrations alike, people imbued with the philosophy of the Council on Foreign Relations—an organization that consistently equates our national interests with those of the American banking establishment—have dominated our foreign policy. In that time we have lost two wars, Korea and Vietnam, and have turned our backs on pro-America allies in eastern Europe, Iran, China, Cuba, Vietnam, El Salvador, Nicaragua, Rhodesia, and in many other places. We have given away the Panama Canal. We have fostered détente and the SALT treaties by which we have disarmed while the Soviet Union has engaged in an enormous arms build-up.

The essential motivation for this has been economic. To a lesser degree, we can blame Marxist influence in our foreign policy mechanism, and, to an even lesser degree, appeasement, ignorance, and misguided liberalism.

The major figures in this disastrous process have been Robert McNamara, who was secretary of defense under President Kennedy, and Henry Kissinger, who figured importantly in the Nixon Administration. Kissinger has long been closely associated with David Rockefeller, former chairman of the board of the Chase Manhattan Bank. Kissinger is the father of détente, author of the Vietnamese surrender, and prime mover of rapprochement with mainland China, the SALT treaties, and the sale of the Panama Canal. No one of Kissinger's status inherited Kissinger's role under Carter, although Zbigniew Brzezinski, as national security advisor, came close. He is a former Rockefeller staffer as well as an intellectual leader of the Trilateral Commission.

In the summer of 1980, Henry Kissinger attempted to assemble a Reagan-Ford ticket under which he would be the new secretary of state. When that failed, Reagan chose as his running mate George Bush—a member of the Trilateral Commission. Then Reagan turned over the running of American foreign policy to people thoroughly indoctrinated into the thinking of the Council on Foreign Relations, such as Caspar Weinberger, William Casey, and Alexander Haig. Weinberger is a liberal, a former Nixon cabinet member, a Rockefeller confidante, and a member of the Trilateral Commission. He is secretary of defense. Casey has long been close to Henry Kissinger and David Rockefeller, and he is a member of the Council on Foreign Relations. He heads the CIA.

Alexander Haig promises to be the most pliable of all as secretary of state. He began his army career unpromisingly by graduating 214th in a class of 310 from West Point in 1947. Nevertheless, fifteen years later, Cyrus Vance spotted him, then a lieutenant colonel, and selected him to be his military assistant. Vance was then secretary of the army. He was a friend of David Rockefeller and later would become secretary of state and a prominent member of the Trilateral Commission. When Vance moved up to become a deputy to Robert McNamara in 1964, he took Haig with him. Haig eventually became McNamara's special assistant. He later served long enough in combat in Vietnam to entitle him to become a brigadier general. In 1968, however, he was back in Washington working for Henry Kissinger, who was then Nixon's national security advisor. He did so well for Kissinger and Nixon that he was promoted to the rank of full, four-star general and thus leap-frogged over the heads of 250 senior officers. In 1973, as Nixon was listening to the death knell of his administration, he also listened to Henry Kissinger and appointed Haig chief of staff at the White House to preside over "the funeral" and the transition to the Ford Administration. Ford then named him NATO commander (upon the recommendation of Henry Kissinger, who else?). It was ideal. The post gave him high public visibility so that his name would become familiar to the American public. And it did not require congressional approval.

Haig's nomination to be secretary of state was strongly endorsed by Gerald Ford, Henry Kissinger, Richard Nixon, David Rockefeller, and Lord Carrington. Carrington is the British foreign minister (and a Trilateralist) who engineered the present Marxist regime in Zimbabwe-Rhodesia. At the very end of 1980 even Zbigniew Brzezinski had endorsed Haig's nomination. Ironically, the big media guns *(New York Times, Washington Post, Newsweek, Time,* etc.) depict Haig as a conservative and a hawk who will stand up to the Russians. I use the word "ironically" because that's how they described Brzezinski in 1977. Haig, however, will serve much the same purpose Spiro Agnew once served. His tough speeches will pacify conservatives while allowing liberal Rockefeller policies to be carried out unimpeded.

The first thing Haig did upon being designated secretary of state by Reagan was to dismiss Reagan's entire and mostly conservative foreign policy transition team. And, according to the *Wall Street Journal,* Haig and Bush will become the chief designers and managers of U.S. foreign policy, because the role of the national security advisor, held presently by Richard Allen who opposes Kissinger policies, will be downgraded in the Reagan White House. And 1980 had barely passed into history when Henry Kissinger was reportedly off on a trip to do a little "shuttle diplomacy" in the Middle East at the request of Reagan and Haig. Kissinger is in a position to become increasingly prominent as a Reagan advisor. The old French proverb may be true in this situation: "The more something changes, the more it remains the same."

As Ronald Reagan gave his inaugural address, the camera briefly panned the Carter family. They were smiling dutifully—at least Jimmy was. I recalled a conversation I'd had with one of his aides the previous year about our nation's relations with Israel.

"It's a mistake to say that the Jews are the good guys and the Arabs are the bad guys. It is not that clear-cut," said Robert Maddox, then President Carter's assistant and religious liaison. He continued to talk about how the Israelis employed intimidation, coercion, and brutality among the Arab population in their midst. I was learning about our government's change of attitude toward Israel.

The thing that struck me most forcibly was that my government no longer seemed to entertain the warm, brotherly attitudes toward the nation which the people of Israel had reestablished on the eastern shores of the Mediterranean in 1948. The thing that stuck in my memory personally was the way we had gone to Israel's aid with outright grants of arms and supplies during the Yom Kippur War in 1973. That exhibited the sort of spirit I deemed appropriate between allies.

Not many days after my conversation with Robert Maddox, I went to Israel to see what more I could learn about this perplexing turn of events. There I had the unique opportunity to meet and talk with Isser Harel. Harel had been chief of Israel's General Security Service and the nation's Intelligence Service and had gained a measure of fame for his capture of Adolf Eichmann in Argentina. That was certainly one of the most symbolic incidents in Israel's brief history as a sovereign state in the twentieth century.

I found Mr. Harel to be a very unassuming man. We had chatted about a number of things before I got around to asking him about America and Israel. Interestingly, he did not speak much of Israel's need for the United States. Instead, he spoke of America's need for Israel.

"You see, this war between Iran and Iraq threatens everything. But America can make a big difference if she will be brave enough to use Israel's strengths."

"What do you mean?" I asked.

"Israel is the only stable democracy in the Middle East. She is very important to the United States and the rest of the free world. Yes, Israel may save the situation at the last moment for the West."

"How?"

"I can only reflect on my experience. Mr. Ben-Gurion's policy aligned us with the free world in the West. That was his intention and he knew it meant we would be confronted by the hostility of the Communist bloc. But I don't think he minded that one bit," the old man smiled.

"In those days, when Ben-Gurion was prime minister, I was the head of Israeli Intelligence. We found that the West, especially the Americans, were rather in a difficult situation with regard to the Soviet bloc—that is, in military, intelligence, and security matters. The United States is a powerful nation, but no nation is so great that it doesn't have weak spots. Anyway, we Israelis helped America very much in those days."

"When was that?" I asked.

"Since the establishment of the State—during the 1950s and 1960s. I am well aware of that era because of my leadership in Israeli intelligence and security. It was all very secret, of course. But the American president and other high authorities knew about it. The cold war was intense then and I think the United States felt somewhat lost in its tensions with the Soviets. And we were in a position to help in a bigger way than our size would suggest. And I would say we helped more than any democracy in Europe.

"It was all kept very secret, as I said. But the Americans were glad for it. We did much for the security of the western nations. In a crisis, the Americans could rely only on Israel here in the Middle East.

"Now today, it may seem that Egypt has become a good friend to the United States. And certainly Sadat is a good ally for America. But, you see, in an Arab country, anything can happen. In Egypt, as in other Arab nations, it is not a question of what the people think. It is a question of what the ruler thinks. Nasser was anti-American, so Egypt was anti-American. *Now* Sadat is pro-American and Egypt is with him. But it might change.

"Israel, however, never has and never will change its policy. It doesn't matter who is the prime minister or which party is in power. Israel is America's only reliable friend in this part of the world. Let me illustrate. In 1956, we took the Sinai from Egypt after Nasser attacked us with weapons he had gotten from the Soviets. We were fighting for our lives. We had to have the Sinai as a buffer between us and Egypt. But what did the Americans do? They forced us to withdraw from the Sinai! They betrayed us and left us vulnerable to more attacks from Egypt. I don't think they much cared what would happen to Israel.

"But then, not long after that, the Americans came to us and asked for help to handle the crisis in Lebanon and Jordan. And we did not refuse out of bitterness over the way they had treated us. We recognized that Lebanon and Jordan might fall into the hands of the Soviets, and so we helped."

I was learning that what I had been taught many years earlier about American sympathy and support for Israel was not the whole story. Some days after my trip to Israel, John Conlin, a former congressman from Arizona, had told me about the nature of American foreign aid to Israel. Between 1977 and 1979 it had remained just under 1.7 billion dollars each year. Conlin explained to me that the votes in Congress to pass the bill authorizing such aid were attributable to "the Jewish lobby backed by the evangelical element." I was amazed as I heard that statement because I realized that the World Council of Churches and various other liberal groups were proclaiming themselves as the voice of Christianity and were trying to intimidate Israel and make them think that they, in fact, could make them or break them. Obviously, the evangelical influence in the matter of aid to Israel was understandable. Evangelicals affirmed the authority of the Bible and most of them perceived biblical prophetic significance in the establishment of the state of Israel. Even before that they held the Jews, by and large, in special regard, much as Arthur Balfour had in Britain at the turn of this century. Balfour had been raised in an evangelical environment which taught that Christianity was indebted to the people of the Book they revered the most.

So, this evangelical sympathy for the Jews had affected more than the U.S. Congress. Balfour was serving in Lloyd George's government as foreign secretary during World War I. It was in that capacity that he addressed what has become known as the Balfour Declaration to Lord Rothschild on November 2, 1917. It said, "His Majesty's Government views with favor the establishment in Palestine of a national home for the Jewish people, and will use their best endeavours to facilitate the achievement of this object. . . ." Because of the Balfour Declaration, the delegates to the San Remo Conference in 1920 gave Britain a mandate to govern Palestine, which was confirmed by the League of Nations in 1922. (See Appendix for entire text.)

President Woodrow Wilson had been consulted about the Balfour Declaration before it was issued. His staunch Presbyterian background likewise made him sympathetic to Zionist sentiments. However, during World War II, our government began to recognize the importance of Saudi Arabia as a source of oil. Since that time, we have deemed it to be in our interests to support Saudi aspirations in the Arab world.

During and after the war, America did nothing to oppose British policy in the Middle East which forbade Jews who escaped from Nazi-occupied Europe to enter Palestine. The Arabs tended to sympathize with Nazi anti-Semitism, and Britain wanted to do nothing that would provoke outright alliances between Germany and the Arabs. America basically stood by and watched until 1948. Then Harry Truman overruled his foreign policy advisors in the State Department and became the first to recognize Israel officially as a sovereign state.

Under Eisenhower, our nation pursued a policy which aimed to diminish British and French influence in the Middle East. It was thought, incorrectly, that this would make us the heroes of the Arabs and Third World nations. However, it tended only to heighten the volatility of the area.

In 1955, Israel appealed, unsuccessfully, to America for arms in light of the fact the Soviet Union had begun supplying weapons and munitions to some Arab states, notably Egypt. Egypt had consistently supported fedayeen terrorist activities from the Gaza Strip and blocked all Israeli use of the Suez Canal, in spite of U.N. admonitions to the contrary, since the War of Independence in 1948. Finally, in 1956, Israel moved to protect itself by seizing the Sinai Peninsula. The operation commenced on October 29. Israeli troops captured Sharm-el-Sheikh in the South on November 5. The next day, a cease-fire went into effect. Israeli forces had also advanced westward to within a few miles of the Suez. The United States persuaded Israel to withdraw from all the territory it had captured, including the Gaza Strip, with assurances that Egyptian troops would be kept out of that sensitive area. Those assurances were not kept, but Israel enjoyed a measure of quiet on her southwestern border after that and her access to Eilat, her seaport on the Gulf of Aqaba, was no longer restricted by Egyptian harassment.

Under Lyndon Johnson our government began to supply tanks and aircraft to Israel for the first time. They were employed in 1967 in the Six-Day War, which electrified the watching world. Israel enjoyed astonishing success against greatly superior numbers of Egyptian, Jordanian, Saudi, and Syrian troops. By June 10, Israeli units had secured the entire Sinai, the West Bank with Jerusalem, and the Golan Heights. The Arabs had clearly provoked the war. Egypt had blockaded the Straits of Tiran at the mouth of the Gulf of Aqaba, and it moved seven divisions—nearly 120,000 men—over a thousand pieces of field artillery and nine thousand anti-tank guns, together with nearly two thousand tanks, into the Sinai and up toward the Israeli border. Arab losses in men and material were enormous. Israeli casualties were 777 dead, 2586 wounded. These figures were much smaller than those on the Arab side. Nevertheless, in light of Israel's smaller population, they were staggering.

I remember the day well when the news came across the wires about the opening of that June, 1967, war. I was sitting in my barber's chair in Philadelphia and we heard it together on the radio. The barber commented, "Israel has had it. It's all over for her."

"Sorry, my friend," I responded, "But you're wrong. Israel is going to win this war—quickly." My barber was astonished by my emphasis and enthusiasm, but I remember the strong assurance I felt that morning that this was not going to be just another war.

And, indeed, it was not just another war. The Arabs took a whipping they would never forget. Some of their spokesmen actually began referring to Israel by that name, something Arab governments had largely refused to do theretofore. Their previous refusal had been another way of denying the existence of the Jewish effrontery of establishing a sovereign state on what they regarded as Islamic soil. But, lest the Arabs sober up too thoroughly after their 1967 defeat, the Soviets rushed in with fresh supplies of arms to replace what had been lost. And, so, by the autumn of 1968, Egypt began to bombard Israeli positions along the Suez Canal. What followed is known as the War of Attrition, which lasted from March, 1969, until August, 1970. It was during that period that Israeli pilots first engaged Soviet pilots at the controls of the MIG-21 fighter jets. Through her air power Israel was able to secure an advantage in the War of Attrition, but not for long. The Americans convinced her to agree to a cease-fire, during which time the Russians and Egyptians, in direct violation of the cease-fire terms, regrouped so as to gain an advantage over Israel. The United States had compelled Israel to agree to the cease-fire by refusing to replenish and strengthen the Israeli jet-fighter capacity in the face of upgraded Soviet anti-aircraft missile installations.

The Soviets and Egyptians had agreed to the cease-fire because they were reasonably certain the Americans would turn a blind eye to their violations of it. And they were right. When the Israelis protested Soviet violations, Melvin Laird, then secretary of defense, said limply that such allegations were "very difficult to prove or disprove." A month passed before the U.S. government was willing to acknowledge the truth, and then it was too late.

All of this taught the Israelis that the Americans could not be counted on to keep their promises—something they had learned before, in 1956. It taught the Soviets that, as Joseph Churba explains, "The United States stood ready to prevent total Egyptian collapse, if necessary even by restraining its one militarily proved client in the region, Israel. This was a profound lesson to be well applied by the Soviets and the Egyptians in their political planning for the Yom Kippur aggression only a short three years later" (*The Politics of Defeat*, New York: Cyrco Press, 1977, pp. 63-64).

So it was that, after Israel regained the initiative in the Yom Kippur War in 1973, she managed to drive the Arabs back on every front. At that point, understandably, the Soviets were ready to sponsor a cease-fire arrangement. "They obtained this," Churba explains, "by threatening to intervene directly and 'end' détente. To avoid this possibility, Washington exerted intense pressure on Israel. In successive moves, during and after the war, a cease-fire halted the Israeli advance, permitted the reprovision of the encircled Egyptian Third Army and introduced the United Nations Emergency Force along the Israeli-Egyptian front" (*Politics of Defeat*, p. 69). American pressure on Israel had taken the form of a U.S. threat to airdrop supplies to the Egyptian Third Army by means of the U.S. Air Force if Israel didn't agree to the cease-fire.

The fact was that, after the Arab oil embargo of 1973, America's already sagging commitment to Israel was compromised more seriously than ever. Thereafter every move had to be measured in terms of how it would affect the certainty and continuity of oil supplies and their prices. Thus, in spite of any support our government might afford Israel, it was decided it must also give heed to Saudi Arabian insistence on behalf of the demands of the PLO (Palestine Liberation Organization) for an independent Palestinian state on the West Bank, predicated upon Israel withdrawing from all the territories it occupied in the Six-Day War, including East Jerusalem. It was Henry Kissinger, by the way, who implemented this policy shift away from Israel and toward the Middle East oil producers. He actually evisioned a stable alliance called the "Teheran-Riyadh-Cairo Axis." It looked to Iran, Saudi Arabia, and Egypt to safeguard U.S. interests in the Middle East by keeping a rein on the radical states of Iraq, Syria, and Libya. They would also serve to frustrate Soviet expansionism directly from the North and, indirectly, from the South through the People's Democratic Republic of Yemen. And thus those three nations have been armed to the teeth with American weapons.

But Kissinger failed to understand the volatility of the Middle East. Long before the Ayatollah took charge in Teheran, the Saudis and the Persians were at odds with each other. The Shah of Iran had used his enormous military might to dominate the Persian Gulf in a way that had caused his Arab allies to lose face. And, of course, Anwar Sadat's romance with Israel has made him anathema to the Saudis, as well as to the rest of the Arab world.

Thus Kissinger, representing the Ford and Nixon Administration, sought to build a bastion against Soviet expansion on the shifting sands of Arab rivalries in the Middle East. In order to do this, Kissinger sought to convince the Arabs—notably the Egyptians and the Jordanians—that the U.S. and not the USSR could help them regain the territory they had lost to Israel in 1967 and failed to regain in 1973. Today we must reflect that Kissinger's castle is in serious disrepair. He failed in his goal to block Soviet expansion by betraying our one serious ally in the region, Israel.

Sitting in a line one day waiting to get into a gas station and feeling stunned by the big jump the price had taken, I noticed a bumper sticker on the car in front of me: "We need oil, not Israel." No doubt about it, the Arabs were conning us into believing that the problem in the Middle East was Israel. It was absurd, but we were angry and searching desperately for simple solutions.

Under the Carter Administration things worsened. The focus shifted so that the goal of foreign policy was to establish economic interdependence among the industrialized nations and to seek to come to some happy arrangement with the underdeveloped Third World nations. Offsetting Soviet influence was not so important any more. Carter called for emphasis on "new global questions of justice, equity, and human rights" (*New York Times*, May 23, 1977, p. 12).

With this shift to economic and moral issues, the important thing for our country became Saudi Arabia and her oil, rather than the extent to which Israel and Egypt might counterbalance Russian aspirations. And the key to the energy problem, in the perception of the Carter government, was the settlement of the Arab-Israeli conflict. If Israel would just acquiesce to Arab demands as a result of U.S. promptings, then the area would stabilize nicely and the oil would flow. Thus, the administration began to believe that a "comprehensive" settlement was possible. By that, they meant a settlement involving, not only Egypt, but also Jordan, Syria, Lebanon, Saudi Arabia, and the PLO. They believed there must be a way for all these nations and the PLO and Israel to be happy together. Furthermore, the administration's accent on Third World matters predisposed it to see the Palestinian problem in that light and to regard it sympathetically. Yasir Arafat began to change his complexion. He was no longer a bloody-terrorist stooge of the Russians. Now, he was a slightly romantic folk hero leading an oppressed and downtrodden people onto a path wherein their human rights could be restored. And so Kissinger's vain dreams gave way to Carter's fantasy as Israel was thrust further into the background.

The surprising moves of Anwar Sadat in his acceptance of Prime Minister Begin's invitation to talk, which eventually led to the Camp David accords, made the Carter people believe more firmly in their dream of a comprehensive settlement. However, Iraqis and Saudis would have none of it and the net effect of the Israeli-Egyptian peace was to drive the remaining Arabs to unite more firmly with the radical elements in their ranks, making conciliation on a comprehensive level more unlikely than ever. In an interesting and amusing sidelight to Sadat's historic trip to Israel, Israeli observers had guessed that, since the Knesset regularly issued such invitations and had for a long time before November, 1977, Sadat may have held up in his acceptance until Golda Meir was out of office. It may have been more than his Islamic soul could stand to pay a conciliatory call on a woman!

The collapse of the Shah's regime in Iran, the Soviet move into Afghanistan, and the Iraq-Iran war have demonstrated how inherently unstable the Middle East is. The Carter Administration was in pursuit of a mirage. No comprehensive settlement was possible and, even if it had been possible and did occur, it would not have guaranteed the flow of oil to Japan and Western Europe.

American performance throughout the time of the Iranian crisis was astoundingly inept. President Carter had expressed support for the Shah on numerous occasions. Nevertheless, as became evident afterwards, the U.S. government had been taking a Khomeini victory for granted since November, 1978. Many believe that it had in fact encouraged, if not instigated, "private" contacts with the Ayatollah and his entourage. In keeping with this, our government learned that the Shah's military leaders had no intention of acquiescing to the Bakhtiar government (which would facilitate the transfer of power from the Shah to the Ayatollah), but planned instead to seize power themselves and maintain a regime loyal to the Shah. It really was amazing—the Shah spent almost four billion dollars on military purchases from the United States alone and encouraged several hundred million dollars in U.S. investments in that country. The Shah's order of eighty F-14s saved the Grumman Aircraft Company, but obviously the picture was much broader than just simply a few good deeds from a country which had been one of America's seemingly strongest allies. One could not easily forget Nikita Khruschev. "We will never have to take Iran," the Russian premier had said, "she will rot away and fall into our laps." Apparently all our public assurances of support for the Shah were shams in order to reassure the Saudis that we would not abandon our friends in the Middle East. It is difficult to imagine that anyone, least of all the Saudis or the Israelis, were fooled.

What has all this meant practically to Israel? Little better than outright betrayal. In 1978, our government sold F-15 fighter planes to Saudi Arabia and Egypt, as well as to Israel. The administration made the sale to the three countries a package deal and, after a bitter fight, kept Congress from vetoing the sale.

President Carter had unequivocally promised Israel that under no conditions would he sell Saudi Arabia offensive equipment for its F-15 interceptors. President Reagan ignored that promise and also proposed the sale of four AWACS to Saudi Arabia (AWACS are the most sophisticated surveillance equipment the U.S. possesses; these have the capability of virtually crippling Israel's security measures.). Reagan sees the sale of this equipment to Saudi Arabia as being necessary to strengthen the Middle East against possible Soviet attack, when in fact, all the sale will do is to accelerate the arms race in the Middle East at a time when Israel's back is already broken in an economic sense.

Ironically, this proposal comes only a few months after Saudi Arabia hosted its fourth summit conference at which they pledged their support to the PLO. In March, 1981, Saudi Arabia presented a check of twenty-eight million dollars to the PLO— one of many substantial contributions.

And how else but as a betrayal could the Israelis interpret our goverment's dalliances with the PLO? The PLO is committed irrevocably to the extermination of Israel.

Our government has repeatedly criticized Israeli settlements in the West Bank as illegal and put tremendous pressure on the Israeli government to discontinue this practice, which the Israelis regard as just, right and essential to their security. This attitude of our government has only been exacerbated by our continued maintenance of two consular offices in Jerusalem. The two stem from the days when the city was divided between the Israelis and the Jordanians. Their maintenance has been a *de facto* refusal by our government to recognize the legitimacy of Israel's capture of the eastern third of that city in 1967 when Israel responded to Jordanian troops which moved against Israel aggressively. Furthermore, from the U.S. consular office in East Jerusalem, American officials maintain contacts with pro-PLO Palestinians on the West Bank in an effort to fortify the administration's case against the Israeli settlements there. Is it unreasonable for the Israelis to regard this as treacherous?

After initially blocking the Israelis from selling their Kfir fighters to Latin American nations, the Reagan Administration has approval the sale of Kfir fighters to Ecuador, setting the stage for Israel's first successful overseas sale of the aircraft.

America's policies at the United Nations with regard to Israel told all the world that we were turning our back on our old friend. Consider this review of the period between March and September of 1980. During that time the United Nations devoted the majority of its time to the Arab-Israeli conflict. It deliberated on a dozen resolutions—ten in the Security Council and two in an emergency session of the General Assembly—which singled out Israel for criticism. The following is a sampling from among those dozen resolutions.

Security Council Resolution 465, March 1: It censured Israel for settlements in the "occupied territories, including Jerusalem." It described Israel's settlements as "a flagrant violation" of international law and a "serious obstruction" to peace in the Middle East. It called for the dismantling of present settlements as well as an end to the planning and construction of new ones. All fifteen members of the Security Council, including the United States, voted in favor of this resolution.

Security Council Resolution 467, April 24: It rebuked Israel for its April 9 incursion into Lebanon and for providing military assistance to "*de facto* forces"—a reference to the Christian militia of Major Saad Haddad in southern Lebanon. Strongly deplored all acts of violence against U.N. forces in Lebanon and in violation of the Israel-Lebanon armistice. Twelve members of the Security Council voted in favor, none against, and three abstained, including the United States.

Security Council Resolution 478, August 20: It censured Israel for its "basic law" on Jerusalem, asserting that "all legislative and administrative measures" taken by Israel to alter the status of the city were "null and void." Furthermore, it called on all nations which maintained embassies in Jerusalem to withdraw them. Fourteen members of the council favored this, while the United States abstained.

This series of resolutions is a clear sign of the escalating diplomatic war which the Arab-Soviet-Third World bloc has been waging against Israel. Action in the General Assembly meeting in emergency session on July 29 called on Israel to withdraw from "all Palestinian and other Arab territories occupied since June, 1967, including Jerusalem" by November 15. It also recognized the PLO as the "representative of the Palestinian people" and endorsed the "inalienable right" of the Palestinian Arabs to establish an independent state. The United States voted against this resolution.

The Arab coalition in the United Nations will continue to maneuver so as to embarrass Israel in the world community. Their goal is to oust Israel from the United Nations altogether. A recent report in the *Jerusalem Post* declares that the United States will fight any effort to remove Israel from the United Nations. State department spokesman William Dyers said, "The U.S. will oppose in the firmest and most vigorous ways any move to expel Israel from any international body and most explicitly from the U.N."

Meanwhile, the United Nations continues to ignore PLO terrorist atrocities while it condemns Israel's retaliation. When the Security Council rebuked Israel for its incursion into Lebanon, they utterly failed to mention the PLO attack on the children's nursery at Misgav Am which provoked that incursion. The U.S. delegate reportedly chose to abstain from, rather than veto, this one-sided resolution because it merely "rebuked" and didn't fully "condemn" Israel.

Similarly, the United States abstained on resolutions condemning Israel for expelling Arab activists but ignoring the terrorist slaying of six Israelis which preceded the expulsions.

All of this aligns with the sort of attitude displayed by the former director of the National Security Council, Zbigniew Brzezinski. In the context of trying to strengthen and support

Saudi Arabian military might, Brzezinski considered Israel a liability to the United States' interests. He recommended that our country take steps to curtail Israel's military capability so as to compel it to be more cooperative with Arab demands.

We must conclude that America has been on a course which has undermined Israel's ability to be strong. That may be unwise for purely political reasons, but I want to propose that there are even more urgent reasons for us to get off this course as quickly as possible.

An Overlooked Asset

"I've got the finest soldiers in the world," Col. Charlie Beckwith said, "I sat there and cried."

That was the reaction of "Chargin' Charlie" Beckwith, the daring American commando leader, when he decided to abort a rescue mission to the American Embassy in Teheran in May, 1980. Reaction to the tragic blunder was immediate around the world, and it gave the world its biggest scare since the Cuban missile crisis.

There was no way to know whether the mission would have been successful in rescuing the fifty-three American hostages held in Teheran even without the mishaps at Desert One in a relatively remote section of the Persian desert, or what the reaction of the Soviet Union might have been when fighting broke out between the ninety commandos and the city's protectors. Estimating how many of the hostages and how many of the soldiers would have been killed is impossible; nor is it possible to ascertain how many Iranian fighters and civilians might have been killed.

But President Jimmy Carter was prepared to take the risk. "There is," the President told a press conference after the fiasco, "a deeper failure than that of incomplete success, and that is the failure to attempt a worthy effort—a failure to try."

The real failure might, however, lie somewhere else: the failure to let Israel in on the planning of the rescue attempt, the failure to learn from Israel some of the treacherous intricacies which might be involved.

If it comes as news to Americans that the Israelis might have been consulted, even though the rescue mission had nothing to do with them directly, it is not news to Europeans. Leonard Davis,

public information director for the Amerian Israel Public
Affairs Committee, an Israeli lobby in Washington, said numerous
European military publications took the United States to task
for not availing itself of the expertise Israel has to offer. The
Israelis, after all, have been used to this type of operation, and
they knew what to expect. Beckwith and his men only knew
partially what to expect, and their mission went awry before it
could get off the desert floor.

Of course, there were other things which went wrong before
the relentless dust storm whipped up and even though Beckwith
ended up with one less helicopter than he needed as a minimum
to have any reasonable degree of success, there had been
breakdowns that hadn't been counted on. Even though the
helicopters and transport planes had practiced in the Arizona
and New Mexico deserts, the Israelis most likely would have
warned them about taking such long jaunts over desert terrain.
The least they would have told the Americans was not to take off
the sand filters from the helicopters. They are an absolute
necessity.

But the Americans, in the interest of getting increased lift
capacity for the helicopters, decided to strip them of the 201-
pound filters. They were fortunate in that none of the helicopters
actually had an engine breakdown, but the lack of the filters
greatly enhanced this possibility.

Meteorologists probably would not have been able to warn
them of the dust that suddenly surrounded the helicopters—dust
so thick, that it made the pilots feel as if they were "flying in a
milk bowl—a darkened milk bowl, at that." The pilots were
buffeted by the sandstorm for three hours. The timing, among
other things, was thrown off.

The Israelis keep the Middle East monitored and seemingly
nothing escapes their notice. It is likely they could have given
some kind of caution that the wind storms might kick up, for
their monitoring probably could have told them of the turbulent
thunderstorms to the west which gave rise to the turbulence on
the desert. Further, they could have given some apparently
much-needed guidance about how to fly through sandstorms, for
they have flown through them many times.

The Israelis were never told of the raid, Davis said. But they
knew of the operation all the while it was going on. They have

such good intelligence equipment that they were able to pick up the American radio signals.

"The Israelis were surprised that the United States failed to mask their transmissions by using regular electronic counter-measures and they feared for the Americans that the Soviets would pick up the signals, too," Davis said.

The Israelis, according to a Defense Department document, without being asked by the United States, voluntarily used their own electronic countermeasures to mask the American transmissions between the U.S.S. Nimitz and the planes. This meant that the Americans were able to transmit their messages between the forces without anyone else picking them up. Without this, instead of half a dozen being lost, possibly all ninety of the commandos would have fallen and the hostages with them, if the commandos could have made it to the embassy.

The Defense Department document indicated that the United States was unwilling to make Israel privy to the rescue attempt, despite Israel's experience in carrying out long-distance rescue missions, because it would tip their hand while the United States was working secretly with Egypt and possibly Oman and other Arab nations in executing the mission. The American Defense Department, Davis said, "bent over backwards to avoid insulting Arabs by consulting Israel."

It is quite probable that the United States would have had very little to fear from the Arabs, because on one occasion Israeli intelligence, transmitted via the United States as the third party, saved Egypt from a possible coup. That was in 1977 when President Anwar Sadat was warned. Davis believes this is part of the reason Sadat made his bold overture to Israel by visiting the country and making a bid for peace. He appreciated the Israeli intelligence, this erstwhile and foremost enemy of Israel, even if the United States hasn't always done so. Under Carter, there was less and less consultation with Israeli intelligence, although the Central Intelligence Agency had officers working in connection with the American Embassy.

The Israelis on two occasions—once a full year before the Shah of Iran fell, warned the United States that the Shah was in trouble. No other intelligence operation—neither the Shah's nor that of the United States—perceived the Shah to be in any danger. But even though Israel warned the United States a year in advance of the impending doom of the Shah, then one of America's strongest allies, the United States did not believe the report. Whether knowing could have averted the Shi'ite revolution, is, of course, not known. But had America heeded its ally's dire warning signals, possibly one of the darkest periods in America's history never would have happened.

Even with the Shi'ites gaining control in Iran, it is not at all unfeasible that with Israeli striking power and expertise, Israel could have been of immeasurable help to the United States in the early stages of the siege of the American Embassy in Teheran, Davis feels. There are numerous Israeli agents in Iran, and Israel has indicated right along a willingness to help her foundering and sometimes blundering ally. But it just was not to be.

The Israeli show of force on occasion has checked the aggressive radicalism, as the *Jerusalem Post* describes it, that threatens American interests in the Middle East. Iraq and Syria are most prone to this radicalism.

"If the United States had been unable to enlist Israeli military support to save King Hussein of Jordan from a Syrian tank invasion in the 'Black September' of 1970, Yasir Arafat's Soviet-trained and equipped forces would probably have overthrown the king, to the disadvantage of both Saudi Arabia, which shares a lengthy border with conservative Jordan, and the United States," Douglas J. Feith wrote in the *Jerusalem Post.*

There can be little doubt that the presence of Israel, with its unalterable orientation to the West and its loyalty to the United States, is the most valuable asset America has in the Middle East, and in the long haul, is more important than what might be the advantage it gains from keeping moderate Arab nations on an even keel to assure their flow of oil to the United States. As columnist Joseph Churba wrote in the *Baltimore Sun*, the reason the United States should proceed with caution on how it views Palestinian autonomy, or more particularly, an independent Palestinian state, is that Israel is essential to American interests. That is but one example.

He wrote, "The difference for us is that democratic Israel, a proven and stable ally, stands as a natural bulwark against Soviet desires for domination in this region. It is also our best investment for guaranteeing the territorial integrity of both

Jordan and Lebanon. We dare not trade this asset for the nightmarish dream of 'Palestinian self-determination.' "

The survival of Israel is vital to the United States, and only the most politically naive person would ever more than for a fleeting moment question why, say, in the election of a president there is so much concern placed on what the candidate's attitude toward the defense and support of Israel is.

Out of necessity, Israel has become the strongest military power in the Middle East, and by and large the Pentagon has been the most ardent supporter of American interests in a strong Israel. By contrast, the State Department support of Israel has not been as stable as Israel would like because of an accommodationist policy toward Arab interests. As a matter of fact, many political analysts consider the most recent statements coming out of the State Department criticizing Israel's settlement policies to be much stronger than those expressed during the Carter Administration. The Pentagon does not lose sight of the importance of Israel to American interests in that part of the world, whereas in appearance at least, the State Department does.

Stability in the midst of a sea of instability is the main benefit Israel offers the United States. Governments come and go in Israel, but they come and go in the orderly fashion of democracies, not by way of coup or assassination or subversion. The United States knows it can count on the government of Israel to be operating on an even keel a decade from now much the same way it operates today.

Iran is an example of how difficult it is to deal in terms of defense and the promotion of American foreign policy in that part of the world, or for that matter, in many other parts of the world. A change in religious mood in Iran, mingled with diplomatic behavior which has outraged the world, has left the United States considerably weakened in the one area in which it cannot be weak, vis-à-vis the Soviet Union. It has humiliated the United States as no other country has ever been humiliated short of being forced into unconditional surrender.

But by comparison, Iran was, on the surface, more stable than some of the smaller Arab states. The United States would be on shaky ground if it were to rely on even the moderate Arab states in the same way it can rely on Israel. As a spokesman for the

Israeli Embassy in Washington put it, there is no equivocation with Israel about whose side it is on. "Israel's open alignment with the West reflects a permanent and unconditional orientation. In contrast, most of its Arab neighbors are officially non-aligned, and subject to the potentially greater influence of Arab unity."

The Embassy spokesman said the revolution in Iran and the resulting loss of American influence in the Persian Gulf demonstrate the inherent political instability and religious ferment characteristic of all the states in the Middle East—except Israel.

"Israel's ties with the United States and its ability to act on America's behalf are not dependent upon one man or one autocratic ruling group," he said. "Its democratic institutions insure that only the ballot—not a bullet—can bring a change in government. Israel has the political integrity on which the United States can depend without hesitation, now and in the future. Israel's government is the one in the region that one can say with certainty will exist in the same form ten years from now."

While the United States has provided Israel with its armaments, and at a considerable price, it is not as if the United States is going it alone. In many countries for which the United States provides armament and defense, it is necessary to have American personnel on hand to assure that the equipment is properly maintained, that the nationals know how to use it effectively, and that it is properly safeguarded against saboteurs, international thievery, adversarial intelligence or forfeiture to friend-become-enemy forces within the nation which has received the aid. Israel can, and does, act on its own, and quite effectively.

Another way the Israelis have helped the United States immeasurably is in turning over captured Soviet-built weaponry which has been used against Israel by the Arabs. This can never be over estimated in its importance because it has enabled the United States to revamp and update its own devices as they have been tested against the latest sophistications of the Soviet arsenal.

There are more Soviet tanks in the area surrounding Israel, primarily from Syria, Iraq, Saudi Arabia and Libya, than are in the entire arsenal of the North Atlantic Treaty Organization (NATO), and in the several major wars since Israel became independent, liberal numbers of them, along with anti-tank devices, including the latest in missiles, have been captured. Israel has turned over entire systems (supplied by the Soviets to the Arabs) to United States military intelligence. The big surge in the Arabs receiving Soviet weaponry came after the Egypt-Czechoslovakia Pact of 1955, and there have been four major wars involving Israel and the Arabs since then. The sharing of data with the United States reached a peak after the Yom Kippur War.

General George Keegan, former commander of the United States Air Force Intelligence, said the information Israel has supplied to this country is "unique in its magnitude" and "crucial in its importance."

Israel supplied the United States with specimens of most of the armored vehicles, armored personnel vehicles and other combat vehicles. Especially important were combat engineers' items, varying from maintenance kits to complete operational and bridging equipment and systems. Also, large numbers of chemical warfare items were turned over to this country, as well as an almost complete array of Soviet artillery systems. Small arms were turned over in such quantities that the United States Air Force was able to establish a series of demonstration units using genuine Soviet equipment, from the AK-47 to tanks and armored fighting vehicles. The new American A-10 aircraft were tested against Soviet systems, as a result of the captured cache. Live fire was used in tests of front-line performance capabilities. Testing in laboratory-type situations, as the captured arsenals enabled, has been of primary importance. This is, in fact, the first time in modern history that a nation could test a whole new generation of equipment still under development against the other side's front-line equipment.

In the 1967 war, for instance, the Israelis turned over to the United States such a complete array of Soviet aircraft, tanks and artillery that some of the information gathered was used to advantage by American forces in South Vietnam. This led to changing certain battlefield tactics.

Also, much American equipment has been modified because of Israeli experience in live situations on the battlefield. For instance, the F-15—a frontline American fighter plane just now going into production and soon to be put into place in Europe—was advertised by McDonald-Douglas Aircraft Corporation as "combat-proven." The truth of the matter is that the only country which had ever used the plane was Israel, but apparently what Israel discovered about the plane's performance was convincing enough that it should be pressed into more widescale production.

Similarly, the Israelis tried out the A-4 Skyhawk, and based on their experience in Middle Eastern situations, the United States manufacturers modified the plane. They then sold it to Kuwait.

General Dynamics in Fort Worth holds the majority of the contracts for Israeli planes. An executive there recently mentioned to me that in a corporate meeting, one of the VPs mentioned, "It's a miracle, it's an absolute miracle." What he was referring to was the fact that Israel, after much insistence, had purchased one of the most sophisticated planes that GD has ever created. It had not been fully perfected and the Israelis had taken the plane, as is, flown it under combat conditions, and modified an extremely technical mechanism in the plane.

So efficient are the Israelis, particularly in communications equipment, that the United States government and American military-supplying industries now have co-production agreements with Israel. Thus, many Israeli-produced and modified types of equipment are making their way into the American military system. The Israelis also provide repair facilities on their homeland for the repair of American aircraft used as part of the North Atlantic Treaty Organization (NATO) defense network, bolstering not only the Israeli economy, but providing a considerable accomodation for the United States.

Extremely important to American defense preparedness have been the aerospace electronic systems which Israel has delivered to the United States in the last fifteen years. Israel has, in fact, been able to capture complete Soviet squadrons, or has salvaged important equipment from aircraft which have crashed after combat. The most celebrated capture was the Iraqi MIG-21, a highly-sophisticated craft, the first to reach Western hands. There are unconfirmed reports that Israel is, indeed, the prime contributor to an American "ghost squadron" which allegedly flies genuine Soviet aircraft.

Among the systems that Israel captured is the most lethal of Soviet anti-tank missiles, the AT3 SAGGER. Israel captured these in such quantities that she could use them in her own operational units. Among the surface-to-air missiles Israel captured and permitted the United States to study, are the SA2 (Guideline), the SA3 (GOA) and the man-held SA7 (GRAIL). The self-propelled ZSUI-57-2 and the highly-sophisticated ZSU-23-24, which is considered the world's most efficient anti-aircraft gun, also have had their secrets bared to American intelligence experts, thanks to Israel. Included in the captured arsenals are the Soviet standard air-to-air missiles, the SA6 and AA2.

Just as important, but less tangible, is the experience Israel has gained in understanding the Soviet military mentality. Israel has been a veritable testing ground for Soviet tactics and it is only because Israel was able to withstand the initial assaults by Soviet-supplied and Soviet-trained Arabs, that it survived and went on to win its conflicts. The first couple of hours of assault, the Israelis have learned, are the crucial ones and the most fearful. The tactics used are sending forth an unrelenting, *blitzkrieg*-like assault of aircraft and tanks and rockets. Israel has learned the secret of repelling the assaults and withstanding their fury and then producing the effective counterattack. This information, though perilously come by and costly, is invaluable to the Western World. Through captured documents, Israel also has discovered the strategy of Soviet-backed warfare.

One of the most important benefits the United States can count on from the Israelis is the knowledge that Israel's bases are available to the United States should the United States ever need them for rapid deployment of forces or for staging areas in the critical Middle East. And since the Israelis need their Airborne Warning and Communications System (AWACS)—which covers virtually everything in the Middle East—to monitor aircraft taking off from Arab state airfields, it is invaluable in keeping Middle East security because Israel shares such intelligence with the United States. This, of course, is not only vital to the United States, but to the rest of the world as well.

Israel is by no means getting a free ride from the United States as far as aid is concerned. As with other countries, there is a liberal grant aspect to the military and economic funds the United States allots to Israel, but most of it is in the form of loans. This is more than just a paper agreement, however. Israel is one of the few nations which pays back its loans, and the interest alone which Israel pays back annually is staggering. This is one of the reasons for the merciless growth of inflation in Israel. Israel does keep its commitments. Israel paid back $550 million in debt service to the United States during fiscal year 1979 and $650 million in 1980. The figure for 1982 is $750 million and $850 million in 1983. Israel's total, worldwide debt will hit $18 billion by the end of 1981. The U.S. portion of this is approximately nine billion dollars—largely incurred as a result of arms purchases. Because these purchases have contributed to our own national strength, it has been suggested that the States should cancel Israel's debt to America, but recent reports indicate that the United States would be unable to do so. Actually, Israel has resisted recent proposals to seek a debt moratorium from the United States because such a waiver of repayment of her loans to the United States could weaken Israel's international credit rating.

Because of what the Israelis are discovering about the military supplies America sells them, improvements, which often save many millions of dollars, hence, American tax dollars, are realized. The money spent on military paraphernalia comes back to the United States through dollar purchases. It provides jobs for many Americans, because there are whole lines of American military production which are open only because of Israel. One example is Chrysler's production of the M-60 tank line. When the F-16 fighter order placed by pre-revolution Iran was canceled, it was Israel which bought them, taking, if not a white elephant, at least a spotted one, off American hands.

Figures for 1979 showed that Israel imported $1.5 billion in civilian goods from the United States, but exported only $700 million to the United States. This translates to a lopsided balance of payments in favor of the United States. This is not a small matter when it is considered that Israel has a population which has not yet reached four million.

Unfortunately it is sad to report such strong statistics from the Holy Land with their weight overwhelmingly in the direction of war, or at least preparedness for war. But that is the main malady for Israel. Israel is making many very positive contributions to science and industry and agriculture which are of value not only to the United States, but to other countries, even the Arab states.

A striking example in a water-starved nation which must do what it can to feed itself is Israel's experimentation in drip irrigation. This method runs tiny tubes into each row of seeds and plants, providing for a constant drip. This means that none of the water is lost due to evaporation, but all of it goes into the soil, giving the plant its necessary boost. By using the more conventional spray method, 30 to 40 percent of the water evaporates, a waste unthinkable in an arid land. The methodology is being adapted to conditions in the United States, and Arabs are using the technique on an increasing scale.

The Israelis also are developing a minigreenhouse system of growing crops, in which plastic tents are used. This system which utilizes the proper amount of water, along with properly treated soil, or even substitute soil, and a shielding from the relentless Middle Eastern sun, is proving to be a boon to the United States. The Israelis don't broadcast it, but they are selling their expertise in this area to many of the Arab nations which are technically at war with them.

How to crack getting oil out of shale rock is one of the big technological problems facing the United States in its drive for fuel independence. Israel is working hard with laser experimentation to bring this valuable source of energy closer to the realm of possibility. If a major breakthrough could be made by Israel, the United States would be the principal country to benefit. And it would not be without benefit to the Arab nations, which abound in shale oil potential.

Israeli firms and scientists are working with American firms in the development of solar energy, long used in Israel and at a relatively high stage of development. The Israelis have just completed tests on a solar pond, a pond of brackish water in which algae are grown. Chemicals in the water cause the water to flow, then the water rises, and as it cools, the water falls. From this method, there can be a harnessing of solar power. For the latter half of 1980, Israeli interests worked with the University of California to co-produce this type of solar pond, which likely will prove to be of considerable worth in supplying certain types of energy needs.

And Israeli technology is being used throughout the world to detect the theft of diamonds or illicit traffic in diamonds. The Israelis have developed a method of "fingerprinting" diamonds by taking laser pictures of them. In case a diamond is stolen it can be pinpointed just as surely as a fingerprint reveals the identity of a human.

Who, in an altogether different realm, can challenge the inestimable value of Israel in archaeological and biblical studies? Israeli archaeologists are not working on purely Jewish archaeological interest, but are just as enthusiastic when the finds pertain to Christian interests and the interests of Muslims.

Despite appearances, often, to the contrary, Israel is the main ingredient for peace in the Middle East, and because she is stable, she enables much more stability in the area than most would realize. Having a strong Israel is a strategic necessity for the United States.

E.R. Zumwalt, a former chief of Naval operations for the United States, put it succinctly, "United States military planners rely on Israel's armed forces to counter Soviet proxy forces in the region as well as to guarantee the U.S. Sixth Fleet air superiority despite the Soviet Mediterranean fleet."

With these, and many other benefits accruing to the United States and to the peace of the rest of the world, Israel's importance should never be overlooked or forgotten; nor should the resolve to see that she is defended.

chapter 2

Explosion in the Middle East

"Baluchistan?"

"That's right. You heard me. Baluchistan," Harry stared at me intently.

"What and where is Baluchistan?" I asked.

Harry Conn, now retired, had been president of the W.A. Whitney Corporation in Rockford, Illinois. The company manufactures fabricating equipment and is a big defense contractor. Before he served as an executive, Harry was chief of research and engineering for eighteen years. He'd published hundreds of scientific papers and lectured at scores of colleges and universities. His work and his travels, together with his natural perceptiveness, made me sit up and take notice when he spoke.

"Baluchistan is a district that sits right on the border of Pakistan and Iran. On the north is Afghanistan and on the south is the Arabian Sea and the Gulf of Oman. Anyway, as I was telling you, the obvious place for the Russians to move, once they consolidate their hold on Afghanistan, is Baluchistan."

"Why?"

"Because from there they can easily reach and control the Strait of Hormuz, through which passes most of Europe's and almost all of Japan's oil. With that kind of control, they can satisfy some of their immediate needs to supplement their own oil production, and it will serve nicely to further their long-range goals. Afghanistan is nothing but a rock. Why would anybody want it? The only way to make sense of it is to figure that the Russians need it to get somewhere else. That somewhere else has got to be Baluchistan."

I could not deny Harry's logic. I had already been hearing a good deal of talk about Soviet economic problems and how their need for oil was going to drive them into the Middle East by the mid-80s. We sometimes forget that Russia has big bills to pay, too. She has poured a lot of money and resources into Cuba, Vietnam,

Afghanistan, and Ethiopia. Problems with Poland have cost her a lot as well. Russia supplies oil to the Eastern bloc nations—East Germany, Poland, Romania, Hungary, Bulgaria—at prices below OPEC levels. But experts say that Soviet oil production peaked in 1980 at twelve million barrels per day, and that by 1985 that will have diminished to around nine million barrels. Meanwhile, the demand goes up. When Vietnam switched its loyalty from China to Russia in 1978, Vietnam lost subsidies worth $300 million a year. The Soviets have apparently had to make that up in huge shipments of oil, gasoline, and grain.

Other areas of the Soviet economy have been suffering as well. Food production is down, labor shortages exist, military spending must increase in the face of American rearmament, and they face the expense of converting oil-burning furnaces to gas and coal. The Soviet citizenry has always suffered a lower standard of living than their American and European counterparts because military expenditures in the Soviet Union have traditionally eaten up a greater percentage of the gross national product than they have in the West. Now, however, the people of the USSR—like their counterparts in the West—are faced with the prospect of a further decline.

One way that Russia has often dealt with shortages is by looting. The Red Army looted Eastern Europe at the end of World War II and then tied those nations to trade pacts that only aggrandized the Soviet homeland. Talk of military adventurism in the Middle East to secure new oil resources really isn't all that far-fetched.

In 1980, I talked with General Huyser, who had returned to the United States after a term as commander of U.S. military units in West Germany. He told me a little about Russian history.

"The Russians have always tended to want to expand their frontiers, at least for the last thousand years. During the eighteenth and nineteenth centuries, they fought in about ninety wars. In only two of them, I think, were they in a defensive posture. Today, that tradition of expansionism has been wedded with communism and we're faced with a real monster that seriously threatens our whole way of life."

Communism is a religion and those who espouse it, especially the Russians, regard it as a necessity for the entire world. They might talk of détente, but that doesn't mitigate their commitment to enforce the Marxist doctrine on all men by destroying capitalism. Détente is, in fact, perfectly in line with that commitment. When Bolshevik hotheads wanted to strike out at once to conquer the world in the name of Communism in 1918, Lenin stopped them. Merciless frontal attack was only in order when conditions were favorable to its success. When they were not, Lenin taught that temporizing tactics ought to be employed to allow time for gathering forces (Lenin, *Works*—London, n.d.—vol. 27, pp. 373, 377). Détente must be construed as one of those temporizing tactics in the face of American nuclear superiority during the 1950s and '60s.

The Soviets are intent upon communizing the whole world, so that all nations will be modeled after Russia. That doesn't necessarily mean a Red Army infantryman will have to stand guard at the end of your block. As grand as the expectations of the Soviets are, even they recognize certain limitations. What they really want, we may reasonably surmise, is hegemony—authority over all other nations not by actual conquest, but by intimidation through the immensity of one's prowess which need be applied only every now and again.

If this is their goal, how do they plan to gain it? Lenin spelled out the guiding principle. It is to enlist allies no matter how temporary or provisional they might be by taking advantage of whatever rifts exist in their ranks. Thus, whoever has a complaint, a grudge, or a grievance in any bourgeois society is potentially a candidate for Communist proposals of friendship and cooperation. We will examine how this is working in the world today in a later chapter dealing with international terrorism and so-called "liberation" movements. For the moment, however, we should observe that it certainly explains the otherwise unlikely alliances between Russia and Islamic nations like Libya. In these cases the Soviets capitalize on Arab grievances against Israel.

In addition to the employment of the principle of divide and conquer, the Soviet Union obviously intends to use its military strength to gain its ends. We have already noted the extent to which the national wealth is employed in support of Soviet military establishment. Fifteen percent, perhaps more, of the gross national product goes for this expense. That compares to more like 5 percent in the United States.

The main obstacle to Soviet influence is the United States.

Today, the United States holds the balance of power in her hands. With her are Western Europe and Japan with their enormous productivity which, combined with America's, greatly outweighs that of Russia and her Warsaw Pact allies. The logical course to follow in order to change this imbalance would be to bring Western Europe and Japan by some means into the Soviet fold. A cursory examination of Soviet activities tells us how they plan to go about it. The ground is being laid in four areas: the North Atlantic, South Africa, Southeast Asia and the Middle East.

The Russians have prepared a sizable fleet of warships, which are anchored at Murmansk and other stations along the Kola Peninsula where Russia's border meets Norway. They are held in readiness to pounce upon American convoys, which would seek to supply men and material to Britain, France, and Germany. Highway construction in Finland points to a probable seizure of Norway's ports and airstrips in the event of war. Another supporting element would be the enormous floating dry dock, large enough to accommodate an aircraft carrier, presently under construction in Sweden at the behest of and for the use of the USSR.

Soviet support for the national liberation movements in Angola, Mozambique, Zimbabwe-Rhodesia, and Namibia has been in the news a great deal. These countries encircle mineral-rich South Africa. Europe, Japan, and America rely upon South Africa for much of their chrome, platinum, vanadium, and manganese. Even if the Soviet Union fails to extend its direct control into South Africa, it can disrupt the flow of these minerals through the kind of guerrilla warfare that ravaged Rhodesia.

That brings us back to Harry Conn's prediction about Baluchistan. The Middle East is obviously a focus of Soviet attention. Three critical passageways mark the flow of oil to Europe and Japan. The first is at the Strait of Bab el Mandeb between the Red Sea and the Gulf of Aden. Significantly, we find Soviet activity and troops on either side of the strait in Ethiopia and South Yemen. The second critical passageway is at the Strait of Hormuz, and even if the Soviets don't move into Baluchistan, they can reach Hormuz readily by air from bases inside Afghanistan. The third critical passageway is at the Strait of Malacca near Singapore, through which tankers bound for

Japan regularly pass. They could be intercepted from bases inside Vietnam.

The United States gets only a modest percentage of its foreign oil from the Middle East. Americans have entertained hopes that a confrontation with Russia might be avoided on two grounds. First was the concept of nuclear deterrent. The phrase was "mutual assured destruction" (MAD) and spoke of the expectation that, if both countries unleashed their full nuclear potentials on each other, the result would be total mutual annihilation. We trusted that the Russians felt this way too and, consequently, would avoid confrontation in nuclear terms. From what we know of their writings and their deployment of ICBMs, however, this would not appear to be the case. They seem prepared to slug it out at the most costly level, hoping to gain an advantage by a surprise, preemptive attack.

The second thought with which Americans and their government have comforted themselves is that war would break out between Russia and China, and that the two giants would bleed each other white. The possibility of this happening seems, however, to have diminished in recent years. The number of Soviet troops deployed along the border with China is considerable but insufficient to launch a real offensive. Besides that, Soviet missile strength is much heavier on the NATO front, than on the Chinese border.

U.S. News & World Report interviewed Daniel Pipes, an expert in Middle Eastern and Islamic affairs at the University of Chicago. They asked him if he thought the Soviets wanted, in the long run, to control the Persian Gulf. They must, he opined, and added that they would thereby control the foreign policies of Japan and Western Europe.

The U.S. doesn't need the oil that much; we can survive without it. But Japan and Western Europe are quite dependent on it. They have shown in the past that they're ready to change their policies in order to suit the Arabs who control the oil. So there's every reason to think that they would change their policies for the Russians if the Russians control that oil. Dismemberment of the North Atlantic Treaty Organization would be one of the first things the Soviets would call for, and this would lead to international isolation of the United States. The stakes are very, very high. (October 13, 1980, p. 26)

What troubled me most was the impression that Soviet strategy was thorough and well thought out. Would we, in the event that things came to a major military confrontation, be able to withstand them?

I ended up talking with five generals, three of them soldiers and two of them airmen, about this question. One of them was retired Maj. Gen. George J. Keegan, with whose remarks I opened the introduction. And I have already shared in this chapter some comments by another of them, General Huyser, about the history of Russian imperialist expansionism. At a later point in our conversation, he offered his personal perspective on our capabilities. "I am as concerned today [about American strength] as I have ever been in the nearly thirty-eight years I've worn this uniform. When I was drafted into the army during the Second World War, everyone was behind what we were doing. Our industrial and agricultural productivity was enormous. There was no question that we were going to win.

"During the Korean War, our military superiority was assured and we had the United Nations behind us. The outcome was never in doubt and we could decide the terms of settlement. It puzzled me that we weren't more forceful though.

"I was deeply involved with our operations in Vietnam. That operation was so frustrating because we did have military superiority, but we seemed to lack the resolve to use it. If we had, I think we could have settled that dispute on terms that would have prevented the grievous and massive refugee problems of the boat people and Cambodians that we have today. It was a shame we didn't.

"In the meantime my concern has grown as I've watched the Soviet arms build-up. They've increased their fire power sufficiently to launch a major offensive. They spend 12 to 15 percent of their gross national product for defense. That has meant that their real military capability has increased by 4 to 6 percent annually over the past several years. Their mobility is way up. They've put everything on wheels and made great technological strides.

"And what have we done? Since Vietnam, we've been reluctant to spend money on the military. Instead of growing, our military has actually declined somewhat, thanks partly to inflation.

"As far as the Middle East is concerned, I fear we may forfeit our sovereignty without a military engagement. They could do it by gaining control of our economy. And I don't mean simply by oil. We only import 41 percent of our oil, and less than half of that comes from the Persian Gulf. We have to see what they're up to in Africa as well. Africa has chrome for steel production, cobalt which we need to produce high-performance engines, and bauxite, which we need to produce aluminum. We need twenty-seven of these sorts of natural resources which we must import. We're really self-sufficient only in phosphate and coal."

I couldn't help but interject, "It reminds me of what Lenin said about the communists gradually pulling the world into their fold so that the United States, as the last bastion of capitalism, would be weakened and bereft of its former power that it would fall into their hands like an overripe fruit."

"That's right," General Huyser replied, "Stalin may have changed his words, but never his doctrine. Krushchev talked about peaceful coexistence, but it didn't mean a thing. Today Brezhnev boasts about the treasures he seeks to control and thus bring us to our knees. Those treasures are the oil and the minerals.

"Taking Afghanistan put them into a very advantageous position. Before, they were 850 miles away. Baluchistan is directly south of their present position. The tribesmen there have no deep loyalty either to Pakistan or to Iran. And the Russians have already been making use of that to influence them. If they can, it will mean an easy path to the warm-water ports. And there is a potential port facility down there that could be developed into something big without too much trouble. It's called Chah Bahar."

I asked him about the specific possibility of open conflict between Russia and the United States in the Middle East.

"The Soviets are prudent planners, perhaps the most prudent military planners in the world today. I don't think they would want to engage us if they thought there was any real possibility that it would come back on their homeland. And, with our nuclear capability, that possibility is very real.

"They calculate things differently than Hitler did. He plunged in whenever he thought the odds were in his favor, even if only slightly. The Russians like to have the odds up around nine to one before they engage in an all-out military operation."

"They're acting pretty aggressive these days," I said and asked, "Does that mean they think their odds are good in case of a fight, or that they think we won't stand behind our words with real force?"

"I'm afraid it may mean the latter. We need to recall that whenever we've spoken firmly and backed our words with strength, they have, more often than not, responded somewhat properly. In 1946 they put troops in Iran and were starting a romance with Turkey and Greece. We delivered them a stiff ultimatum to take the pressure off Turkey and Greece by getting their troops out of Iran within forty-eight hours, and they complied with our wishes.

"In 1948, they blockaded Berlin. We didn't just argue with them. We launched a massive and expensive airlift to sustain the Berliners and frustrate Soviet intentions. It worked.

"In 1949, they moved into Czechoslovakia. We responded by promptly organizing NATO, and they haven't come any further since then. In fact, if anything, they've lost ground in Europe since then.

"We met them head-on in Korea and got a reasonable settlement. Again we exhibited military force in 1962 during the Cuban missile crisis and got the desired results. When the Israelis began to throw the Arabs back in 1973, the Russians started to load up their airborne troops, but we came to the alert and they backed off. And when they started into North Yemen in 1979, we started to help the Yemeni to resist—and, again, they backed off. We have to show them we mean business. They really don't care about anything except power."

On October 2, 1980, I talked on the phone with Maj. Gen. Jerry Curry, a key Pentagon spokesman. I wanted to get his views, especially because he has a doctorate in international affairs and he wrote his thesis on the Middle East. I mentioned that I had felt disturbed by the impression I drew from the White House that there was little to be alarmed about in the Middle East, especially in Israel.

"When I was in the Middle East in 1970 doing research for my thesis, I became convinced things are moving more rapidly there than people would care to believe," said General Curry. "Today, ten years later, that conviction has only been deepened. As geared as

I became to the volatility of that region, it was still unthinkable ten years ago that the Shah would fall from power and that Iran would so quickly lose its place as the principal military power in the Persian Gulf. It was equally unthinkable that the Russians would deploy troops in Afghanistan. After all, what would anybody want with it? Its rugged geographical terrain, its fiercely independent people, its lack of natural resources make it a pretty unlikely target. And it certainly represented no threat to the Soviet Union's territorial integrity.

"The biggest surprise of all, though, was Sadat making that trip to Jerusalem in 1977. No one expected that. Now, in time, I think Iran will settle into a generally neutral role. When the dust settles we're going to be faced with a new situation there. I don't see Armageddon happening next year, but we cannot be complacent. We need to focus our attention on the Middle East, both as a government and as an entire people."

I spoke also with Lt. Gen. Richard Schaffer, USAF (retired). He expressed concern over our readiness to meet a serious Soviet threat and over the erosion of the quality of military personnel, which he attributed to our failure to offer sufficient incentives to keep qualified people on active duty, especially those in highly technological roles.

General Freeze heads up the operations of military intelligence for national security. He, like General Huyser, saw reason for concern both in the Middle East and in Africa. He emphasized the role of the Cuban military detachments in Africa, and he spoke of Castro's influence in Latin America. In an interesting sidelight, he observed, that while Jews and evangelicals seemed interested in Middle Eastern events—he called the whole region a tinderbox—he felt that the American people at large did not realize the significance of these events.

In Israel, on the other hand, I found no one who was indifferent to these matters. Everyone I talked with had strong opinions and firm ideas about the significance of the Middle East and Israel's role there. Brig. Gen. Ephraim Paran, chief military assistant to Prime Minister Begin, talked about events in the Middle East "leading to a catastrophe for the Western World. If Russia makes a move toward Iran, I hope that the United States will not stand aside and do nothing." He speculated that Russia might invade

Iran outright, but it seemed to him more probable that they would foster revolution from within the country. "The Communist party of Iran," he said, "is not big, but it is well-organized. And they are heavily armed since the Shah fell. America needs to recognize that her only reliable ally in this region is Israel."

Abraham Schechterman is chairman of the Likud Party in Israel. He thinks that the United States ought to feel a debt of gratitude to Israel for the way it helped the United States in the past in its struggle against Communism. "We helped the Free World very much when we held the Suez Canal. We wouldn't let the Russians through to transport arms to Vietnam. So, they had to go all the way around Africa. It took each ship seventeen days longer to reach Hanoi that way. In a war, that kind of time counts a lot. And, you may not be aware of this, but back during our war in 1973, we brought down four planes in fifteen seconds. Later we learned those fighters had been manned by Russian pilots. This gave the Russians a hint that they should be very careful." Schechterman's eyes glistened with pride as he recalled the event. There was no doubt in his mind who would stand with America if she came to grips with the Red Army in the Near East.

Reuben Hecht is one of Begin's advisers, like General Paran. I was explaining to him that some leaders in American government belittled the idea of the United States standing staunchly with Israel in the Middle East because, if we did, the Arabs would cut off oil deliveries to Europe and Japan. Hecht chuckled, "What does your government think, that the Arabs will use their oil to drink? The Russians will not give them dollars for it. The only reason the Arabs have so much power is because the Europeans and Americans are not united. The Arabs can blackmail them because if your American president wants to draw the line, the French president will go along with whatever they want. If the French president wants to draw the line, then the West German chancellor will gladly put up with their demands. Their might is illusory. It is there only because your disunity grants it to them.

"Naturally the Arabs will protest and threaten you with dire consequences if you are completely pro-Israel. But the question for you is who will be your ally to stop the Arab-Communist assault against Europe? Is it not true that you had one deception which cost you untold billions? That was the Shah of Iran. The terrible things they did with your hostages shows the weakness of American foreign policy. Those Arab fanatics tried to humiliate the whole world. But does America learn a lesson? No. They keep handing over arms to strengthen the hand of the Arabs. Instead they ought to recognize that Israel needs enough territory to stand on so that her military might can really help America. But no, they hand over the Sinai to Egypt and want us to give up the West Bank. Mr. Sadat will not live forever, and who knows who will come after him? Perhaps another Nasser. Then where will we be? I'll tell you, the Sinai will become a Russian base."

Some people might think what he was suggesting was preposterous. But, to me it made perfect sense. Which of the Middle Eastern nations would really be much help in a serious fight? The Saudi fighter pilots were unproven. Egypt's performance in previous wars had been unspectacular. The Israelis alone have shown themselves time and again to be a resilient and sturdy fighting force in the air and on the ground.

And what about Hecht's arguments that the Arabs really gained their leverage more through American-European disunity than through their oil? It would be hard to test his theory, but it made some sense. And what if we did solidly align ourselves with Israel? Would it really make things any worse for us in the region than they presently are? I doubted it. A lion with a fang missing and a paw bloodied after a fight in Vietnam might find a ferocious cat of considerable value in a fight with a bear.

Benjamin Netanyahu lives in Jerusalem and directs the work of the Jonathan Institute. The institute is named after his son who led and died in the raid on Entebbe Airport to rescue the Israeli hostages from the Arab terrorists. The institute is devoted to the study and exposure of terrorism. Benjamin taught at Cornell for seven years and is professor emeritus of Near Eastern studies there. We'll hear more from him in later chapters dealing with the PLO and international terrorism. But I want to insert here some comments he made to me which are relevant to the focus of this chapter.

"The Soviets are after nothing less than domination of the whole world. And only one thing stands in their way—the United States and its atomic weapons. If that were not there, they would have taken the whole world over in a matter of days.

"The Americans may look weak right now, but you can never tell what emotional outburst may develop among them overnight. That's the nature of the Americans. They are like the water of the ocean. Calm now, but furious in a storm. Kaiser Wilhelm thought they were just quiet water that would do him no harm. But they were the outraged waves of the storm that finally drove the Imperial German Army out of France in 1918.

"The Russians are smarter than Kaiser Wilhelm and much smarter than Hitler. They don't want to tackle America head-on. They would prefer to destroy America slowly. They want to strangle it by capturing one portion of the world after another. This is why terrorism is so important to them. Years of terror wear a nation down. Then it falls easily, like Vietnam, and no Russians even need be there. That's the way they're working on Africa to surround and destroy South Africa. They also want to surround and isolate China by controlling Southeast Asia. To control Europe they need the Mediterranean. So, they have Libya. But they need the whole Middle East, and especially the bridge to Africa which is Israel. The Middle East is the strategic center of the whole world. It's been that way throughout history. The world's greatest empires have always controlled the Middle East: the Medo-Persians, the Macedonians of Alexander, the Romans, the Arabs, the Turks, the British—and now the Russians want their turn at it.

"You see, I'm not talking about the future of Israel, but about the future of America and of the whole western world. The task before us cannot be overestimated.

"And, if it had not been for us Israelis, the Russians would already have moved in here just as they did in Angola, and Yemen, and Ethiopia, and twenty other places. Without Zionism here, Russia could cut through this region like a knife through butter. And they would establish one pro-Russian regime after another, and nothing would remain of the whole area. What I say has to be true. Otherwise, why would they work so hard to eliminate Israel? If we were not so important, as so many would like to say, why does the Kremlin spend so much of its money to support the constant terrorist attacks on Israel?

"And I want to tell you the Russians are better chess players than the Americans have been recently. They know the game better. They are more familiar with the issues and with the forces at work in this area. The Americans are so naive, for example, that they are ready to negotiate with the PLO, if only the PLO will affirm resolution 242 of the United Nations, which says Israel has a right to exist. The PLO will gladly say anything they have to say to get what they want. It is sickening."

Listening to Benjamin Netanyahu was a sobering experience. Some people would call his remarks alarmist claptrap, but to me, it was the clear, unfiltered vision of an especially perceptive mind trained in logic and analysis. I knew, after listening to him, that I could not rest until I had learned all I could about this tangled subject. One thing I needed to learn more about was the PLO, though I never imagined down what murky lanes my quest would lead me.

chapter 3

The PLO

I decided to ask Isser Harel about the PLO. Mr. Harel is considered to be an expert on this terrorist group. Harel had been chief of Israeli intelligence during the 1950s and was the man who captured Adolf Eichmann.

He began, "Their ultimate goal is to root out Israel. Everything else they do and say is leading up to that somehow, you can be sure. They want to destroy the Jewish people and everything that pertains to them.

"They get their money from the Arabs. All the Arab states of the oil country supply them with money." That statement rang a bell; a very reliable source in the United States had told me something that I considered quite impossible. He had said, "For every barrel of oil that Saudi Arabia sells to the U.S. it channels approximately $2.00 into the hands of the PLO."

My mind raced back over the chronicle of Arab terrorism. It had been increasing steadily since the mid-1960s. After the humiliating defeats dealt to the Arabs in 1967, they began to promote the terrorists much more avidly. Obviously their regular armed forces were no match for the Israelis. And they needed time to rebuild for the next fight. Most important, they needed a way to take revenge on the Israelis for humiliating them. The PLO became the fang for their venom. Their viper had struck often and horribly after Sadat's trip to Jerusalem, late in 1977.

In mid-February, 1978, a time bomb exploded in a crowded bus in Jerusalem. Two people were killed and forty-six were injured.

A month later, on March 11, a band of terrorists plied their way toward a beach fifteen miles south of Haifa. They had numbered thirteen when they started out. Already they had lost two of their number by drowning. Finally they reached the beach, where they came upon an American tourist with a camera. She suddenly realized who and what they were, but too late. A blast of automatic fire and she was dead. They quickly moved past her body and up onto the highway where they commandeered two busloads of Israelites returning from a holiday.

They crowded everybody into one bus and ordered the driver to continue moving south toward Tel Aviv. Word of what was happening quickly reached authorities because the terrorists fired on passing cars.

Meanwhile, security men had erected a roadblock seven miles north of Tel Aviv. Finally the bus came into sight and opened fire. This was obviously no hostages-for-ransom situation. The Israelis steeled themselves for the worst and tried to return fire without firing indiscriminately into the bus. The screams and sobbing of women and children reached their ears in spite of the noise of gunfire. Then it happened, the horrible report of a tremendous explosion and the whole bus erupted in flames. The terrorists had detonated an incendiary bomb. More than thirty died in the inferno. By some miracle, seventy people survived. The security men rushed in and actually managed to take two of the terrorists prisoner. Nine others lay dead in and about the remains of the bus.

It is remarkable what Israel does with their terrorists. Not one captured terrorist has ever been sentenced to death in Israel. They are imprisoned and the Red Cross is permitted to visit them regularly. Most are imprisoned for life or for indefinite terms. The law in Israel calls for capital punishment in the case of terrorist murders, but the Israelis believe more strongly in the principle of restraint. Only Adolf Eichmann—and that because he was a Nazi war criminal, not a terrorist—was executed after trial and sentencing.

A group named Al Fatah, the strongest constituent member of the umbrella Palestine Liberation Organization, claimed responsibility for the bus atrocity, saying that it reflected their decision to step up "revolutionary armed violence against Zionist occupation." Saudi Arabia's state radio applauded Fatah's act of brutality and cowardice as "courageous" and said it "had a noble aim." Kuwait and Libya officially joined the chorus, as did two daily newspapers in Jordan. Yasir Arafat, who founded Al Fatah and gained his dominance over the PLO through it, acknowledged that he had personally approved the massacre.

On May 7, 1978, Arab terrorists fired off a Russian-made Katyusha rocket which exploded in Jerusalem and injured a woman. This was the PLO's way of marking the thirtieth anniversary of Israeli independence—at least that's what they explained afterward.

Thirteen days later, 150 French passengers were lined up to board an El Al (Israeli airlines) jet at Paris's Orly Airport. Three Arab terrorists managed to get within range of them and opened fire. The French authorities responded alertly. The three terrorists were killed, as was one of the policemen. Three of the police were seriously wounded, together with a stewardess and one passenger. Others were injured, but not seriously. Though grotesque, this compared favorably to a day at Lod Airport in Israel six years earlier. There Japanese Red Army gunmen in the employ of the PFLP (Popular Front for the Liberation of Palestine, another constituent of the PLO) machine-gunned defenseless passengers, killing twenty-six of them, wounding eighty.

The day after the Lod massacre happened I was flying into Lod. Next to me on the plane was a Puerto Rican tour host. He was obviously distressed and, when I asked him why, he explained to me that he himself had originally been scheduled to escort the tour group which had been gunned down the day before. Almost in tears, he went on to say he had traded duties with a friend in order to accommodate his personal schedule. Because of that change in his schedule, he had been spared the enormous grief of hosting the ill-fated tour group.

When we arrived at Lod, the evidence of the preceding day's incident was still much in view. Israeli soldiers were everywhere and they were heavily armed. The wall of one building bore the scars of the automatic gunfire which had not found its target in human flesh. I shuddered.

To return, however, to our survey of terrorist activities in 1978, in June the PLO planted another bomb in a bus on the outskirts of Jerusalem during the evening rush hour. It was their gesture of hatred in the midst of preparations for the celebration of the eleventh anniversary of the retaking of East Jerusalem from the Jordanians. The explosion in the bus killed a twelve-year-old boy, two girls aged fifteen, a seventeen-year-old and an eighteen-year-old boy, and a thirty-year-old American medical student. Twenty other people were wounded. Fatah took credit from their headquarters in Beirut. This marked the eleventh incident of terrorism in Jerusalem in 1978.

Three Arab terrorists working for the PFLP ambushed an El Al crew as they were getting out of their minibus at the entrance of the Europa Hotel in London. Using grenades and machine guns they managed to kill a stewardess and to injure nine other people, some of whom were members of a wedding party that had been standing in front of the hotel. The stewardess, Irit Girdon, aged twenty-nine, was killed as she was running for cover toward the hotel entrance. She collided en route with one of the terrorists who had just pulled the pin on a grenade. The collision prevented his intended toss and both he and Irit died in the explosion. Two other stewardesses sustained injuries. One terrorist was captured; one escaped. Irit Girdon was buried with honors adjacent to the graves of the athletes who perished in the 1972 Munich Olympics massacre.

As the Camp David discussions approached at the end of the summer, terrorist activity reached furious levels. Numerous bombs were planted throughout Israel. Twenty-six of them actually exploded, often killing and maiming people. But many of them were found and dismantled or exploded by authorities in a safe place, thanks to alert citizens who responded to official requests to keep an eye out for suspicious parcels and objects. And thanks to men like Steve Auster. Steve had served in Vietnam and later on in the Los Angeles Police Department. He was a bomb expert who had emigrated to Israel in 1973. Thereafter he had rendered invaluable service to the Israeli government by dismantling over twenty-five explosive devices. On September 5, 1978, he got a call to come down to a storage facility for propane gas cylinders in Jerusalem. They had found a device planted there evidently in hopes of getting the propane to go off as well. But Steve never got his hands on the bomb. It exploded when he was just walking up to it. It tore off both his legs and one arm. He died in the hospital a week later. The hoped-for chain reaction of propane explosions did not occur. The PLO claimed credit for the incident.

On the last day of that same month, an armed Israeli patrol boat spotted a ship proceeding north in the Gulf of Aqaba. Thousands of Israelis had flocked to Eilat at the northern end of the gulf to celebrate the Jewish New Year. The beaches and hotels were crowded, so Israeli patrols were on extra alert. Thus, the fast-moving, unidentified vessel aroused considerable suspicion. The Israelis hailed it, but were ignored. They gave pursuit and it soon became evident the ship was manned by terrorists. The Israelis finally opened fire and, before long, the ship was dead in the water and beginning to list. The Israelis approached cautiously, acutely aware of terrorist extremism. However, they surrendered readily enough and the Israelis boarded their ship to inspect its cargo before it sank: forty-two Katyusha rockets and an estimated three tons of explosives. Three of the seven captured terrorists had been wounded in the fight. From the four uninjured men they learned the terrorists had intended to fire the rockets into Eilat's business district and then run the ship aground on the public beach as an enormous bomb. Rubber dinghies would have carried the terrorists to the nearby Jordanian port of Aqaba and safety. They had set sail from Latakia on the Syrian coast of the Mediterranean a month before, under the flag of Cyprus. False papers indicating they were bound for a port in Saudi Arabia helped them pass through the Suez Canal. They had come within seventy miles of their target.

November 19 marked the first anniversary of Anwar Sadat's now-celebrated trip to Jerusalem. The PLO marked it with several bomb plants, the most lethal explosion occurring in a bus packed with tourists and Israelis in Jericho. Four persons died and thirty-eight were injured, including Swedes, Canadians, and Americans.

Bombs continued to explode, especially in the capital city of Jerusalem, throughout the rest of the year. Both Arabs and Jews—men, women, and children—suffered death and injury. Many will spend the rest of their lives with permanent injuries— amputations, scars, loss of sight or hearing, severe burns, countless impairments. Worse, in many cases, are the emotional scars. Twenty years ago, terror was a word that was not frequently employed in the English language. We might have described any number of mildly distasteful or unpleasant things as "terrible," with no sense of terror. But today the impact of terror with all its grotesque implications has reached around the globe. No air passenger can board a plane any longer without being searched by metal detectors and X-ray. The effect of terror is enervating. It takes the heart out of a person. Only the most resilient and sturdy can endure it for long.

I have only given the highlights of 1978's terrorist scenario. But it goes on week in and week out, month after month, year after year—and, if you're an Israeli, it goes on with fierce intensity. I am reminded of a scene I saw when I was in Eilat during a trip to Israel. A schoolteacher was on an outing with her class. It was a normal, casual lark, except for one thing—the automatic weapon the teacher carried at her side.

But, as we have already seen, these attacks have hardly been limited to any one group. Indeed Arab terrorists experience a good deal of internecine strife. Iraqi-backed terrorists, led by a former comrade of Arafat named Sabri al-Banna (code name: Abu Nidal), regarded Arafat and the PLO as altogether too soft on the Israelis. Their quarrels have created considerable bloodshed within the ranks. The PLO has charged Abu Nidal with masterminding the murders of its London and Kuwait representatives. A number of assassinations and attempted assassinations of Iraqi government officials have occurred in 1978 in London, Paris, and Karachi. Local police are frequently wounded or killed in these melees. Then, on August 5, 1978, terrorists broke into the PLO offices in Islamabad, Pakistan, and opened up with machine-gun fire on all occupants. A Pakistani policeman, a medical student, a PLO terrorist undergoing training in the Pakistani army, and the telex operator all died.

U.S. diplomats have been killed or taken hostage by Arab terrorists. Al Fatah calls itself Black September when inflicting blows outside Israel. Thus, eight Black September gunmen broke into a Saudi Arabian embassy party in Khartoum in 1973. Two American diplomats and the Belgian chargé d'affaires died in the gunfire. Another member of the American foreign service, Michael Konner, was kidnapped by Palestinian terrorists in Beirut in 1975. He was beaten and held for fourteen hours. Two months later Col. Ernest R. Morgan was seized in Beirut by members of the "revolutionary Socialist Action Organization" who held him for ten days. Less than three months later, in

October, terrorists kidnapped two employees of the U.S. Information Agency in Beirut and held them for four months. The next year, in June, Francis E. Meloy, Jr., America's ambassador to Lebanon, was kidnapped with two of his aides in Beirut. All three of the men on this occasion, however, were killed.

Other targets of Arab terrorism have included the Swissair jet that blew up in midair in February, 1970. Its thirty-eight passengers and nine crew members all perished. The PFLP claimed credit. Black September gunmen attacked an airport lounge in Athens in 1973. Their machine guns killed four and wounded thirty-five hostages. The list could go on almost interminably. Travelers in airports in Nairobi, Rome, Athens, Istanbul, Paris, Amsterdam, Cairo, Beirut, and Tel Aviv have been assaulted with machine guns, grenades, and bombs. Terrorists have fired on planes while taking off. The favorite weapon on these occasions is the one-man bazooka rocket launcher. Passengers of virtually every nationality have been affected. And most of the major international airlines have been struck. The only notable omission is that of Soviet citizens and the Soviet airline, Aeroflot.

Indeed, the terrorists have often tangled with their fellow Arabs, even to the extent of taking the Arab oil ministers hostage at an OPEC meeting in Vienna in 1975—and demanding and receiving $25 million ransom from Saudi Arabia and Iran.

To understand this better, we need to examine briefly the structure of the Palestine Liberation Organization. It is loosely comprised of a number of different groups which have emerged under the leadership of one or another individual, sometimes under the sponsorship of a particular Arab government. The latest document in my hands, *The Palestine Liberation Organization*, published by the Israel Information Centre in Jerusalem in November, 1979, lists nine groups which, they explain, emerged as "the result of a gradual process in which various factions arose, joined forces with other groups under different names, split and regrouped again" (p. 4). The following table is taken from pages 4 and 5 of that publication.

Faction	*Leader*	*Characteristics*
Al Fatah	Yasir Arafat	The largest terrorist group in the PLO. At the fifth meeting of the Palestinian National Council in February, 1969, Fatah gained control of a majority of the Council seats and has remained in control ever since.
Black September	Abu Iyad	The cover name used by Fatah when carrying out terrorist operations outside of Israel.
Al Saiqa	Issam Kadi	The second largest terrorist faction in the PLO. Al Saiqa was established by the Syrian government to carry out terrorist raids against Israel and to represent Syrian interests within the PLO. To this day it is financed, trained, and controlled by Syria.
Popular Front for the Liberation of Palestine	Dr. George Habash	Originally formed by the merger of various Egyptian and Syrian-sponsored groups in 1969, this-neo-Marxist faction opposes the "less extreme" position of Fatah.
Popular Democratic Front for the Liberation of Palestine	Naif Hawatma	Sponsored by Iraq, this extremist Marxist faction split away from the PFLP in May, 1969.
Popular Front for the Liberation of Palestine—General Command	Ahmad Jibril	Supported by Libya and Syria, this group also broke away from the PFLP. It specializes in committing dramatic operations.
Palestine Liberation Front	Talaat Yakoub Abu Alabas	A pro-Iraqi splinter group which broke away from Jibril's faction.
Arab Liberation Front	Abd Airhim Ahmed	Founded and run by the Iraqi government .
Popular Struggle	Samir Gawsha	Leftist, with a strong pro-Iraqi tendency.

The name of the Iraqi and Syrian governments appears often on this list, and both governments are known to have substantial ties with the Soviet Union. Naif Hawatma, for example, advocates the overthrow of Jordan as well as Israel. In fact, a number of the leaders regularly attack the old-line conservative sheikhdoms and monarchies of nations like Saudi Arabia, Kuwait, Oman, and the United Arab Emirates. Their pronouncements call for the overthrow of these reactionary regimes. The Soviets have clearly capitalized on the sentiments of the Arab terrorists and gradually drawn them more into their camp. We can see this particularly in Arafat's recent cosmetic attempts to achieve a more moderate image which we will examine shortly. In the meantime, it serves nicely to keep everyone confused by having the more outspokenly Marxist leaders of the terrorist movement, like George Habash, decry Arafat's gradualism, loudly protesting that the Jews ought to be annihilated without further ado. This sounds properly radical and appeals to Arab temperaments, but it is Arafat, clearly at the helm, who proceeds with the caution and deliberateness of a man who has been reading and heeding Lenin.

Roaming the Streets

The PLO was first organized in Cairo in 1964 (three years before the 1967 war), under Arab League Egyptian auspices. They drew up a document called The Palestine National Covenant (see Appendix 6). The use of the word "covenant" conveys more of a holy sense rather than meaning a charter or a constitution. It has been revised several times and presently contains twenty-three articles which reject the Balfour Declaration, the U.N. Partition, and even the Jews' biblical claims on the land; most important, they deny the Jewish right to be a nation, a free people. They insist instead that all the territory properly belongs to the Palestinians, and only those Jews living in Palestine prior to the "Zionist invasion" can be regarded as legitimate Palestinians and thus allowed to stay. The covenant does not say it, but if you ask any PLO spokesman or leader when the Zionist invasion began, he will tell you that it started in 1917. In spite of the lengthy rhetoric, it does not oversimplify the matter in the least to say that the covenant essentially calls for the physical eradication of Jewry and the state of Israel and the establishment of a Palestinian state instead—in place, incidentally, of both Israel and Jordan.

In light of present Soviet proposals for a "sovereign" Palestinian state in the West Bank, we do well to note that in 1964 the West Bank and all the other presently disputed territories were in Arab hands and had been so since 1949. There was no move during those years to establish a Palestinian state in those districts. The Arab goal then, as now, was and is to take the land away from the Jews, not to give the Palestinians any rights.

Thus, things began in earnest after the Six-Day War in June, 1967. By 1970, Arafat and his Al Fatah were in control of the PLO. He has chaired the organization ever since. Arafat maintained his base of operations in those days in Jordan, as had his predecessors in the PLO. King Hussein had welcomed them warmly, but they repaid his welcome by intrigue and treachery inside Jordan itself. They invited the Bedouins to join their ranks and oppose the king. They erected roadblocks to harass the citizens and collect fees from them, and they terrorized the Palestinians to intimidate them into embracing their call for the liberation of Palestine.

We should note in passing that, while the PLO claims to represent the Palestinians, they in fact do not. The largest number and percentage of Palestinians today live in Jordan and Kuwait, not in Israel. Besides that, the PLO has appointed itself to this task. No election was ever conducted among the Palestinians to establish a representative body. The original appointments were made by the representatives of the Arab League, among which there are no democrats.

In any event, the PLO continued to stretch King Hussein's patience while they enjoyed the refuge of his country. They nearly established a rival capital for Jordan at Karamah a few miles north of the Allenby Bridge over the River Jordan. From there they exchanged artillery fire with the Israelis. Hussein tried to put a stop to it because he feared Israeli retaliation, but his efforts were in vain. The PLO were a law unto themselves.

The Israelis did retaliate finally, in 1968. They warned civilians to evacuate Karamah. That, in turn, alerted Hussein, who dispatched forty-eight tanks, eleven artillery batteries, and two brigades of infantry, but not until after the Israelis reached Karamah. Approximately 320 members of the PLO were involved. The Israelis surrounded and destroyed the Al Fatah installations, killing about 200 terrorists and taking 120 prisoners. But, as they withdrew from Karamah, they met Hussein's troops and a pitched battle ensued. Israel suffered stiff casualties, twenty-six dead and seventy wounded. And they lost a considerable number of armored vehicles. Arafat escaped to the town of Salt on a motorcycle. Whereupon, Al Fatah declared a great victory on Radio Amman, and there was dancing in the streets of the city.

Now, however, the terrorists stayed in Amman and Hussein really had trouble on his hands. They roamed the streets of the city brandishing their weapons and defying local police. Amman became a site of virtual anarchy. Finally, in June, 1970, Hussein ordered his troops to drive the PLO—or Fedayeen (kamikazes), as they were still known at that time—out of the city. In the bloody fighting that followed the terrorists murdered Maj. R.J. Perry, military attaché at the U.S. embassy in Amman. Then they occupied two hotels, the Intercontinental and the Philadelphia, and held thirty-two American and European guests as hostages. With that, George Habash announced that they would kill the hostages and blow up the hotels if the Jordanian troops didn't back off. Habash and Naif Hawatma, who was there too, both received funding from the Soviets. They could afford to attack an Arab head of state. Arafat's money came from the Arabs, so he sought to be more conciliatory. Nevertheless, the fury of the confrontation pushed Arafat more and more towards Habash and Hawatma.

Hussein did back off after Habash's speech threatening to kill the hostages. That was on June 12, 1970. After that, things continued to be relatively quiet, but tense, until September when Habash's men managed to hijack two jumbo jets (Swissair and TWA) and bring them to Jordan's Dawson Field. Three days later, on September 9, they hijacked a BOAC plane and brought it to Dawson, too. Altogether they had 445 hostages whom they threatened to blow up in the planes if imprisoned terrorists in Israel and Europe were not released within seven days. By September 12 they had freed all but fifty-four of the hostages. Arafat, speaking for the central committee of the PLO, fully endorsed Habash's PFLP demands.

All this, needless to say, infuriated Hussein, who was suffering untold embarrassment as the rest of the world looked on. He

surrounded Dawson Field with tanks and compelled the terrorists to give up their remaining hostages. However, the planes
were all destroyed. Still Hussein restrained his Bedouin troops,
who wanted desperately to avenge Jordan's honor.

On September 16, Hussein announced a military government
on Radio Amman to restore order to his troubled land. The next
morning he unleashed the Bedouin Arab Legion in a full-scale
operation against the PLO. Tanks demolished every building
in Amman from which there was firing. Before Hussein was
finished, he had killed around 3,000 of the Palestinian terrorists
and broken the PLO power in Jordan.

Hussein's action prompted an immediate reaction from his
northern neighbor, Syria. Men and equipment poured over the
border to reinforce the terrorists. Syrian commandos struck and
captured two Jordanian border villages on September 18, and
Hussein stiffened for all-out war with Syria, which greatly out-
numbered him in tanks and aircraft.

Israel and the United States mobilized their forces, thereby
giving notice to Syria that if she launched a full-scale invasion
she would encounter more than Jordanian troops. It worked.
Syria held back and the Jordanians were able to drive out what
Syrian forces had been committed without much ado.

From Jordan, the PLO moved on to Lebanon. Lebanon is the
only Arab nation with a significant Christian (Syrian, Orthodox
and Catholic) population.

When the French discontinued their mandate of Syria and
Lebanon in 1946, the Christian majority in Lebanon worked out
a delicately balanced arrangement with the Muslim minority
under a democratic constitution. The results were largely happy
enough and Beirut became a bustling and prosperous commercial
center whose citizens enjoyed probably the highest per capita
income in the Middle East.

When Palestinian Arabs fled Israel during the 1948 war, sev-
eral thousand were admitted to Lebanon—not more lest the
Christian-Muslim balance of population be seriously disturbed.
Disturbing that balance was always a matter of grave concern,
especially to the Christians who stood to lose the most from it.
They had felt safer from Muslim antagonism under the French
and had been reluctant to see them go. And, all the while, the
Muslims argued for unification with Muslim Syria. They did not

have much regard for Lebanon's pre-Islamic past, the days of the Phoenicians and the enormous wealth of Tyre and Sidon. For them, all significant history commenced with the advent of Islam in 632CE. And so the tension continued, just beneath the surface.

However, the Palestinians did disturb the balance in Lebanon, out of proportion to their actual numbers. That was because agents of the PLO worked actively in the refugee camps and established bases within them from which to launch terrorist attacks into Israel. The Lebanese government was faced with a dilemma. To drive the PLO out would anger the Muslim population and to let them stay would enrage the Christians. Therefore, the Lebanese prime minister denied their existence in public and negotiated with Arafat to limit raids into Israel so as not to provoke Israeli reprisals. This arrangement, however, worked only briefly, until the PLO in Lebanon commandeered an El Al airliner. The Israelis promptly dispatched jet fighters to Beirut's airport, where they destroyed Arab airliners on the ground.

While Lebanon was thus knocked slightly off balance, its Muslim neighbors applied pressure to secure for the PLO the sole right to supervise and police the refugee camps in southern Lebanon. In addition, the Lebanese were persuaded to release PLO terrorists whom they had imprisoned for their subversive activities against the Lebanese government. Consequently, terrorism inside the Lebanese borders revived considerably. On November 15, 1970, to cite but one example, terrorists surrounded a house, apparently at random, in the town of Aitarun. It was occupied by Mahmoud Faiz Murad—his wife who was in her ninth month of pregnancy—and his father. All three were gunned down in cold blood when they resisted terrorist attempts to remove them by force.

The Lebanese Muslim community sided with the PLO and, in 1975, civil war erupted between the Christians and Muslims in that country. Christian apprehensions were expressed by several spokesmen. Dr. Albert M'khebar, a member of parliament, declared, "I will renounce my Lebanese nationality, acquire an Israeli one, and go around the whole world to proclaim my apostasy from the Arabs and Arab nationalism, if its true nature is what we see in Lebanon" (*Al-Hawadeth*, July 11, 1975). Raymond Edde, head of the Christian National Bloc Party in parliament, complained, "The western world no longer is concerned with the defense of the Christians in Lebanon" (*ibid.*). And Pierre Gemayel threatened, "For the sake of the defense of Lebanon, we shall seek help from the Devil, even if that Devil is Israel . . ." (*ibid.*).

That same week, *Time* magazine carried this statement by Elis Marvun of Beirut: "Now I can understand why Israel is refusing the suggested 'democratic Palestine' where the Israelis and the Palestinians would live together. The outstanding example the Palestinian people are giving now in Lebanon is, I believe, more than enough to warn Israel of such a trap. . . . I am a Lebanese citizen whose brother and two cousins have been coldly shot down by the Palestinians in their own homes in a Hitlerian style. I can already see the day when, in order to survive, our people will join Israel. . . ."

As fighting between Muslims and Christians intensified, the President of Lebanon, Suleiman Franjieh, publicly announced, "The Lebanese had given them a refuge, and our reward was the destruction of Lebanon and killing of its people. I have served the Palestine cause for thirty-five years. I never expected the day would come when I would ask God to forgive my sins because I served a people who did not deserve to be served or supported" (*Los Angeles Times*, January 21, 1976).

Official appeals for help were made to the United States and the United Nations, both of which remained aloof while Syrian-trained and Soviet-equipped troops of the Palestine Liberation Army (*Al Saiqa*) poured across the border from Syria into Lebanon. They were accompanied, as we now know, by regular Syrian troops. The net result to date has been a near-takeover of Lebanon by Syria. A new government is struggling to gain a footing in Beirut at this writing and, presumably, to throw off the Syrian domination. Meanwhile, in the south of Lebanon, a strange thing has happened. The leader of the Lebanese Christian Army in southern Lebanon, Maj. Saad Haddad, has established an enclave in which the Lebanese people in southern Lebanon can dwell in relative safety. Haddad and his troops tangle frequently with PLO terrorists moving from camps in his area toward the Israeli border.

The Good Fence

While I was in Israel I went to see Haddad. I had been to Lebanon once before, in 1972. Then I had visited Beirut, a beautiful, peaceful city. A taxi driver had talked at length about how Lebanon had become one of the most beautiful resort spots of the Middle East. What a contrast with today's devastation.

My visit with Major Haddad took place inside Israeli territory, in Metullah to be exact, late in September, 1980. I told him there were some who considered the Israelis to be involved in terrorism in southern Lebanon. Haddad looked sad and said, "I would like them to come here and see who is controlling the area. Then they will know that the PLO terrorists are making the rules. The south has become a big base of terrorists. If we are shooting, it is to defend ourselves against these terrorists. For five years we have been cut off from all sides, except the south. The PLO wants to exterminate our people and nobody cares."

"Have you captured many of these PLO Arabs?"

Haddad's eyes narrowed seriously. "Do you think I'm fighting Arabs on the front line? Far from it," he said. "I'm fighting terrorists from all over the world. North Korea, Cuba, South America, and just a month ago, two Czechs got killed in a fight. The PLO has people from almost all the Communist countries. And from all the Arabic Islamic countries, too—Libya, Iran, Egypt. These are the PLO your state department is supporting. Your country, the Europeans, and all the Arab countries support them."

"Why do you think we support them?" I asked.

"I'll tell you why. The terrorists are frightening the rich Arab countries, so they give the PLO money, as much as they want, because they are desperate to keep them away from their country. Then the rich Arab countries turn around and put pressure on America and Europe to say the PLO is good or something like that.

"But they are not good," Haddad's eyes flashed. "They are criminals. Look at Lebanon. It used to be a paradise. They burned it. They killed a whole country. And they want to destroy the whole Middle East. They have said many times that they consider all the old regimes as reactionary and they are going to make progress by making them Communist. That's why they don't attack Israel from Jordan any more. And the Syrians won't allow them either, unless they are in Syrian uniforms. The Jordanians stopped them in September, 1970. That's where they got the name Black September. Only Lebanon allows them. Why? Because

Lebanon is a weak country. And it has a Christian president which the PLO wants to get rid of.

"The Christians of the world should wake up and help their brothers in Lebanon. If the Christians in Lebanon are exterminated, so will all the other Christians in the Middle East. The large Christian population of Lebanon is what guarantees the safety of the Christians in other Arabic countries. And what the terrorists have done here in southern Lebanon they will do to churches wherever they go. People should see what has happened to the villages in southern Lebanon which the terrorists have occupied. They ruin them. They are making a toilet of Lasherish (one of the towns in southern Lebanon occupied by the PLO). And they would do the same to Jerusalem if they got their hands on it. They would turn the churches into mosques."

"What about the U.N. forces north of you?" I asked. "Are they helping to keep peace?"

"The U.N. is doing nothing. They are just there for show. Worse than that, sometimes they are covering for the PLO. The area where the U.N. troops moved in used to be clean of PLO, but not any more. The PLO moved in and they have camps inside the U.N. area from which the PLO make terrorist actions. They came from there to one of the villages and planted mines. Four people were killed in that village. And last night, at exactly eight o'clock, they fired rockets from Dar Amish, which is in the U.N. area. If we trusted the U.N. forces to protect us, we would all be dead. We have to count on ourselves."

"What about Israel?" I asked.

"That's the only country which cares for us. Without Israel we would have been exterminated a long time ago. Four of the main Christian villages were almost completely wiped out by the terrorists. In El Damour there was a terrible slaughter. They just lined up the little children and killed them all. Can you imagine that? We are not ready to face that. It must not happen to our children and our families. That is why we are so thankful for Israel. They are supposed to be our enemy, but they are helping us. But the people who are supposed to be our friends are leaving us because we are poor people. We have no oil. We have nothing to sell to them."

"How did your people first get in touch with the Israelis and find out they were not the enemies you thought they were?"

"Well, it happened because we are poor and we are farmers. We are soldiers because we have to be, but we don't have any doctors or hospitals. Sometimes, when our men are wounded, they die because we cannot give them proper care. The Muslim terrorists have driven us into a corner here with no way out because the Israelis had put up a fence at the border between Lebanon and Israel.

"But one day one of our women had a sick baby. And she felt so desperate because she saw it was very sick and might die. So she sneaked out of her village and went down to the fence. Pretty soon she saw some Israelis. People had always said Israelis shoot women and children, that they are monsters. But that woman had no other chance, so she waved and yelled. She couldn't speak their language, so she made signs and they came over to her and saw her baby was sick. One of them ran off somewhere and, pretty soon, he came back. He had gone to get approval to bring the baby to the hospital. So, they got the woman to hand her baby over the fence to them and they took the baby to their hospital.

"Well, that mother, she just sat there by the fence day and night, waiting for them to bring her baby back to her. After a day or two, the Israelis cut a little opening in the fence and took her to see her baby. Pretty soon her baby got better, and she came back here and told all of us what happened. At first people doubted, but little by little they began to try it.

"When someone is dying of thirst and you give him even a drop of water, it gives hope. And more and more people found help. Pretty soon they started calling that fence the 'Good Fence.' Everybody calls it that today. Now they've even let some of our people have jobs down there during the day. And we began to ask them for ammunition to fight the PLO. The humanitarian help was good, but they had to help us militarily, too, or we would all be dead. Today it is like regular relations between two countries who have a common enemy."

"Is that common enemy the Muslims?" I inquired.

"Not really," Haddad answered. "There are a lot of Shi'ite Muslims in my area. And they are cooperating with us. There is no difference between us. We share the same kind of life. We face the same enemy. They realize the terrorist program is political. The terrorists are not going to help anybody, Muslims or Christians. They are coming to make their own war. They don't treat the Muslims any different than the others. They make slaves of everybody they conquer.

"Please tell the American people that we are on the same line as America. The terrorists call us pro-American, and they think we are really supported by the Americans. So, it is sad to see the state department putting pressure against us. They are helping our enemy which is also their own enemy, if they only knew it.

"One time I met a member of a Hungarian TV crew who came over from the U.N. lines, and we talked. I asked him why they are fighting against us because we are only Lebanese defending our land and our homes. He said it was because we are supported by the Americans. I wish the Americans would support us instead of opposing us! We're going through a holocaust. The PLO has killed over 60,000 of our people, shooting them in the streets like animals. Why are the nations of the earth closing their eyes to our plight?"

"The PLO terrorists have plenty of money, don't they?" I suggested.

"As I told you earlier, we are fighting against mercenaries. Most of the fighters on the front line are paid mercenaries. That's one of the big differences between them and us. We fight for our faith, for our country, for our principles, for our families. What are they fighting for? Money. But we don't make any money by fighting. Instead, it costs us everything. When the fighting goes badly for them, they can pull back. What have they got to lose? But we cannot pull back. We must risk our lives to protect our wives and children."

His courage astonished me. He was obviously a simple farmer, but he was also an extraordinarily brave man. He had brought no bodyguards with him. As we sat in a public restaurant drinking tea, I had to remind myself from time to time that the PLO hated him and would love to kill him. At any moment a jeep could have roared by and a terrorist could have hurled a bomb from it into our midst.

I confess that I felt stirred as I watched Saad Haddad cross "the Good Fence" back into southern Lebanon. In fact, I knew I had been with a good man—simple, courageous, kind. There had been a time in my life when I believed such men no longer existed, if indeed they ever had. But, in this humble Lebanese soldier, I had met one.

What I was seeing and hearing in Israel ran head-on into American foreign policy. Haddad was saying that we Americans were helping our enemies and hurting our friends. Was he right? An acquaintance of mine who was on the White House staff made an appointment for me to speak with the deputy director of Israeli affairs at the State Department, John Hirsch. He sought very carefully to explain and justify the nature of our policy toward Israel and the rest of the Middle East.

He began by reviewing the progress since the Camp David meetings in 1978. Israel and Egypt signed a peace treaty in March, 1979. Then they began to discuss the question of self-government for the residents of the West Bank of the Jordan River (Samaria and Judea). "We hope," he said, "those negotiations are on track . . . [because], in our judgment, the Camp David process is the only realistic way to solve the Middle East problem, which includes these various differences between Palestinians and Israelis. We want to find a solution in which Palestinians can live their lives while Israel finds a way to meet its very legitimate and real security problems—a way that is convincing and plausible to them, not simply to us who live six thousand miles away.

"Our goal is to obtain treaties of peace between Israel and her neighbors—Egypt, Jordan, Syria, and Lebanon. And we want arrangements which assure Israel's security and which deal fairly with the Palestinians in the West Bank and Gaza. In the Camp David accords we don't say how those final arrangements should look. What we do say in them is that things as they are must change. The three parties to the accords [Egypt, Israel, and the United States] agreed to try to change it for the better by ending the occupation and by allowing the Palestinians to participate in the determination of their future. The Arabs object that we intend to maintain Israeli control under another label which will not allow the Palestinians to truly express themselves politically. So, the Arabs are calling for an independent Palestinian state and for recognition of the PLO as the sole legitimate representative of the Palestinian people. However, the U.S. government will not recognize or negotiate with the PLO until it accepts Israel's right to exist and until it accepts Resolution 242. That is a fundamental impasse which means the PLO is not a participant."

"Didn't the PLO," I inquired, "meet recently in Damascus and reaffirm its commitment to destroy Israel?"

"That's right," Hirsch replied. "Although there's been a lot of controversy over the significance of what emerged from that meeting. Arafat subsequently gave interviews to various journalists. The gist of what he said to them was that the conference had been misunderstood. That the resolution to destroy Israel was only one of many resolutions and did not represent a net consensus of all the members of the organization. The PLO, according to Arafat, is a more or less democratic organization in which various groups have differing views. It sounded to me like he was walking away from it obliquely as far as Israel was concerned. It was not a very clear restatement of the PLO's determination to destroy Israel.

"The Camp David accords try to grapple with problems like these in another way and to avoid a head-on impasse. That's why we talk about involving the people who live on the West Bank and in Gaza in the negotiations. You see, these people have been living under someone else's government for centuries—the Turkish, the British, the Israelis [and, a significant omission, Jordan 1948-67]. They've never had a chance to have a voice—and having a voice is different from having your own way—in their own affairs. And we think an experiment in self-government would have a salutory impact on both sides. It would give the Palestinians a stake in what is happening. And once they have their experiment in self-government, we believe they'll begin to understand the problems of government differently than would be the case if they were out in exile somewhere. At the same time, if this experiment works, we hope it will convince the Israelis that the Palestinians can think about things other than attacking Israel. Our philosophy is to try to build confidence on both sides, which is not something that can happen overnight. It will only come by experience because the roots of this are so deep and the antagonism is very intense."

The thing that made me sit up and take notice as I listened to John Hirsch was what he said about the PLO's "not . . . very clear restatement of [its] determination to destroy Israel." I could tell by that, that he wanted to see the PLO as changing its position.

PLO Doubletalk

Beginning in 1976, Henry Tanner, a veteran *New York Times*

correspondent in the Arab world, began to report a shift in the
PLO position as a result of the declaration it issued after its meeting in Damascus that year. He noted that while the declaration
talked about a Palestinian state in the West Bank and Gaza, it did
not refer to a secular state in all of Palestine. That was important
because a state in all of Palestine would imply the disappearance of Israel. Perhaps the PLO was at last coming to grips with
reality and had decided to moderate its position.

According to The Associated Press (Damascus, November 26,
1978), when Illinois Republican Congressman Paul Findley met
with Arafat for four hours, Arafat told him, "The PLO will accept
an independent state in the West Bank and Gaza with a corridor.
At this point we will renounce any use of violence."

Earlier, in May, 1978, both the PLO observer at the U.N. and
the head of the PLO office in Paris spoke of the reality of the
existence of Israel. That would seem to indicate they were gradually coming around to the idea of peaceful coexistence with Israel.

That same month, correspondent Anthony Lewis summarized
several statements Arafat had made in conversation with him.
Arafat said that the only solution to the Middle East problem
would be guarantees given by the United States and the Soviet
Union to Israel and the establishment of a Palestinian state, and
that the joint U.S.-Soviet declaration of October 1, 1977, could be
a basis for a realistic solution to the problem.

At a press conference in Rome, held during a meeting of Israelis
and Palestinians, Ahmed Sidki Dajani said, "The PLO could begin talks with Israel if a strip of land for an independent state
were made available." Reporters asked him if this meant recognition of Israel, and he replied, "Of course, something of the sort
follows" (Reuters, Rome, September 25, 1979).

On March 20, 1980, in an interview with *Die Presse*, Austria,
Arafat was asked, "Now, very concretely, Chairman Arafat: Is
your goal a Palestinian state only? A homeland for your people?
Or the destruction of the Israel of today?" He answered, "The
most important goal is that my people live in peace, in a land of
peace. In a free state, in a democratic state. I do not intend to kill
or destroy anybody. Our people wish to establish its state in their
homeland. We don't conduct war because of a will of war, we
do not conduct wars in order to kill anybody; we are attacked.
Sixty percent of our people are refugees; 40 percent live under

occupation. The Palestinian tragedy is unique in history. Never-theless, we don't educate our children to hate anybody. Therefore, we suggested the first solution, which was turned down; that was a civilized solution. We are ready to have a democratic state where Muslims, Jews, and Christians live together in equality, justice, and fraternity. Then we brought up the second proposal, that was also accepted by our National Congress: We are ready to establish our independent state on any piece of land in Palestine from which Israel retreats."

Then, on April 22, 1980, Reuters (dateline: The Hague) quoted a five-point program for a political settlement which PLO spokes-man Khaled el Hassan claimed had been adopted by the Palestine National Council:

1. Israel should withdraw from all the areas it occupied in the 1967 Six-Day Arab-Israeli war.
2. The occupied zones should come under the trusteeship of the U.N. for a period of up to one year.
3. The U.N. should organize a referendum of the Palestinian people on whether they wanted to exercise their right to self-determination.
4. If the Palestinians chose independence, a state should be established. This would consist basically of the West Bank and Gaza Strip.
5. Negotiations should then begin under U.N. auspices, in-volving the U.S., USSR, the EEC (European Economic Community) countries and all concerned countries in the re-gion, including the governments of the new state and Israel, to deal with various problems.

These statements, and others like them, which appear rather frequently in the press, seemed to give some basis for John Hirsch's sense of hope. But all the press releases and interviews I've quoted above are taken from a publication of the Israel Infor-mation Centre in Jerusalem, entitled "PLO Doubletalk." Each of its eight typewritten pages puts together a statement and a denial of that statement as recorded by the press. Often it would seem that the PLO says one thing to the Western press and another thing to the Arab press. For example, when Khaled el Hassan, who announced the five points listed just above while he was in Holland, returned from Europe to Beirut in May, 1980, he was quoted by *Al Safir*, an Arab daily. His statement there denied the existence of the five-point program and blamed the news agencies for distorting his words. Here are his exact words, according to *Al Safir* on May 15.

> The Palestinian state must be established with a political rather than a geographic purpose. Were territory alone to be the goal, this would be treason—for he who forfeits half of his homeland is not worthy of the other half.

> Neither I nor the delegation accompanying me carried a concrete program for discussion in Europe. Arafat did not know in advance of these ideas.

> In the ideas I outlined, I referred to the Palestinian people, and by this I meant the PLO, the Palestinian National Council and the entire Palestinian people, including the inhabitants of the territories occupied since 1948.

> The dialogue with the Europeans focused on three points: recognition of Israel; changes in the Covenant; and cessation of violence. We replied to these points through adherence to the Palestinian National Covenant, for it calls for the destruction of Zionism and we continue to seek the obliteration of the Zionists in order to liberate our lands and our people.

Gil Carl Alroy, an expert on the Middle East, explains this propensity for doubletalk in his very interesting and informative book, *The Middle East Uncovered* (Princeton Publications: Princeton, New Jersey, 1979). He explains that the patriarchal system of clans on which Arab society rests allows for almost no cooperation or trust between groups larger than the extended family. Thus, Alroy explains, "Arab society resembles a seething mass more than a working organism" (p. 24). Consequently, the Arab personality is plagued with deep and real feelings of insecurity. This has given rise to the typically Arab trait of excessive politeness and flattery. "Frankness in face-to-face dealings must be avoided at all cost, since slight may engender extremely dangerous response. This encourages indirectness, formality, and resort to subtlety and double meaning. Arabs quite naturally carry many habitual traits into their contacts with outsiders. Especially marked has been their tendency to suggest agreement where none really exists and to euphemize intent that might antagonize foreigners in statements concerning such touchy issues as Israel or the use of oil as a political weapon" (pp. 24-25).

In 1974, the PLO was under pressure from Moscow, with which Arafat had become increasingly associated, to alter its position in order to participate at the negotiating table with Israel at the Geneva Conference. To meet this challenge, the PLO issued its Ten Point Transitional Program. This document reaffirmed the PLO's commitment to destroy Israel, preferably in one fell swoop. But, failing that, the organization affirmed that it would settle for control over part of the land it covets and use it as a base to destroy Israel gradually.

An Arab summit meeting convened at Rabat, Morocco, late in 1974 and designated the PLO as the "sole legitimate representative of the Palestinian people." It was shortly after that that Arafat spoke to the U.N. General Assembly, delivering his "gun and olive branch" speech. It included his call for a "democratic and secular state in all of Palestine" in which Muslims, Christians, and Jews could live together in justice, equality, and fraternity. This slogan was first published by the PLO in 1969 in order to obscure the clear commitment of the covenant to the destruction of Israel.

One will search the Arab world in vain looking for a secular and democratic state. Lebanon once came close, but the PLO has managed to destroy that nation in a bloody civil war as we noted in the previous chapter. To think that Yasir Arafat would head up a government that was either secular or democratic is the height of folly. The standard pattern for Arab government is the autocratic national socialism that ruled Germany under Hitler. No other broad heading more aptly characterizes various political systems of all the nations from Morocco to Iraq.

Yasir Arafat

In 1976 Thomas Kiernan wrote a biography of Yasir Arafat. It is a revealing portrait, although Kiernan got little real cooperation from Arafat himself. "Not because Arafat wouldn't see me, but because I learned that his concept of cooperation had all along been diametrically different than mine. So unwilling was he to go into the factual details of his life, so hopeful was he instead of getting me to re-create the mythological life he had invented for himself, that had I concurred in his notion of cooperation this book would have emerged not as biography, but as press agentry" (*Yasir Arafat*, London: Abacus, p. 2).

Kiernan, after a vivid account of the sordid course of Arafat's childhood and youth, portrays Arafat in 1966 as a man single-mindedly determined to wipe Israel off the map. He had renounced wine, women, and other temporal pleasures to devote himself to this one mission. Within seven years after the great Arab debacle of the Six-Day War (June, 1967), Arafat had passed along a torturous route, which included a brief imprisonment in Syria, to become the titular head and spokesman of the entire PLO. And he had become so prominent in that position that a United Nations General Assembly now heavily populated by representatives of governments which had gained independence by revolution in the years since the end of World War II, invited him to address them. Kiernan describes the event:

To the old-line Western nations which had dominated the U.N. in its early years, the invitation to Arafat was an embarrassment they could do little about. To Israel it was, of course, an outrage. To the majority of nations, however, many of them born of terrorism and guerrilla warfare, the Palestinian cause was a kindred one and Arafat a kind of spiritual brother. Indeed, the very man elected as president of the General Assembly during the session in which Arafat was to speak was himself a former Algerian terrorist.

As Arafat stood before the General Assembly and accepted its welcoming ovation he was, in the eyes of many, a sympathetic figure. Dressed in his familiar soiled khaki windbreaker and checked kheffiyah which hid his totally bald pate, and with a holster on his hip, he read his carefully prepared speech—the product of the combined efforts of his closest Fatah colleagues—in alternating compound of stentorian and pleading Arabic. It was a speech of contrasts— truths and untruths, historical accuracies and inaccuracies, threats and mollifications—all symbolized by the image he used to conclude it: the gun and the olive branch.

As a speech it told the world everything it could want to
know about Palestinian aspirations. It told the world everything it could want to know about Yasir Arafat. At the same
time, it told the world nothing about either. (p. 220)

By far the most intriguing section of Kiernan's book, however,
is the epilogue. In it he marks Arafat's decline after the U.N.
appearance. It did not bring the glory and recognition Arafat
had hoped for. Kiernan explains that this was entirely predict-
able. The U.N. speech had revealed the vacuity of Arafat's politics. He speaks loftily and loudly of liberation and revolution, but
he is unable to speak with any clarity about what system of government he would institute in Palestine if ever he gained it. Talk
of a democratic and secular state is sufficiently vague so as to
mean anything.

In recent years Anwar Sadat is the more familiar face among
the Arab leaders. And Arafat, according to Kiernan, sensed in
some measure that he was being eclipsed. His rise to glory had
made him show his true colors and he was consequently passed
over by the United Nation's—and the whole world's—political
sophisticates as a rank amateur.

This placed him once again where he had often been before, on
the horns of a dilemma. Should he follow the statesmanlike path
of patience and perserverance with moderation, or should he go
with the radical program of violence and terrorism that had
proven so effective in the past? Kiernan thinks the answer is
inevitably the latter because "on his desk, wherever it might
be located on any given day, lies an Arabic translation of *The
Protocols of the Elders of Zion*, that famous counterfeit tract
manufactured by the secret police of nineteenth-century Czarist
Russia to justify their anti-Jewish pogroms. [It was one of Adolf
Hitler's best-loved books, one that obviously fueled the evil
flames within his heart.] It is a volume he opens frequently and
earnestly quotes from to visitors, and if for no other reason than
that he is not a stateman" (pp. 222-23).

And so, concludes Kiernan, Arafat and his cohorts will resort
to violence as they have in the past because it has become their
habit and because it automatically assures the authentication of
their Islamic manhood. And finally because they believe a lie.
"Arafat and most of his colleagues believe without a doubt that

they were exclusively responsible for bringing about the wars of
1967 and 1973. It has become the conventional wisdom within
the movement that the provocation of these wars was funda-
mentally instrumental in advancing the Palestinian cause. As
Arafat and his cohorts revert to their basic instinct, they will
doubtless endeavor to bring about another war, using the tactics
they believe were so effective previously. But this time their
ambitions will not be limited to an Arab-Israeli war. They are
already looking beyond the frontiers of the Middle East" (p. 223).

chapter 4

World Terrorism

Something Major Haddad had told me in Metullah was haunting me. I had asked him, because he was a man who fought head-on with terrorists in southern Lebanon almost every day, who the PLO were. His answer had shaken me. Yes, he had spoken of Palestinians. But the first words out of his mouth were, "They are working with the Soviets and terrorists from throughout the world." Then he went on to name Cuba, North Korea, and South American countries as sources of their manpower. And there were the two Czechs who had been killed. What did it all mean? I wanted to find others who could corroborate and explain what Haddad was talking about. I was pretty sure the answers I would get would explain what Kiernan meant about the PLO and Arafat looking beyond the frontiers of the Middle East.

While in Jerusalem we had interviewed Jews who had escaped from Iran after the fall of the Shah. Things had gotten very rough for Jews in that country once the militant Muslims took power. What I learned about jailings and extortion was pretty disturbing, but the thing that disturbed me even more was their mention of the PLO. These people claimed that Palestinians had confiscated their money and the money of lots of other Jews, and that they had taken it in turn to Libya. All of this was done out in the open. It did not seem to trouble the authorities at all.

One of the fifty-two hostages, after having left Iran, said the day after the takeover he realized there were others from another country involved in the takeover. Khomeini's first official act in Iran had been to give the Israeli embassy to the PLO.

Isser Harel was the first to help me get a broader perspective on the terrorist problem. It was, indeed, the first thing he talked about when I broached the subject.

"They have plenty of money from the Arab states," he explained. "And they are equipped by the Russians. In fact, they

71

are equipped even by the West."

"By the United States?" I asked.

"Yes, if your country supplies arms to any Arab country—and it does—then you can be sure those arms will reach the PLO terrorists."

I realized there was a lot of truth to this statement. On January 30, 1980, Saudi Arabia spent one billion dollars on their third Islamic conference, playing host to sheiks and prime ministers of the Islamic world. These were leaders of thirty-seven countries and the PLO. It's obvious that the Arab world is using all of its influence to try to bring respectability and recognition to the PLO. I was shocked as I witnessed on national television, one of the heads of Saudi Arabia making a bold threat, that if President Reagan and our government do not reduce our foreign aid to Israel by at least 50 percent, the Saudis could eventually lose faith in the United States and decide to cut back oil exports to America drastically. He threatened that our rate of unemployment would at least double, and the price of oil would double. He went on to say that we would not be talking about a recession, but a depression. He ended his little talk with a statement that Saudi Arabia is not threatening the United States; it intends to use the oil weapon as a part of the rudder to guide the world's economy.

Mr. Harel continued, "Would you like to know something even more unbelievable? They actually have used the diplomatic pouches of some of these Arab countries to transport arms and explosives into Europe or wherever they want them to go. [Diplomatic pouches are customarily used to transport confidential materials between embassies and their sending nations and are exempt from search and seizure or customs inspection.]

"The PLO is organizing terrorism all over the world. They are behind the Italian terrorists, the Irish terrorists, the Baader-Meinhof gang in West Germany. They train Africans, South Americans, North Americans. They are the heart of international terrorism, a thing that will destroy civilization if it is not stopped."

"I understand that some of the Arab countries don't like the PLO," I interrupted.

Harel smiled, "Who told you that?"

"Well, what about Jordan? Didn't King Hussein drive them out of his country and inflict severe casualties on them?"

"That was ten years ago. They have reconciled since. Today they are working together."

"Tell me more about the Soviet Union and the PLO," I urged.

"They are training them. We caught some people not too long ago who murdered some women and children on a terrorist raid. One of them confessed to us that he had been trained in Russia. You see, the Russians at first didn't want to support terrorism. They had a doctrine which said terrorism was dangerous to big organizations. However, they have found, contrary to their doctrine, that the PLO works very well for them. So, they started training them, not only in Russia, but in East Germany, Czechoslovakia, all over the Soviet Bloc."

"Are the PLO leaders and terrorists Communists, then?"

"Not particularly. If you ask them, they often don't support Marxism or Communism. They just want to destroy Western civilization. An old-fashioned Marxist would like to destroy you so he can build his Communist state instead. But these people are unable to build anything. Look at Iran and Khomeini. The terrorists are crawling all over that country. They helped kidnap the American embassy people. Eventually they will destroy Iran simply because they know how to do nothing else.

"Still that doesn't make any difference to the Russians. They don't necessarily care if the terrorists they train are good Communists. It makes no difference because those terrorists do what they want them to do—destroy."

"How is the United States handling the terrorists?"

"Well, they are handling it differently than the Europeans. The United States has a weak policy toward them on a political level, but not on a security and intelligence level. In Europe, on the other hand, the security and intelligence people are acting, I would say, just like their governments who are afraid of the terrorists. What do the Germans or Italians or British do when they capture these people? Do they put them on trial? No! They release them, they bargain with them, they make deals.

"But I'll tell you something else about the United States. When the Iranians took those hostages from the embassy and America didn't act immediately with all their strength, even military strength, the Russians knew they could take over Afghanistan without fear of the Americans. It was a sign for the Russians that Americans cannot protect their rights."

Isser Harel is a sobering man to listen to. He had told me a lot in a very little time. I needed to follow up on the things he had said, to find out more about them, and set them in order. I got my first help from Moshe Yeager, Israel's Assistant Director General of Foreign Affairs, who handed me his latest report on the subject, sixteen typewritten, legal-size pages entitled, "The PLO's Role in World Terrorism."

The most striking thing about this report was its matter-of-fact tone. As I read it, the horrible scene of the bloodshed in the nursery at the kibbutz in Misgav Am came to mind. There, on April 6-7, 1980, these valiant "commandos," as the press sometimes dubbed them, had ferociously murdered a two-and-a-half-year-old child and a secretary. They managed also to take the life of a soldier, and they wounded another adult civilian, four children, and eleven soldiers. By themselves the statistics were agonizing, but, if one ever paused to think of them as people with mothers, fathers, siblings, spouses, sweethearts, or children, it became nearly unbearable.

Perhaps this document was written by a person related to one of those Israeli soldiers whom the Syrians had captured and then literally eaten alive. The report had come from the Syrians themselves. A leader had proudly boasted of the soldier from Aleppo who had leapt on the first Israeli, who was tied and defenseless, and devoured his flesh until the man died. Still the Israeli report remained steadfastly statistical and analytical.

It noted the the PLO had, at first, limited its activities to Israel between 1965 and 1968. Then, between 1969 and 1974 it attacked targets indiscriminately throughout the world (at the Munich Olympics, for example). "From 1974 to early 1979, the PLO concentrated more intensely on its political strategy as an additional means of attaining its objectives, and, seeking to appear in Western eyes as a suitable negotiating party, it reduced the scale of its spectacular terrorist activities on the international scene, although continuing its attacks inside Israel as before." The Israeli-Egyptian peace treaty in 1979 provoked renewed terrorism on an international scale, as the PLO's most vocal form of protest.

As I read on, the report began to turn its attention to the PLO's links with large numbers of foreign organizations. I saw the names of Latin America and Nicaragua, the Dominican Embassy in Bogotá. Close to home, I thought.

As Harel had said, ideology was not a controlling factor. Neo-Nazism and Marxism mixed easily in these circles. Western Europe suffered most from their atrocities because of its geographical proximity to the Arab-base nations.

Then I came to a statement that helped me to understand the situation. "The PLO has become a central factor in international terrorism and world-wide political extortion owing to a rare combination of financial and political support. . ." (p. 4). Money, the most essential ingredient, was coming from oil-rich Arab states. I was paying more for gasoline in order to finance terrorism against Israel and the West. In addition the PLO was accorded extra-territorial status (that means exemption from the application or jurisdiction of local law or tribunals) by Lebanon, South Yemen, Libya, Algeria, and Syria. These and other countries helped them out with passports, use of diplomatic pouches, and shelter.

Many other governments grant the PLO legitimate status within their borders when they feel compelled to do so in order not to offend Arab states and their diplomatic missions. Thus the PLO has opened offices in approximately seventy capitals around the world. Austria and Malta have, in fact, granted the PLO full diplomatic status. In other places they find diplomatic immunity in various Arab missions.

In an interesting subpoint, the report notes that the PLO "has contrived to exploit these sources of strength to further its aims in spite of the fact that it is a roof organization over eight groups which often feud among themselves violently, even slaughterously. Indeed, the internal differences between the components are turned by the PLO to its advantage, so that it can both practice terrorism and operate as a political group—to pose simultaneously as a strict adherent of its basic terroristic aims and as a factor seeking to moderate them" (p. 5).

At any rate, with the help it receives from others, the PLO can turn around and extend help to still others. One way they do this is by training terrorists in their camps to perform murder and sabotage more expertly. According to Robert Moss of the *London Daily Telegraph*, several hundred members of various organizations were undergoing training at the Al Fatah camp (Hamuriah Camp) in southern Syria in June of 1980. It was an international conclave of Germans, Italians, Japanese, Basques, Argentinians, Brazilians, Armenians, Iranians, Africans, and Filipinos.

Once a would-be terrorist gets his diploma from a camp like this one, he or she will go back to practice the trade nearer to home. And, if they encounter the authorities in the process, they can readily find refuge from them in one of these camps again. The people who assassinated Hans Schleier, the German industrialist, as well as Italian Premier Aldo Moro's murderers, found such refuge in Lebanon. Incidentally, this sort of thing has led to the formation of a special school in Summit Point, West Virginia. There Bill Scott, an ex-champion, Formula-Super-Vee race-car driver, trains chauffeurs and corporation executives to foil attempts to kill or capture them on the road. One of Scott's graduates, a corporate chauffeur, was confronted by a man pushing a rack of clothes across a downtown street in New York. His training taught him to be alert, so he was immediately suspicious. Instead of taking chances, he gunned his car onto the sidewalk to circumnavigate the obstacle, taking several parking meters with him. "It was not an attack," explains reporter Robert Wurmstedt. "Luckily no pedestrians were injured. Though trying to drive around a roadblock is the worst thing to do—it exposes you to broadside fire—the chauffeur's startled boss gave him a $5,000 bonus and paid for the parking meters" ("In West Virginia: Driving for Dear Life," *Time*, October 6, 1980, pp. 10, 15).

Back to the sands of the Middle East. The chief culprits among the nations who are presently sheltering terrorists are Lebanon, Algeria, and Libya.

When the PLO is not sheltering fellow terrorists, it might be joining them, for example, to sabotage the petroleum storage installation in Singapore in January, 1974. That was carried off by a joint squad of Palestinians and Japanese. The Entebbe highjacking was done by Palestinians and Germans.

Arms, money, lodging, and forged papers are also forthcoming from PLO stores to European and other terrorists. And, sometimes, one group will do another group's dirty work. It was Japanese terrorists who massacred the passengers at Lydda Airport in 1972 on behalf of George Habash's Popular Front for the Liberation of Palestine. The Wadie Haddad Palestinian terrorists, on the other hand, highjacked a Lufthansa jet for the

Baader-Meinhof German terrorists.

The Soviet Connection

The Israeli report may have been dryly written, but it was packed with information. Still, I knew I needed to learn more. The report had carefully refrained from mention of Soviet involvement. However, Benjamin Netanyahu, with his mane of white hair and piercing blue eyes, was not so reticent when I went to visit him. I have already listed his scholarly credentials, noted his brilliance, and related his vision and understanding of Soviet global aspirations in the second chapter. But now I want to dip into another part of our conversation the day I visited him in Israel. It began when I asked him to tell me about the Jonathan Institute.

"You have probably heard about the raid on Entebbe? Our son, Jonathan, led that raid and was killed in it. The institute is named after him. He was thirty years old.

"Neither I nor my family created the institute. Instead, many people, here and overseas, believed there should be a center devoted to the study and exposure of terrorism. They raised the money and they suggested that it be named in honor of our son. We, of course, were pleased and honored by their proposal, and we immediately joined in the effort wholeheartedly.

"And, since we started to study and pool our information, we have learned much. Terrorism is spreading around the world like a great disease. And the question we have kept asking ourselves is: Are all these numerous incidents of terror isolated or are they related in some way? Does terrorism just happen, much as grass appears after the rain? Or is it an organized movement performing the wishes of some superior group?

"So the Jonathan Institute convened an international conference in Jerusalem devoted to the study of international terrorism. It took place July 2-5, 1979. Fifty speakers from nine countries— people prominent in government, the news media, and academic fields—addressed the conference. We have already printed some of their talks in brochure form. There is one here that I think will interest you particularly."

He handed me a forty-eight-page pamphlet with a glossy cover simply designed in red and black. Its title: *International Terrorism:*

The Soviet Connection. It contained the brief speeches of seven men, two academicians, two writers, an Air Force general, and two politicians.

I was particularly impressed with the opening statement of still another document Netanyahu had handed me, a quote from Paul Johnson's *Seven Deadly Sins of Terrorism.* The quote could serve as an introduction to *The Soviet Connection.*

> Terrorism is not neutral in the political battle. It does not, in the long run, tend toward anarchy: it tends toward totalitarianism. Terrorism actively, systematically and necessarily assists the spread of the totalitarian state. The countries which finance and maintain the international infrastructure of terrorism—which give terrorists refuge and havens, training camps and bases, money, arms and diplomatic support, as a matter of deliberate state policy—are, without exception, totalitarian states. The governments of all these states rule by military and police force. The notion, then, that terrorism is opposed to the "repressive forces" in society is false—indeed, it is the reverse of the truth. International terrorism, and the various terrorist movements it services, is entirely dependent on the continuing good will and the active support of police-states. The terrorist is sustained by the totalitarian tank, the torture chamber, the lash and the secret policeman. The terrorist is the beneficiary of the Gulag Archipelago and all it stands for.

I turned to the first chapter, then, of *International Terrorism: The Soviet Connection,* "The Roots of the Involvement," by Professor Richard Pipes of Harvard University. He traced the birth of modern terrorism to the establishment in 1879 of an organization in the small Russian town of Lipetsk. It was called Narodnaya Volya, or "The People's Will." With only about thirty members, it decreed and plotted the murder of Czar Alexander II, which it accomplished on March 1, 1881.

There had been nothing quite like it before, explains Pipes, because they perceived that the enemy was not only the autocrats, but also the capitalists, the religionists, the law—the entire system and all that holds it together. Their efforts and those of their successors, Pipes claims, destroyed the awe with which the Russian people had regarded the regime and paved the way for the revolution in 1917. The Bolsheviks recognized this and have ever since maintained an ambivalent attitude toward terrorism. On the one side they oppose it because they are extremely vulnerable to it since their authority rests on the impression, held by the people whom they rule, that they are omniscient and omnipotent. On the other side it is a relatively inexpensive way of achieving their end, global domination. And, since they believe that the West's sources of power are in the Third World, they like terrorism because it works quite effectively in the Third World.

Because they are vulnerable to the effects of terrorism themselves and because they don't want to jeopardize their trade relations with the West—after all, much of their military supremacy can be attributed to systems they have developed as a result of acquiring American computers and the advanced American technology that went with it—the Soviet Union prefers not to identify with terrorism openly.

Brian Crozier points out that, "although Soviet spokesmen have condemned hijacking (presumably because the Soviet Union itself has suffered the inconvenience of this form of terrorism), the organs of Soviet power—in particular, the International Department of the CPSU's (Communist Party of the Soviet Union) Central Committee and the KGB—support many terrorist groups." They do it, he says, because it enfeebles non-Communist regimes. But they also support groups that are or might be critical of the USSR (e.g., the Baader-Meinhof gang) in order to make those groups dependent on them and perhaps eventually bring them under Soviet control.

The Russians are more open in their associations with local groups that can be successfully rated as "national liberation" groups. Otherwise, if supporting local terrorists would embarrass the local Communist Party, they keep their support for the terrorists quite secret, if possible. Thus, in Portugal, the local Communist Party can criticize revolutionary violence and appear to be a sober and responsible group which ought to be permitted to participate in government. And, still, the Soviets can quietly support the terrorists who work to destabilize the government.

Crozier describes the nature of the support. The big item is training. The Soviets have set up camps for this in Moscow, Baku, Simferopol, Tashkent and Odessa. Two streams of students come to study. The first are from orthodox Communist sources. The second is the national liberation stream. The Communists study for six months at the Lenin Institute in Moscow. The national liberationists start out in academic courses at the Patrice Lumumba People's Friendship University in Moscow. Then, those selected for terrorist training are sent to one or another of the camps to study agitation, propaganda, target practice, bomb making, sabotage, street fighting, assaulting buildings, and assassinating.

Then Crozier turned his attention to the Middle East. The Soviets had bestowed twelve billion dollars worth of military hardware on Libya. It was more than enough to equip every living creature in Libya a hundred times over. The probable purpose was to create a stockpile for dispersal to the PLO (this explains the satchels of money that the Iranian Jews in Tel Aviv told me about, which they say were taken to Libya by PLO men; it was evidently a shopping trip for weapons). Other recipients work in Japan, Turkey, Yemen, Iran, Lebanon, Eritrea, Chad, Chile, Uruguay, Nicaragua, and the Philippines.

Crozier sounded an especially somber note as he concluded. In 1974, he explains, the Soviets invited the PLO to open an office in Moscow, an honor they rarely accord to such groups and which bespeaks a long-term commitment. It corresponds to their invitation to the Viet Cong to do the same thing in 1964. That was, says Crozier, "the prelude to a massive commitment of Soviet arms to the Communist side, sustained until the defeat of the Americans and their South Vietnam allies in the 1970s" (p. 18).

Ray S. Cline of Georgetown University reviewed the "Strategic Framework" for the Soviet involvement in terrorism. He outlines the roles of the Communist Party of the Soviet Union, the Soviet Security Police (KGB), and the Soviet Military Intelligence (GRU). "Moscow," he says, "is evidently playing roulette with international terrorism, calculating on picking up some of the chips on the board from time to time and some day walking off with the whole board and everyone's chips" (p. 20).

Robert Moss spoke of signs that the most aggressive faction in the Soviet leadership—"the group that centers around Mikhail Suslov, Boris Ponomarev and certain elements in the KGB—has seized on the political uncertainty that stems from Brezhnev's failing health to promote a more adventurist line in dealings with the international terrorist movement" (p. 25).

Moss also observes that, because the PLO has become so closely linked with the Soviet Union, the "creation of an independent Palestinian Arab state on the West Bank under PLO domination would not simply constitute the addition of one more terrorist state to the already lengthy list: it would represent a quantum leap in the *capabilities of the international terrorist movement*" (p. 27).

Later I came across more evidence to support the statements of the men which were published in *The Soviet Connection*. On February 17, 1981, President Sadat told a press conference in Cairo that the PLO was entirely controlled by the USSR. In a recent broadcast, Radio Monte Carlo aired a report on PLO-Soviet ties by citing a lecture given by the PLO's representative in Moscow, Muhammad El-Shair. El-Shair made the following points:

1. PLO-Soviet relations are excellent and they maintain close political contact.
2. Many hundreds of PLO officers have been trained in Soviet military academies. (More than 2,000 PLO members are presently studying in the Soviet Union.)
3. The PLO enjoys special diplomatic privileges in the USSR.

Congressman Jack Kemp, who represents the thirty-eighth district in New York, says that the problem of international terrorism calls for a concerted effort by the United States, West Germany, Britain, France, Israel, and others "to take more direct, and where desirable, joint action against the Soviet Union and its conduits for terrorism" (*The Soviet Connection*, p. 33). He adds that, although few Western governments will acknowledge Soviet participation in terrorism in public, it remains a fact none of them can afford to ignore.

Maj. Gen. George J. Keegan, USAF, who was chief of Air Force Intelligence from 1972 to 1977 (the same man whose comments open the introduction on this book), notes that the Soviets have long regarded "terror on an international basis as the single most cost-effective adjunct to their global efforts" (p. 37). He cites Soviet documents in 1919, 1927, and 1929 which established guidelines for the covert establishment of revolutionary terrorism. The program of training guerrillas and terrorists got under way in Russia in 1932, and, by 1936, more than a hundred military academies and service schools featured courses designed for terrorists by the Lenin School of Revolution in Moscow. Stalin established the present system which "involves thousands of full time KGB, GRU and military personnel and the use of over 100 major facilities within the Soviet Union for training of foreign terrorists and cadre" (p. 38).

Sen. Henry Jackson reviewed the problem and asked, "What can be done?" He suggested five things. First, the Western democracies need to recognize that international terrorism is their collective problem. Second, these same nations must resist any efforts to define terrorism as some form of "freedom fighting" or "national liberation." Third, we ought to loudly expose the Soviets and others who sponsor terrorism. Fourth, the Western democracies must work together to apply sanctions against countries that help or harbor terrorists. Finally, each democracy needs to seek ways to combat terrorism within its own borders—ways that are consistent with our democratic principles.

Another document to emerge from the Jerusalem conference is *International Terrorism: The Darkening Horizon*. It reviewed many of the same things I had read in *The Soviet Connection* and it scored the press for being taken in by terrorist propaganda and, worse, for giving the terrorists so much media coverage whenever they managed to carry off some new outrage. Using the word "commando" instead of "terrorist" in the press aroused this pertinent response which was published in the *London Times* in 1973. "Those of us who had the honor of serving with them, and as guardians of their honored and distinguished record, deplore the debasement of the name [commando] as now applied by both the national press and radio to refer to any gang of politically motivated thugs of any nationality who resort to murder of innocent civilians by the most despicable means" (Anthony Smith, Honorary Secretary, Commando Benevolent Fund, April 17, 1973).

Elsewhere the booklet noted that ABC television had broadcast an hour-long study of PLO raids on Israel. During the program they made much of the "suicidal" nature of the "missions." However, during the entire hour they failed to mention that not one of these supposed missions was ever carried out against a military target.

But certainly the thing that pointed most disturbingly to a darkening horizon was a brief section of *International Terrorism*, entitled "Terrorism in a Nuclear Age" (pp. 29-30). It warned that terrorist arsenals are becoming increasingly sophisticated. They are already using heat-seeking, anti-aircraft missiles against civilian planes. At least fifteen light anti-tank missiles have been stolen from U.S. Army storage depots in Europe. A 1976 *Baltimore News* dispatch said terrorist groups were out shopping for nerve gas. *The Boston Globe* reported that U.S. postal officials had intercepted shipment of a nerve gas bomb.

Considerable amounts of strategic nuclear material have been reported missing in recent years. A congressional hearing uncovered the fact that several hundred Libyan students—10 percent of all Libyans studying in the United States—are majoring in nuclear sciences.

CIA and West German intelligence sources report that German terrorists were being trained in the use of chemical and biological warfare at PLO camps in the Middle East.

Perhaps the Soviet Union, its allies and some Arab states have recognized the truly global threat of equipping terrorists with nuclear, biological or chemical weapons of mass destruction. Nevertheless, there are national leaders who may indeed be prepared to hand over such tools of destruction. In any case, state support for international terrorism has opened a Pandora's box, and the demons unleashed may never be recaptured. (*The Darkening Horizon*, p. 30)

I didn't sleep well that night. I was almost sorry I had begun my quest for information. Now I was virtually overshadowed by an ominous sense of doom. What had started as a local fight in tiny Israel had surely fostered the spread of a disease around the world. Benjamin Netanyahu had not been exaggerating.

Everywhere I looked, some source of internal unrest—a feud that wouldn't have amounted to much in previous centuries— was being fanned by Soviet money, arms, and training (often channeled through the PLO) into a nasty and protracted conflict. Before we conclude this chapter, we need to review the extent to which this is happening around the world, sometimes unnervingly close to our shores.

A Crumbling World

Evidence is strong that the Puerto Rican nationalist movement is being renewed with the help of the Cubans. El Salvador is crumbling in the face of terror and insurrection. Nicaragua is long gone. And links between the victorious Nicaraguan Sandinistas and the PLO are assured.

Ireland has been in agony for a long time, but the stakes have grown higher now that Soviet arms shipments are arriving in the hands of the Irish Republican Army. Meanwhile, in Spain, Basque terrorists tie time bombs to the bodies of rich businessmen to secure ransoms for the safe removal of the bombs. Political violence took over a hundred lives in Spain in 1979, in spite of democratic reforms after Franco's death.

Italy is severely being rocked. Terrorist incidents occur as often as 300 times a week there. More than seventy prominent Italian leaders have been assassinated since 1977.

Turkey is still a member of NATO. In fact, its troops constitute the largest single unit on station in Europe today. It makes plenty of sense for the Russians to promote old Armenian grudges against the Turks. The plan has worked well. Thousands have died and the country may be on the verge of anarchy.

The stories of Iran—once the symbol of stability in the Middle East—and Afghanistan are too familiar to repeat. And we have reviewed the plights of Israel and Lebanon elsewhere in this book.

In the Western Sahara, Moroccan troops battle Polisaro guerrillas. After the Spanish left this region, Morocco and Mauritania divided this mineral-rich region between them. But Algeria and Libya spotted the local Polisaros and started shipping Soviet-made weapons to them.

Chad, a former French colony, lies directly south of Libya. Muslims in the north don't get along well with Catholics in the south. Naturally Colonel Qadaffi of Libya has been pleased to dispatch some of his arsenal into the hands of his fellow Muslims in Chad. Only the presence of French troops in the south kept the nation from being overrun. But, French determination to resist was not great. Qadaffi has gotten the upper hand and has already taken over Chad. It is amazing how the world press has kept this so quiet. A half-million-square-mile nation twice the size of Texas could never have been taken over without the assistance of the Soviet Union. The USSR has 3,500 Soviet and

East German advisors training the Libyans in the use of Soviet weaponry while Russian pilots show Libyans how to fly the latest MIG 25s and MIG 27s. Despite its size, Libya is becoming quite a powerful nation. Obviously twenty billion dollars in oil profits every year does help and so does the fact that this tiny nation sells 700,000 barrels of oil to the United States every day.

Ethiopia, now fully and openly backed by the Soviets, faces insurrection from Muslim separatists in Eritrea and guerrilla warfare in Ogaden, a district claimed by Somali tribesmen.

In Yemen the Communists in the south would surely love to absorb the U.S.-backed tribesmen in the north. The civil war drags on.

Uganda may be cooling down with the departure of Amin. However, we may rest assured that it will take long for the nation to heal from the wounds Amin inflicted.

In Angola, pro-Western UNITA forces still fight against Soviet-armed, Cuban-supported forces of the Marxist government. One may suspect UNITA gets a little help from South Africa.

Directly south of Angola is Namibia, where the South-West Africa People's Organization has battled for Namibia independence from South Africa for fourteen years.

Things are momentarily quiet—no headlines, at least—in Zimbabwe-Rhodesia. The Marxists have won the elections. Robert Mugabe is in power and South Africa watches warily. Zimbabwe will likely serve as a launching pad for terrorist raids headed south.

In Thailand government forces have battled for years against Chinese-supported rebels. Thailand's problems stemming from the Cambodian refugees may complicate this matter for them. And, in Cambodia, the Russians back the Vietnamese invaders while the Chinese back the ousted Pol Pot regime. It's something of a proxy war in which everybody loses. Prospects of famine are especially ominous.

In the Philippines, President Marcos is beset by lots of unrest, especially from Muslim insurgents in Mindinao. Funding, arms, and training from the PLO keep them going strong, utterly implacable in the face of Marcos's best conciliatory efforts.

Documentation is now available on PLO subversion in El

Salvador. On February 23, 1981, the U.S. Department of State released a report on Communist activities there: "DLU representatives also met with visiting PLO leader Yasir Arafat in Managua, July 22, 1980. Arafat promised military equipment, including arms and aircraft. (A Salvadoran guerrilla leader met with Fatah leaders in Beirut in August and November and the PLO has trained selected Salvadorans in the Near East and Nicaragua.)"

The Consulate General of Israel released a more detailed report on Soviet and PLO subversion in El Salvador. They pointed out that a delegation of members of "The League of February 23" (one of the leftist, subversive movements in El Salvador) visited Beirut in August, 1979, and met with the head of the Popular Front for the Liberation of Palestine, Dr. Habash, who promised them support and aid (*El Liwa*, January 21, 1981, Beirut).

The PLO News Agency, *Wafa*, reported in May, 1980, that a delegation "of the Revolutionary Coordination Council in El Salvador" had visited Lebanon at the invitation of the PLO and met with leaders of Al-Fatah, the Popular Front and the military wing of Fatah, who promised assistance in weapons, military equipment and training in order to aid the revolution in El Salvador. The Popular Front also promised its help in acquiring weapons.

In June, 1980, a group of Salvadoran underground fighters arrived in Lebanon for military training and this group was received by members of Fatah.

Where will it all end? The Russians are clearly out for big stakes. They stir unrest and conflict across the entire globe as they stand steely-eyed, watching the roulette wheel spin. How far can we go before the whole fabric of Western civilization begins to unravel? What would happen if a Qadaffi, or an Amin, or an Arafat actually got his hands on nuclear weapons?

The BBC aired a report in 1980 of its lengthy investigation into Pakistan's entry into the nuclear arms race. Funds for this inordinately expensive undertaking were traced straight to Colonel Qadaffi, who was also helping the Pakistanis get the uranium they needed from his Muslim neighbors in Niger. Of course, all that Qadaffi wants in return for his brotherly (the Pakistanis are Muslims, too) largess is an atom bomb or two.

On February 9, 1981, the Associated Press released an article entitled, "Soviets Supporting Revolutionary Movements, Turner Claims" (New York AP). The article reads:

A former director of the CIA says the Soviet Union is supporting revolutionary movements in Central America and other parts of the world, threatening the United States and its neighbors.

Adm. Stansfield Turner said Sunday the Soviets are "all over the world causing difficulties."

He blamed the Soviet Union for the "internationalization" of revolutions through connections with Libya—"a real troublemaker"—and sponsorship of the Palestine Liberation Organization.

Interviewed on CBS' "60 Minutes," Turner said the Soviets are helping the Libyans "in the supply or the sale of excessive amounts of military equipment, far beyond what the Libyans can possibly use on their own."

The excess, he said, is funneled through Cuba to revolutionaries in Nicaragua, El Salvador, Guatemala and other Central American nations.

"The Cubans don't have the resources to provide much of anything to anybody," said Turner, CIA director under the Carter administration. "They're getting that from the Libyans, from the Soviets, from others."

Expanding international terrorism is posing a great danger "to our friends" Mexico and South America, he said.

But he added that Soviet sponsorship of terrorism is worldwide, including that of "Moslem liberation groups in the Philippines."

Surely, if there was ever a time for serious alarm, it is now. The West must stand to form an unbreachable wall of denunciation and effective counteraction in order to preempt the Soviet-inspired international terrorism that menaces us all, especially Israel.

Will it happen? It is not guaranteed, but I refuse to accede to a helpless pessimism which says that people such as you and I can do little about it, that we must leave it entirely to the politicians. That is the counsel of passivity and defeat. The quiet waters of the American populace can still be aroused into a storm that will make the Soviets and their cronies quail. And what I say is not simply patriotic rhetoric. I believe Israel is the key to America's survival.

chapter 5

Jews

As a child, I often heard that expression "You Jew," or "What are you trying to do, Jew me down?" Obviously, it was a way of insulting another child in a schoolyard. But that's where it begins. And from a bunch of cruel, childish words it moves steadily to the kind of thing I was hearing on my car radio this morning—a bombed synagogue in Paris. Fatalities. Maybe I was dreaming; I turned up the volume. It had really happened and this was October 4, 1980, not November 9, 1938.

I was only mildly reassured when, in the next few days after that, I heard reports of massive demonstrations in the streets of Paris and other French cities to protest the bombing. Actually I had begun to grow alarmed during my research into the background of Yasir Arafat. He was clearly more of an anti-Semite than a nationalist. His uncle, it turns out, was closely associated with Hitler, insomuch that he directed the extermination of Jews in Bosnia during World War II. The Arabs had been openly sympathetic to Hitler during the Second World War. I had even come across Anwar Sadat's famous "letter to Hitler" reprinted in a collection of documents from the Fourth Conference of the Academy of Islamic Research. Sadat wrote the letter in 1953 for a Cairo weekly, *Al Musawwar*, which had asked him and several other Egyptian notables, "If you wished to send Hitler a personal letter, what would you write to him?" The first three sentences of Sadat's letter set the tone sufficiently: "My dear Hitler, I congratulate you from the bottom of my heart. Even if you appear to have been defeated, in reality you are the victor. You succeeded in creating dissensions between Churchill, the old man, and his allies, the Sons of Satan" *(Arab Theologians on Jews and Israel,* ed. D.F. Green, Editions de l'Avenir: Geneva, 1976, p. 87). "Sons of Satan" is a common and longstanding appellation for Jews among anti-Semites. I was told in Israel that Sadat had never repudiated his letter, even when embracing Menachem

Begin. This concurs with Joseph Churba's assessment of Sadat in *The Politics of Defeat*. Churba wrote, "A man of determination but proved tactical flexibility, Sadat, ever since his assumption of power upon the death of Nasser in September, 1970, has had as his foremost objective an Israeli return to the 1967 lines by one means or another. Far more than did his predecessor, Sadat focused on the United States to achieve his objective even as he moved on the parallel fronts of war and peace" (p. 129). A few paragraphs later Churba claimed that observers have "underestimated Sadat's capacity for duplicity" (p. 131).

At home I read the morning newspaper to get more information about the attack on the synagogue. It turned out not to be an isolated event. On February 23, 1979, the Bordeaux headquarters of the League against Racism and anti-Semitism had been sprayed with machine-gun fire, fortunately injuring no one. But a month after that someone hurled a Molotov cocktail into a Jewish old-age home in Paris. Thirty-two people were injured that day.

I tried to make sense of it. France had been the first country to authorize an open PLO information and liaison office within its borders. Could it be that French deference to the oil-rich Arabs had somehow created an atmosphere in which neo-Nazism might blossom anew? The more I had studied and read about the Middle East—the oil, the Arab-Israeli conflict, Soviet intentions, terrorism, Iran and Iraq, Egypt and Libya—the more my mind boggled at the impossible complexity of it all. All of us, not just the Russians, were standing around that roulette table, and none of us could predict with any reasonable degree of certainty where the little ball would be resting, if and when the wheel ever stopped spinning. In the face of such complexity and tensions, one's mind begins to search frantically for some simple solution— like anti-Semitism.

A friend sent me several copies of a little monthly tabloid out of Dandridge, Tennessee, called *The Battle Ax N.E.W.S.* All of them were loaded with anti-Semitism, talk of violence, racism, and lots of pictures from NEWS social events. NEWS stands for National Emancipation of our White Seed. The members wear paramilitary uniforms. In some of the pictures they were toting sixshooters on their belts. The articles were sprinkled liberally with Bible quotes.

I confess the whole thing was difficult to take seriously. These men represented a tiny lunatic fringe in our society, hardly the sort of thing to get unduly alarmed about. Or did they?

Maybe it was time to take another look right in my own American back yard. Things were changing for us more dramatically than ever before. Neither of the world wars had really touched our shores. Nor did they seriously damage our economics. Our strength and resilience had been unmatched by anything that tried to oppose us, until Vietnam and the ensuing inflation of the 1970s. At the opening of this ninth decade of the twentieth century, Americans could no longer take comfort in thoughts of our national imperviousness. The climate was right for a reaction that could include an outbreak of anti-Semitism.

It is especially sickening to know that clergymen are being used in a manner that could encourage anti-Semitism. On January 7, 1981, the Associated Press released the following article:

Clergymen Want Israeli Aid Cut

NEW YORK (AP)—About 400 American clergymen, including several bishops and some celebrities, are calling for the United States to reduce its aid to Israel because of alleged violations of human rights.

In a statement released Tuesday, the clergymen also said the United States and Israel should each open talks with the Palestine Liberation Organization.

The statement, whose signers included some previous critics of Israel, was to be delivered today to the Israeli Embassy in Washington, and sent to President Carter, President-elect Reagan and other officials.

It charges Israel with violations of various principles of the U.N. declaration of human rights on the occupied West Bank and in Gaza, including torture, annexation of territory, property seizure and destruction, arbitrary arrests and collective punishment.

Israel has denied such charges in the past.

Noting that Congress in 1975 prohibited economic aid to any country engaging consistently in "gross violations" of human rights, the statement said: "We . . . call upon our government to reduce aid to Israel until she recognizes the human rights of the Palestinian people."

Signers of the statement included four United Methodist bishops, two of them retired; a retired Episcopal bishop; and Antiochian Orthodox metropolitan, Philip Saliba.

Also, Catholic anti-war activist the Rev. Daniel Berrigan; his brother, ex-priest Philip Berrigan; and civil rights leader the Rev. Jesse Jackson, who have previously criticized Israeli policies.

The PLO has an agent who is working in Christian church circles in the United States. An old hand at Arab propaganda, Yusuf El Bandak influences American clergymen in behalf of Arab causes. He operates out of the Tunisian Embassy in Washington. His entire career has been marked by anti-Semitic activity and terrorism, and he has called for a "Christian crusade" against Israel.

It would even appear that the Pope himself, John Paul II, has, in some measure, been duped into becoming an unwitting spokesman for PLO propaganda. On October 5, 1980, during a homily delivered in Otranto, Italy, he said, "The terms of the Middle East drama are well known: the Jewish people, after tragic experiences connected with extermination of so many sons and daughters, driven by the desire for security, set up the State of Israel. At the same time, the painful condition of the Palestinian people was created, a large part of whom are excluded from their land. . . ." On December 20 of the same year, the Pope met with the minister of foreign affairs for Saudi Arabia, Saud Al-Faisal. The Vatican later issued a communique outlining their discussions of the Middle East, the Palestinians and Jerusalem. Saud informed the Pope of his government's concern "about the illegal action by which Israel annexed the Holy City." The Pope reiterated the Vatican's attitude of opposition to "any unilateral change in the political status of Jerusalem" in hopes that it would become "a meeting point of the three monotheistic religions—Christianity, Islam and Judaism."

In a similar vein, we need to take note of the Archbishop Hilarion Capucci affair. Israel sentenced the archbishop to twelve years in jail after they caught him smuggling arms for the terrorists in 1974. Pope Paul VI was able to secure his release by promising that he would refrain from further involvement in Middle East politics.

In 1978, however, the archbishop was in South America speaking out against Israel. Later he was involved in setting up the PLO office in Venezuela, much to the embarrassment of the Holy See. The archbishop denounced the Camp David Accords and, in January, 1979, he showed up in Syria to address a group of Palestinian guerrillas. Inquiries at the Vatican indicated that he was there without its permission. Nevertheless, the churchman has continued to travel widely and to espouse loudly the cause of the Palestinians. Recently, Michael Metrinko, former U.S. hostage in Iran, told of his Easter, 1980, meeting with Archbishop Capucci. When he tried to explain the treatment the hostages were receiving in Iran to the clergyman, Metrinko reported, "he [the archbishop] immediately gave me a lecture on America's support of Israel and that I am there [in Iran] because my 'government is a criminal government.' " As a matter of fact, in March, 1981, the Vatican Secretary of State, Cardinal Agostino Cassaroli, held an official reception for a PLO representative, Farouk Kaddoumi.

Such incidents as these coupled with total endorsement of the PLO by the Council of Churches, which rejects Jerusalem as the capital of Israel and does everything in its power to assist the PLO in obtaining their "human rights," are more disturbing to me than almost anything else I am observing in our society today.

But before I try to assess the present climate any further, we need to take a brief look at the past to get some idea of the history of anti-Semitism so that we can more readily understand what it means.

Bleeding Wafers and Plagues

Jews had been vilified in some so-called Christian writing during the first eight centuries of the common era as "the killers of Christ," as "degenerates," as "children of the devil." By the time of the Crusades, which began in 1096, the Jews entered the first period of ferocious and systematic anti-Semitism. It began somewhat casually. The knights on their way to fight the Saracens logically concluded it would only be right to do some damage to the infidels in their midst, the Jews. And so, the

Crusaders attacked Jewish settlements on their way east. It grew thereafter into something more intense and horrible, with full-scale massacres. These slaughters were often opposed by local burghers and churchmen, in vain nevertheless, since they were powerless in the face of the heavily armed Crusaders and the mobs who accompanied them.

One of the accusations often hurled at the Jews in medieval days was that of "ritual host murder." This meant that the Jews were supposed to have sneaked into a church and stolen the sacred wafers that had been consecrated by the priest for communion. The Roman church taught that such wafers were the true body of Jesus. Hence, the story goes, the insidious Jews would take the host (consecrated wafer) back to their synagogue and there cut it open with a knife. And, behold, when they did, it would bleed! This sort of superstitious fiction picked up on the more serious and longstanding accusation in the church that the Jews had killed Jesus. For most people, however, that was part of remote history. The "ritual host murder" stories had a way of bringing it close to home. And, occasionally, unsolved murders were blamed on the Jews, especially if it was near the time of Passover. In this case, the story was that the Jews had murdered the victim as a form of human sacrifice which they were alleged to practice in relation to Passover.

The Jews suffered severely again during the incredible rampage of the bubonic plague that devastated the population of Europe during the fourteenth century. Everyone sought an explanation for it. Some more thoughtful souls even surmised that a form of contagion was involved. But for the mass of the people, it was one of two things: the judgment of God or the work of the devil. Many went on to reason beyond that. If it was the work of the devil, then he would surely use evil men, particularly the Jews, to poison the wells. Greed often motivated this sort of thinking as much as or more than piety. Many who were members of churches, though they were not men of real faith, recognized that Jews were singularly vulnerable to extortion. The Crusaders had enriched themselves off the Jews in that way. The plague presented another opportunity to kill them in the name of God and, meanwhile, quietly collect their wealth. Churchmen might object, but the church's control of society was much less thoroughgoing than some historians would have us to believe.

In any event, out of two great upheavals in the eleventh and fourteenth centuries—the Crusades and the Black Death— serious anti-Semitism emerged with a life, a literature, and an art of its own that was to make a lasting impression on all of Europe, from Moscow to Brest. And thus it continued, somewhat dormant in its violent aspects, until the end of the nineteenth century.

It was at that time that Russia was undergoing enormous upheaval. Terrorists assassinated the Czar and the regime, aware of its enormous vulnerability, cast about for some way to focus public attention away from itself. Their answer was a series of systematic and deadly anti-Semitic pogroms that drove vast numbers of Jews to the shores of America. The history of Russian anti-Semitism is ancient and it continues to this day in quite the same tradition. Historians have often noted that the Soviets differ little from the Czars in the things that count. Thus it is not surprising that their policies represent a solid continuity.

It was in Germany and Central Europe that the most Jews had perished at the hands of the Crusaders. Therefore, when Germany suffered defeat in World War I and a subsequent inflation that dwarfs anything happening today (workers had to be paid daily in nearly worthless paper money which was disbursed literally in bushels), the resort to anti-Semitism was a well-established tradition. When the second blow of the Great Depression fell, it ushered in Hitler and his radical programs. Encouraged and spurred on by his demonic leadership, the latent forces of anti-Semitism came broiling to the surface as never before in the history of the world. To speak of the six million victims of Nazi anti-Semitism is impossible.

Nazi anti-Semitism reared its grotesque head in this century, wearing as usual, a Christian mask. The Nazis had no love for Jesus Christ. They used Christian slogans only to lend respectability to their program. But they themselves disdained Christianity almost as much as they hated Jews. They knew that membership in the Nazi Party and membership in the church were quite incompatible. Adolf Eichmann tells his experience in this regard.

When I first joined the Party they asked me to leave the Church, but I did not wish to do so. I remained a church member and did not at first see why I could not be a member both of the Party and the Church. I was married in the Church in 1935 and the Party was very angry. They became more and more opposed to my church attendance and insisted that I give up my membership. . . . Later I saw that there was a serious conflict between the Party belief and the Church. (*Struggle for a Soul*, pp. 34-35)

We can safely surmise something from this about the murderous anti-Semitism of the Crusades and the fourteenth century. The people who actually perpetrated the acts then were no more sincere and pious Christians than the Nazis of this century. They may have told themselves they were good Christians, as Eichmann did, but, in fact, they merely capitalized on the ill-advised remarks of some church leaders as a cloak for their greedy and murderous intents. So it was that Eichmann told his captors it was a source of great joy to him and that he would descend into his grave laughing to know that the deaths of five million Jews would be on his conscience.

Leon Poliakov remarks about the cry heard among the Crusaders, which said that they ought to start their work first among the infidels in Europe: "Especially for the scum that always rises to the surface during great revolutionary movements, it served as a pretext for easy and lucrative pillaging. Thus the perpetrators of the chief massacres of Jews were not the organized armies of the barons but the formless mobs that preceded them" (*History of Anti-Semitism*, Shocken: New York, 1974, p. 42).

I recognize that this review of the history of anti-Semitism doesn't even begin to sketch the shape of the beast, let alone give any kind of thorough picture. Because of the limitations of space I have sought only to select incidents which I trust, in the retelling, will evoke images that are generally accurate. I have limited myself to only the most extreme and bloody expressions of this malignancy, omitting such signal episodes as the Dreyfus case at the turn of this century in France or the eviction of the Jews from Spain in 1492. I do want, however, to remark on the experience of the Jews in America.

The Jew in America

Several Jews accompanied Columbus in his explorations of the

Caribbean, and twenty-three Jews arrived in New Amsterdam in the seventeenth century. Peter Stuyvesant, however, only tolerated them, denying them almost every conceivable sort of liberty. Nevertheless, Jewish population in the colonies grew. By 1664 they numbered 300, and by 1776, 2,500. Haym Solomon, as is fairly well known, helped immeasurably to finance the revolution.

What anti-Semitism there was, was mild in comparison to the experience of Germany and Russia. For example, small-minded accusations in the 1890s that no Jews had fought in the Civil War were readily rebuffed by a quick check of the facts. Really, the greatest threat to the Jewish community in the United States was that of assimilation. The absence of serious persecution, the generalized "melting-pot" milieu of the population, and the remarkable degree to which most people enjoyed genuine civil liberties all worked together to motivate many Jews to let down their guard, so to speak.

And that trend to assimilation only began to change with the enormous influx of Russian Jews after 1880. These people were foreigners in the most radical sense. The American response grew to first-class xenophobia. Nor were the Germans and Englishmen who constituted the bulk of the American Jewish community from the early nineteenth century altogether over-joyed at the arrival of their fellow religionists from Russia. The American Jews tended to favor Reformed and Conservative Judaism, free, as they saw it, of the superstitious and narrow practices of the Orthodoxy which the Russians practiced.

If anything, these new Russian immigrants were an embarrass-ment to the old Jewish community in America. Nevertheless, in time, the things that drew them together proved stronger than the things that drove them apart. And, acting somewhat like a catalyst was the increasingly unkind response of the American Gentiles. By 1900 the Jewish population in the United States had more than doubled. Before the coming of the Russians, it had numbered about 400,000. Now it stood at one million. By 1917, Congress had put the clamps on this immigration by the institution of quotas and literacy tests. With that the older Jewish community worked hard to apply pressure to reopen the doors at Ellis Island. They did manage to get the literacy test conducted in Yiddish and Hebrew, and to have the literacy requirement waived in the case of those who could prove they were fleeing from religious persecution. By 1920, the Jewish population in this country stood close to four million.

Thereafter, however, immigration trickled off to almost nothing. And American Jews began to hear rumblings of a more strident anti-Semitism. The Ku Klux Klan grew to enormous numbers in the 1920s, and Henry Ford sponsored a vicious collection of anti-Semitic tracts which he published in the *Dearborn Independent* between 1920 and 1927. Throughout the 1930s, pro-Nazi and anti-Semitic voices began to be heard in the land. Most notably there was Father Charles Coughlin. With him were men like Gerald L.K. Smith and Francis Townsend. Their followings were not small. The Great Depression represented enormously complex problems. When men like Coughlin and Smith criticized the Keynesian economics of the Roosevelt Administration, they were engaging in legitimate politics. But such talk was largely above the heads of their listeners who needed to think in simpler terms. Anti-Semitism was just the thing. So, Coughlin and others told them, it was the international Jewish bankers who were selling them down the river. Now there was something a man could get his teeth into.

Thus were American sensitivities to the dangers of anti-Semitism lulled. No one was proposing that we do anything so nasty as killing them. It just became fashionable to blame our problems on them.

Only the shock of the horror of the concentration camps—with newsreel footage of bulldozers filling mass graves with emaciated corpses—began to awaken Americans to the dangerous implications of what subtlety had been injected into their own system.

But today it would seem we need to learn that lesson more seriously. For once again we are in danger of being led by subtle diversions down that same path. The conditions are right. We are faced by frustrating problems as a nation, and as individuals. A malaise has come over us, a kind of mental depression on a societal level. And what is depression? Only anger which we think, truly or not, we have no safe way of venting. But this anger is looking for a way of release, and it will come out somewhere. It cannot be suppressed. We must stand up to the Arabs, who are soaking us for their oil, and turning us away from Israel. But the Arabs seem quite invulnerable. Likewise,

the Russians. Alas, who can we get our hands on? If we are not on
our guard against it, tradition will lead us back down the trail of
anti-Semitism just far enough so that we will stand by un-
concerned and unwilling to help while the Arabs try to finish in
Israel what the Germans began in Poland.

In fact, perhaps we are already doing that very thing to some
extent. On July 23, 1980, Yehuda Blum, the Israeli ambassador
to the United Nations, addressed the seventh emergency special
session of the General Assembly. The Arab delegates, of course,
promptly rose to their feet and walked out of the hall when Blum
came to the podium. They should have stayed to listen. If for no
other reason, they could have enjoyed the quiet humor Blum was
able to display as he ridiculed their incessant efforts to embarrass
and humiliate Israel in this international amphitheater. I quote
from his opening remarks:

Mr. President:
    Anyone reviewing the business of the United Nations
since the beginning of the year would be bound to conclude
that there are hardly any international crises, or threats to
peace and security in the world other than the Arab-Israel
conflict. The Soviet Union has withdrawn from Afghanistan.
Its troops have stopped slaughtering thousands of ordinary
Afghanis. Sweetness and light radiate from Southeast
Asia. There are no threats to the sovereignty, national
independence and territorial integrity of States in that
region. The huge flow of refugees from Vietnam and
Cambodia has ceased. A hundred and twenty thousand
individuals were not driven out in recent months from Cuba
and turned into refugees. All has been and remains quiet in
Africa, from the top to the bottom of that continent,
including the Sahara, the Maghreb and the Horn of Africa.
In the Middle East, there are no tensions between Iran and
Iraq. The two Yemens have been acting as model neighbors.
The Syrian army of occupation has pulled back from
Lebanon. Stability and tranquility reign in the north of that
war-torn country. International terrorism, with its concomi-
tant features of indiscriminate murder and the taking of
hostages, has been brought under control. Apparently,
were it not for Israel, international harmony would reign

all over, and it is only Israel that prevents the advent of the Messianic era.

Indeed from the apparent dearth of emergencies throughout the world, the outside observer might even conclude that the human condition is a happy one. But, as we all know, nothing could be further from the truth. When one looks at the vast assemblage of nations gathered here and tries to compute the sum total of human misery that most of them represent, one is forced to a quite different conclusion. Indeed, as one contemplates the very real threats to the existence of literally hundreds of millions of human beings, the wars, the lack of freedom, the brutal suppression of minorities, the mass death sentences, the persecution and torture of dissidents, the cruelty and the degradation, the disease, the malnutrition and the poverty in the world today, one can only conclude that the lawless majority in this Assembly shamelessly turns its back on the real problems facing mankind by indulging so much of its time in barren anti-Israel exercises.

The fact is, Mr. President, that many of the States represented here regularly violate every human standard and international norm in the conduct of their affairs, both domestic and external. They regularly practice every crime that they mendaciously attribute to Israel, but the Assembly is not convened into Emergency Special Session. The international crimes and the threats to peace persistently perpetrated by totalitarian and dictatorial regimes which rush to harrass Israel are legion, yet the General Assembly passes over them in silence.

The reason for this hypocrisy, cynicism and bias is not hard to explain. In everything to do with the Arab-Israel conflict, a majority of this Assembly lets itself be led—in some cases willingly, in others under duress—by a coalition of extreme Arab States, in conjunction with the Soviet Union, its satellites and the radicals in the non-Aligned Group of Countries.

Virtually all of the Arab States are still obsessed with Israel. Most of them still refuse to recognize Israel and its right to exist. Most of them are still committed to the destruction of Israel, and to the use of "all means" to achieve that objective. Among those "means" are the manipulation of this organization, the monopolization of its time, the abuse of its means and machinery, and even the harnessing of the Secretariat, so that the whole UN system can be exploited in the relentless Arab campaign of political warfare against Israel. What is happening here in this session, and for that matter what is happening at the UN World Conference on Women in Copenhagen, are only the latest manifestations of the ceaseless Arab warfare against Israel.

The United Nations has become, quite literally, a forum for the expression of anti-Semitism. The vocabulary may be altered slightly with the usage of words like "Zionist" and "Israel" instead of "Jew," but the intent is the same. And what has been our government's official response to all this? I asked John Hirsch at our State Department to answer that question. He gave me a lengthy explanation for a somewhat generalized policy of abstention. I'll try to paraphrase it in capsule form. Our government, he said, is committed to a negotiated settlement of the Arab-Israeli conflict. It is, therefore, opposed to any acts or resolutions in the United Nations or elsewhere that might be construed as unilateral or one-sided. Since the Arabs promote unilateral resolutions in the United Nations which tell Israel to get out of the West Bank or condemn it for occupying Arab territory, and since the Israelis act unilaterally by building settlements in the West Bank, our government wouldn't want to appear to be taking sides, so we abstain.

Our commitment to a negotiated settlement sounds very reasonable and even-handed. But it is based upon the assumption that each side in the conflict is essentially sincere and imbued with goodwill. Such an assumption is unwarranted.

The net effect has been that our government has stood by and abstained time and time again in the face of anti-Semitic thrusts in the United Nations. Are we not, then, fast developing a posture of unconcern and unwillingness to help as the Arabs muster their forces to complete Hitler's "final solution"?

Franklin Littell recalls the sorry witticism about a Berlin resident who remarked to a friend in 1935 that he "missed the good old-fashioned anti-Semitism." Surely in the face of the Nazi atrocities that were already beginning to take place in 1935, one might have longed for the "gentlemanly anti-Semitism" of former days.

Nevertheless, it is precisely that soft anti-Semitism of religious and culturally refined people which, we have seen, prepares the way for the murderers and thugs. The great danger to Jews in our society is not the lunatic fringe members of National Emancipation of our White Seed in east Tennessee. It is instead the fuzzy thinking of our policy at the United Nations that fails to notice insidious anti-Semitism because it's so concerned about unilateral actions.

A former congressman who asked me not to use his name told me, "Mike, in-depth polling shows that, while they wouldn't talk about it publicly, two-thirds of the people in America think the left-wing Jews are ruining the country, morality-wise." I shuddered. We have not yet really taken to heart the lesson of the Holocaust.

The list of atrocities related to the Holocaust becomes increasingly disgusting and barbaric. But we must not shrink from at least a partial list of them. We have to speak up in the face of those who would acquiesce to anti-Semitism at the United Nations, or wherever it might spring up. Those who claim to be Christians must not allow liberal church groups, which have actually become so deceived that they believe raising money for the PLO is an act of Christian charity. This fact came to my personal attention through a man who found himself on an airplane, sitting next to a courier who was transporting money raised from a church group to help the Palestinian refugees. Little did they know that that money would probably end up buying arms with which to kill women and children in Israel.

I'm really not overly concerned about another Holocaust in America. I don't believe that type of thing is going to happen. But the thing that concerns me most is the subtle religious anti-Semitism that takes place in the name of Christian love. This I believe is the most dangerous because it appeals to the emotions and can turn an individual away from a strong commitment in behalf of Israel under the guise of "human rights" and the love of Jesus.

Let me show what I mean by citing part of a letter I received from the American Arab Anti-Discrimination Committee. The lady who wrote the letter claims to be a loving Christian. "Your witness to the need for love in the war-torn Middle East is quickly tarnished by the claim that God's attention is reducible to financially supporting the modern political state of Israel. How many times I have felt my soul wrench at how easily Christian faithful make the facile transposition of biblical Israelites into the present-day rulers of the state of Israel. Old Testament covenants and blessings are conveniently yanked into the twentieth-century political arena of the modern Middle East—right past the gaze of the Church, the body of the very Savior who preached a new covenant: of the unconditionality of love, of the challenge to forgive, and of the universalization of God's chosen people.

"What should disturb us most is the uncritical and unchallenging Christian view that since the political/secular ideology of Zionism took its symbolism from Scripture, and its state's name from the twelve tribes, that it automatically qualified to fulfill the God-centered 'consecrated nation.' Or, that since the Israeli army occupies Jerusalem, the Holy City is only *now* holy. I challenge you, lovingly, to examine the worldly manifestations of the Israeli state that defy its claim to be the Spirit-filled nation of God. Accompany one Israeli soldier on his daily round of duty on the occupied West Bank and assess for yourself how pleasing are his actions to the Prince of Peace. Witness the expropriation of a Palestinian family's home and farm, or the collective humiliation of the men and boys of an Arab village by Israeli soldiers or settlers, and assess for yourself how this fulfills God's sacred covenant.

"Perhaps you are now convinced that I must be an anti-Semite, or oblivious to the historical tragedy that befell the Jewish people of Europe forty years ago. Perhaps you wonder why I dare challenge the commonly held Western Christian support for the Israeli state. I dare to challenge this support because I have witnessed the un-holy violence that political Zionism has bred in its creating an exclusionist state. I have witnessed the horrifying instant-replay of a tortured people slowly wielding the instruments of torture. I have seen the results of official and unsanctioned displacement of villages, towns and cities of Palestinian families, the uprooting of generations of a proud, simple people, all in the name of my God. I have witnessed the testimony of young Israeli soldiers confessing their moral agony over the orders they must follow to maintain national security among the people whose land they now control by rule of the gun. I have read in the eyes of mothers—both Israeli Jews and Palestinian Arabs—the pain of unknown futures for their children, reflecting the sickness which military occupation has spread into the souls of all their children."

The letter reflects a subtle anti-Semitism that is often masked by a profession of Christian love. It overlooks God's special commitment to Israel and the need to stand with the nation He established. We must be careful to avoid this kind of mistake.

chapter 6

Arab Blackmail

Following the defeat of their invading armies in the disastrous Yom Kippur War of 1973, Arab leaders met in Kuwait to lick their wounds and formulate still another strategy in their unending battle against Israel. They were well aware that the Jewish forces were rescued from annihilation by the action of the United States, which organized and operated the largest airlift in history. That fragile flow of supplies and military materiel was the lifeline that kept the small but ferocious Israeli war machine in action, and once again cheated the Arabs of victory.

Angry and grim, the Arabs announced the formation of a united front against Israel and vowed to punish the Western nations whose "meddling" had spoiled their plans. "Starting now," they declared, "we will unsheath the sword of oil."

A new era of political warfare began with the first oil embargo and massive price increases.

In their first battle using the new weapon, the Arabs won! A nation of American drivers lined up to pay inflated prices for rationed supplies of gasoline. The stock market shuddered and sank to its knees. Industries cut back, shut down, and laid off workers. Western powers reconsidered decisions not to sell arms to Arab nations. The so-called Palestine Liberation Organization was hurriedly recognized at the United Nations.

Smiling and cheerful in the exhilaration of their newly discovered power, leaders of nineteen Arab nations flew to Morocco to plan their next strategy. What they came up with was a new world monetary system whose primary currency would be "petrodollars." Again they proclaimed their new policy to the world. From that point on, they said, all oil-and-monetary negotiations with consuming nations will be inseparably linked with "other issues."

Among those "issues" were: lower prices for Western goods and services; and "full Israeli withdrawal from our territory."

105

Since that time, the Arabs have fought their new quiet war in board rooms, on campuses, and in government suites. They have bided their time, patiently working to exert control and influence in a wide range of situations, and buying controlling leverage over Western business and government figures with an inexhaustible supply of petrodollars. A marvelous example of this is Japan. In 1980 third and fourth quarter increases in deliveries from both gulf states raised their share of Japan's oil imports from 37 percent to 52 percent. It also sharpened Japanese anxieties over peace and stability in the region in 1980. More than 70 percent of Japan's total oil imports pass through the Strait of Hormuz, so now out of Tokyo are coming special meetings with Arafat, including declarations that peace in the Middle East cannot be achieved without a solution to the Palestinian problem. The foreign minister of Japan, Masayoshi Ito, stated in October that Israel must recognize the PLO's rights. The Japanese met with Yasir Arafat on December 13, 1980, and with Anwar Sadat on December 17, 1980.

Ironically, by limiting the supply and increasing the price of oil, the Arabs have used our own money to acquire their new position of power and influence. The citizens of the West contributed to their cause each time they filled up their automobiles with gasoline.

In a very real sense, the two great weapons in the Arabs' war against Israel and the West are the vault and the valve. Every week that passes places the nations of the West more and more at the mercy of the Arab League because of their money-filled vaults and their control of the shut-off valve to the flow of oil. We are seeing the evolution of a kind of warfare that might be termed econo-conflict. As one observer and analyst has noted, "What the Arabs failed to do with their tanks and troops, they are now attempting to do in board rooms and brokerage houses. They are continuing to battle Israel by applying pressure on its allies—and never firing a shot."

A former high official in two U.S. government agencies, who is now an international trade consultant, compared the development of this new war strategy to the sad experience of America at Pearl Harbor. Speaking off the record to a Philadelphia investigative reporter, he said, "Just prior to World War II, there was a controversy over the question of using airplanes and aircraft carriers as primary weapons of war. It had never been done and Americans did not want to think about the crazy idea. . . ." The official said that for years the American military ignored the controversy and simply did nothing. "We sat there, confident in our own battleships, and watched the horizon for the enemy battleships to come—because that is how war had always come in the past."

But, as everybody knows, Pearl Harbor changed all that. In a matter of hours, a handful of planes crippled much of the U.S. Navy and forced America to take note that the art of war had changed—battleships did not matter so much any more. The official shook his head sadly and exclaimed, "You see, it took a catastrophe to bring home that simple realization."

He followed up his point by observing that the old heads of the Jewish movement in Washington are still thinking in old terms— still watching the horizon for the next wave of Arab tanks to come. But that is not how the Arabs are operating now. The weapon now is money.

The unspoken moral to his story might well be expressed by saying, "Let's hope it does not take another catastrophe to wake us up this time."

During the past six years, Arab nationals have been involved in hundreds of billions of dollars worth of financial activity. Arab officials, operators and entrepreneurs have bought their way into America's highest social, financial, military, and political circles. No one is sure exactly how extensive the Arab holdings are because of the tight cloak of secrecy they have drawn about their activities. Another hindrance is the lack of federal laws requiring the recording or disclosure of such investments. Also, the Arabs often hide their identity as investors by hiring local "front men" to represent them, or by "washing" their money through complex webs of multinational corporations.

But more and more often, when they wish, the Arabs can make their presence felt. The amount of pressure they can bring to bear can often be devastating.

A special report, *The Arab Takeover* (Jewish Press), dated July 11, 1980, revealed that Libya was involved in Idaho. It also revealed the involvement of petrodollars with political leaders and corporations, who are cooperating to some degree with the Arab world, and have a lot to lose by being overly sympathetic to Israel.

Late in 1976, Sen. Stuart Symington was part of a five-member subcommittee investigating foreign deposits and their possible influence over the U.S. banking system. As the subcommittee prepared to subpoena records of American banks, they were warned not to continue their investigation by representatives of Kuwait and Saudi Arabia. The two countries said they had about eleven billion dollars in American banks, including well over seven billion dollars in short-term deposits. They threatened to transfer the money immediately to European institutions if the Senate probe continued. Such a move would have crippled and possibly even collapsed the entire Federal Reserve System.

The subcommittee backed down, explaining that they really had no choice. Senators Frank Church of Idaho and Clifford Case of New Jersey were in favor of forcing the issue. But Symington and Charles Percy of Illinois felt that it was "simply not worth the risk."

Interestingly enough, Stuart Symington later became a registered foreign agent for Saudi Arabia, Kuwait, and Abu Dhabi, as well as for some individual Arab investors like the former director of the Saudi Arabian Intelligence Agency. He represents the financial interests of his clients as they purchase interests in American banks.

Frank Church, on the other hand, once said, "We have had our neck in the OPEC noose since 1973, and thus we tend to catch cold whenever the Saudis sneeze." He was regarded as one of the most powerful men in Washington for many years, and bumped heads with the Arabs on several occasions. As chairman of the Senate Foreign Relations Committee, he consistently opposed moves to sell sophisticated military hardware to the Arabs. He led the fight against the controversial sale of F-15 fighter planes to the Arabs. He also held up granting the export license Libya needed to add five C-130 Hercules planes, two 727s, trucks, and spare parts to the two-billion-dollar weapons arsenal the country had purchased from Russia, which included 100 MIG jets.

Although I, like, many conservatives, do not support Frank Church because of his liberal position on many issues, I certainly found agreement with him on one important point—his strong stand in behalf of Israel.

Failing to persuade Church and his committee to change their

minds, the Arabs set out to neutralize or destroy the senator in
his home state of Idaho. First, Kuwait bought one of the largest
land and cattle companies in the sparsely populated state. Then
Libya moved in with ingratiating charm and fat bankrolls. A
seven-member trade delegation toured the state, talking about
their desire to buy huge quantities of local products and how
difficult Senator Church was making it for their country by holding up delivery of their cargo planes.

Three separate expenses-paid junkets to Libya for Idaho officials, farmers, and educators were set up for the stated purpose
of discussing the possibility of new trade programs.

Arab officials arranged to buy some forty million dollars worth
of wheat, and expressed interest in buying Idaho corn, soybeans,
and lamb products. They announced their intention to give the
University of Idaho an agricultural studies grant of $500,000.
And Libya suggested to the state's most powerful political group,
the 22,000-member Idaho Farm Bureau, that it might consider
locating its U.S. trade mission office in Boise if the nation felt
"welcome."

Charles Percy of Illinois, mentioned already in the introduction to this book, succeeded Church as chairman of the Senate
Foreign Relations Committee. Percy, when he was in Moscow in
November, 1980, told the Russians that he favored a Palestinian
state with Yasir Arafat as its ruler. *The New York Times* quoted
him as saying, "This would permit Arafat to realize his wish to
be a chief of state before he dies."

Libya's courtship of influential American businessmen and
government-connected figures gained considerable notoriety
during the so-called "Billygate" scandal during the 1980 presidential election campaign. News reporters discovered and made
known that President Carter's brother, Billy, had become increasingly involved with the Libyans, hosting the visit of an
Arab "trade delegation" to Georgia, accepting two expenses-
paid trips to the North African nation to discuss setting up a new
American corporation using Libyan money, and receiving a
half-million-dollar "loan" and other personal gifts.

Arab petrodollars have also been spent to retain the "services"
of the firms of numerous other public figures and former top
government officials. The list includes: John Connally, former
secretary of the treasury; Spiro T. Agnew, former U.S. vice

president; J. William Fulbright, former U.S. senator and chairman of the Senate Foreign Relations Committee; Clark Clifford, former secretary of defense; Richard G. Kleindienst, former U.S. attorney general; Richard P. Helms, former director of the U.S. Central Intelligence Agency and U.S. ambassador; Raymond Close, former CIA station chief in the Middle East; John O'Connell, former CIA station chief in the Middle East; Frederick G. Dutton, former assistant secretary of state; Linwood Holton, former assistant secretary of state; Willis C. Armstrong, former assistant secretary of state; Gerald Parsky, former assistant secretary of the treasury; Patrick Caddell, close friend and pollster for President Carter; Crawford Cook, close friend of the American ambassador to Saudi Arabia, John West; and many others (*The Arab Takeover*, Jewish Press, July 11, 1980).

A veteran Washington observer said recently, "The Arabs have become a major force in Washington. A few years ago their lobby was a joke—they didn't know what they were doing. The progress they have made is incredible. They are now well organized, highly polished and—it goes without saying—extremely well-financed. They have good staff people who deliver well-documented position papers. They also have some dynamic law firms and former Hill people—ex-senators, representatives, and aides—pounding the drum for them."

During the controversial F-15 debate, which involved the issue of linking all arms sales to Israel with an equal sale of the same equipment to Arab states, the experienced and formidable Jewish lobby came head to head with their Arab counterparts in one of the first all-out tests of strength. And the Arabs won. The vote was 55-54. It was a major victory because it clearly demonstrated that the Arabs now have the know-how and connections to affect the passage of legislation.

And they also have the clout—the bargaining pressure points that can no longer be ignored! Members of the U.S. Congress are constantly aware of the ever-present Arab threat. If they want to keep the oil flowing and the money supply stable, they have to take a careful look at American relationships with all Arab countries. They can't move on any issue involving the Middle East until they take Arab oil money into account.

There is an interesting side note regarding the U.S. effort to achieve "balance" by selling an equal number of F-15 jets to

Israel and Saudi Arabia. With the fall of the regime of the Shah
of Iran, Khomeini pledged full support to Arafat's PLO campaign
to destroy Israel. Part of that support involved all the American
weapons the new Iranian government had inherited, including
a fleet of F-15s. Overnight the balanced shifted in favor of the
Arab League.

Again and again, the motivation and purpose of Arab financial
transactions can be linked back to their unrelenting hatred of
Israel and their avowed intention to hurt and destroy the Jewish
state by every means available. Their diabolic plans are often
aided by the avarice and greed of individuals and corporations
within the Western community of nations.

For example, arms and munitions manufacturers are eager to
supply large quantities of modern weapons to the armies of the
world. If they can sell to their own governments, they bask in the
glow of feigned patriotism and count their money. If their own
government is not buying, then they must look around for other
paying customers. Far too often the conditions of the sale are
dependent not on the intended use of the arms but on the amount
of money the potential purchaser is willing to pay.

Enterprising Arab representatives agree to find customers
for the weapons manufacturers, and they bring the vast oil profits
of the Arab countries to bargain with as they outfit entire armies.
Then they charge the manufacturing firms hundreds of millions
of dollars in "commissions" for arranging the deals.

What happens to the "commissions"? They are used to buy up
America! Literally. The money is used to acquire ownership
or controlling interest in billion-dollar banks, office buildings,
hotels, manufacturing plants, construction companies, cattle
ranches, farms, financial brokerage houses, etc.

One such Arab entrepreneur is a man named Adnan Khashoggi, who had close personal ties to the Saudi Arabian royal court.
In fact, it is said that this man carried a personal message from
King Faisal to President Richard Nixon in the October, 1973,
war. This message asked that America stop the airlift and stay
out of the Arab-Israeli conflict. Nixon ignored the request (*The
Arab Takeover*, Jewish Press, July 11, 1980).

Khashoggi established himself as a multimillionaire by setting
up billion-dollar military equipment sales between American
and European manufacturers and Saudi Arabia. He became a

prime channel for the sale of HAWK missiles made by the Raytheon Corporation. Pentagon files indicate that he received as much as forty-five million dollars at a time in commissions from various American companies.

Khashoggi set up the world's first Arab multinational corporation, Triad Holding Company, and began to purchase banks, ranches, businesses, and real estate. He also set up offices and homes in California, Arizona, New York, Geneva, London, Beirut, Riyadh, Jeddah, Brazil, and Indonesia.

In 1974, he was opposed during a takeover attempt of a three-hundred-million-dollar bank in San Jose, California. Calling himself a spokesman for the Arab world, Khashoggi threatened that if the "fanatics" who were blocking the sale of bank stock to him did not give in, the flow of Arab oil money into the American business community would stop. When he was still refused, he charged that he had been the victim of "a Zionist-inspired wave of anti-Arab hatred."

Since that time, Khashoggi has continued his financial activities and acquisitions. He bought a 7,000-acre ranch in California, acquired another bank, and formed an investment company as a front for further investments in fifteen San Francisco-area companies. He also set up an agency on the campus of a California college, purportedly to "train banking and finance experts for developing nations."

His company has been involved in an investigation and legal action regarding investment fraud schemes in connection with a forty-million-dollar townhouse and industrial park development project. And in 1975, he was personally subpoenaed by Frank Church's Senate subcommittee on multinational corporations—in an investigation of bribes.

This is the activity of just one man, representing just one of the twenty-one Arab countries. There are no doubt hundreds—perhaps thousands—of other such representatives funneling Arab money into the country to buy influence and control.

The Arab investments have also been channeled into stocks, bonds, and commercial paper investments. Treasury Department records indicate that Arab investment in U.S. bonds, bills, and notes soared from $2.2 billion to $10.7 billion in a two-year period. Nontreasury stock holdings went from $365 million to $1.4 billion, and other bond purchases went from $685 million to

$1.7 billion in a four-year period ending in 1977. Of course, these figures include only those transactions which can be traced directly to Arab investors and may be only a small portion of the total amount involved.

Based on studies of economic trends and indicators over the past several years, bureaucratic and independent economists have concluded that the Arabs have invested in excess of fifty billion dollars in the United States in the last five years. Of course, only a small part of this can be identified, the rest having been surreptitiously invested through subsidiary corporations. No one can be sure what vital American interests are even now controlled by Arab funds.

But some of the things we do know are alarming. For example, the Federal National Mortgage Association, with forty billion dollars in assets and the sixth largest corporation in America, is the major supplier of home mortgage loan money in the country. The largest holder of financial "paper," or notes, for that association is Saudi Arabia.

The Arab petrodollar strategy also involves a "linkage" program designed to draw segments of top U.S. industry close to Arab governments. Is it working? New studies show that just before the 1973 Middle East war, U.S. exports to Arab countries were less than one billion dollars a year. By the end of 1978, that figure had jumped dramatically—to more than fifteen billion dollars.

Also, there are now 167 dues-paying members of an organization called the Arab-American Association for Commerce and Industry, which represents the member nations of the Arab League. Who are the American member companies? Eighteen of the top one hundred defense contractors, including Western Electric, Westinghouse, and General Electric; twenty-one of *Fortune* magazine's list of the top one hundred U.S. corporations, with combined annual sales totaling 400 billion dollars—companies like the Ford Motor Company, IBM, ITT, Union Carbide, and U.S. Steel; and ten of the nation's top twenty banks, with combined assets of about 280 billion dollars, including the Bank of America, Chase Manhattan, and Bankers Trust Company (*The Arab Takeover*, Jewish Press, July 11, 1980).

Arab "linkage" programs have also been extended to American colleges through educational grants and endowments. This kind of activity has increased tenfold since 1973 as at least seventy-five universities and colleges have accepted gifts from Arab states. But the gifts always came with strings attached—usually the requirement being the establishment of an "Arab Studies" program.

When the University of Southern California accepted a million-dollar gift from Saudi Arabia to fund a professorship in Arab studies, the school had to agree to allow the Saudi government to approve the instructors chosen for the program (*The Arab Takeover*, Jewish Press, July, 11 1980).

An Arab-endowed $1.5 million grant to MIT for engineering studies of problems in desert societies stipulated that no Jews be allowed to work on the program. When MIT refused to sign the agreement, the Arabs hired away all the non-Jewish MIT experts they needed to set up the program as a private business.

On February 23, 1981, Georgetown University returned to the government of Libya a gift of $600,000 it had received to finance a professorship in Arab studies. Georgetown's president, the Rev. Timothy S. Healy, cited their reason for returning the gift as follows: "Libya's continued accent on violence as a normal method of international policy and its growing support of terrorism as a tool of government has made it increasingly impossible for Georgetown University to feel comfortable in having its name associated with the Libyan Government."

Nonetheless, Georgetown has held on to various donations from other countries in the Middle East. These nations include Kuwait, the United Arab Emirates, Oman, Egypt, Jordan, Qatar, and Saudi Arabia.

The University of Texas received a three-year grant from Libya to support programs in its Center for Middle Eastern studies. This grant expired last year.

The University of Michigan is another institution that has received money from Libya. To conduct summer institutes in 1978 and 1979, Michigan accepted approximately $90,000 from the government of Libya.

It has become increasingly obvious that the Arabs look upon all business deals and "linkages" as direct political tools. They have become very straightforward in asserting this principle. In an editorial in *Middle East* magazine in October, 1978, the editors declared: "The day when you can do business with the

Arab world and not take note of what they believe in and fight for has long gone. The Arab world is sufficiently strong today not only to fight for what it believes in, but to expect that its friends and allies will stand up and be counted."

The editorial went on to say, "Today, politics and economics not only mix, but are totally interdependent. There is a consensus among the Arabs that to do business with the Arab world means taking a political stand not incompatible with Arab interests and legitimate rights."

If that statement sounds suspiciously like a threat, it is only because it is meant to. The Arabs feel they now are in a position to blackmail the rest of the world into agreeing to any demands or terms they wish. And they are already making demands on a regular basis.

We've already examined some of the ultimatums handed to the United States relative to banking regulations and trade agreements. But America is not the only Western nation facing such Arab pressures. Walter J. Levy, probably the leading oil expert in America, wrote an article in *Foreign Affairs* magazine which stated that one by one, oil-importing countries are succumbing to the blackmail terms of OPEC for continued oil supplies.

Levy noted that the demand included: "more and more political and other extraneous conditions, related, for instance, to the interest of the producing countries in the Palestinian problem, or in their nuclear capabilities, or in the political postures of their governmental customers."

As a direct result of Arab pressure, the members of the European Economic Community are now calling for "association" of the PLO in the peace process. France had been forced to offer Iraq enough high-quality uranium to enable that radical regime to manufacture nuclear weapons by July, 1981; but on Monday, June 8, 1981, Israeli fighter bombers, in a daring strike 600 miles into Arab territory, destroyed Iraq's nuclear reactor Osiris, named after an Egyptian god.

Denmark capitulated to the insulting and humiliating demands of the Saudis that they agree, in an oil contract, to language that forbids the Danes to criticize any of the customs or political actions of that supersensitive country.

What are the "Arab interests and legitimate rights" which they refer to so often? Make no mistake about it—to the Arab that phrase is synonymous with the annihilation of Israel. To them, coexistence is not a viable option. Even the partition of Israel's already-small territory to allow a Palestinian Arab state would not be acceptable for long.

The poorly kept secret that two dollars from the sale of each barrel of crude oil purchased from Saudi Arabia by the Western powers is donated to the PLO to support and further their stated goals is evidence of the Arab's true design. With their own extensive land holdings in the region and their unlimited oil wealth, the Arabs could long ago have resettled all of the refugees and solved the Palestinian problem once and for all. Their constant and continuing exploitation of the human suffering of the so-called refugees for political purposes is the most cruel kind of hypocrisy.

Yet, Arab leaders like Saudi Arabia's foreign minister, Prince Saud al-Faisal, continue to parrot the official line endlessly. A recent article in *National Geographic* quoted him as saying, "The thing that prevents this being a stable region is the Israelis' occupation of Palestinian and Arab territories and the making of refugees. This has created the turmoil in the Middle East. The United States has a responsibility to resolve the issue with justice, not on the basis of what Israel will accept. Israel cannot continue to refuse to allow Arabs to return to their homes. What is meant by 'the commitment of the USA to Israel'? Is it a commitment to continued Israeli occupation of Arab lands, or to the fulfillment of human rights and stability in the Middle East?"

Apparently the Arabs believe that by following Hitler's example of telling "the big lie" over and over until people begin to believe it, they will ultimately convince the rest of the world. And some nations have begun to adjust their policies accordingly.

What seems to be forgotten by many of the so-called Middle East experts is that even before the establishment of the State of Israel, the Middle East was in a state of constant turmoil. Instability would remain endemic in the region even if Israel were to disappear.

The conservative *New York Times* recently editorialized: "The Iraqi-Iranian conflict should deflate the simple-minded thesis that only the Palestinian question stands between the United States and secure oil supplies."

Nevertheless, the Arabs continue to brandish the "sword of oil" in attempting to force the rest of the world to comply with their demands. This is clearly blackmail.

Law enforcement officials have found that it is never wise to pay a blackmailer. And a growing number of world leaders are privately wondering if this is not a sound principle for international politics as well.

The Arab Trade Boycott of Israel was intended to shut Israel off from trade with all Arab nations, and limit her economic interchange with all other nations. The Arabs threatened to retaliate against any nation failing to observe their illegal and complicated system of rules. The boycotts also attempted to influence the internal policies of various companies as to the hiring of Jews, supporting "Zionist" activities, etc.

In June, 1977, the United States adopted an anti-boycott law in the face of the most dire Arab threats. But the promised retaliation never materialized. Indeed, it has been observed that even Arab League nations ignore the boycott when it is in their own economic interest to do so.

Perhaps the key to relieving the stranglehold the Arabs are using to press their blackmail demands is to use their own weapon against them. Reuben Hecht, as I noted in the second chapter of this book, suggested this very thing to me, stressing that the West's weakness lay in its lack of unity. His vivid remarks about the Arabs' inability to drink their oil and their lack of paying customers in the Communist bloc or the Third World were convincing arguments for his point of view.

This idea seems to find support in a comment made by Dr. Ghazi Algosaibi, Saudi Arabian minister of industry and electricity, in a recent speech. He said, "The new Arab world is interdependent with America. Your industrial way of life . . . will collapse without Arab oil. The independence of the Arab countries in the face of expanding Communism cannot be maintained without your strength and resolve."

In recognition of this interdependence, Saudi Arabia has been willing to sell its oil cheaper than other members of OPEC. A potential conflict of interests exists within OPEC because of the differing national interests of its members. The high-population members need to sell all the oil they can produce to meet their current financial requirements. On the other hand, the low-population members do not need to produce all the oil they can sell.

All this means is that a relatively minor reduction in world demand for OPEC oil would create pressures within OPEC by increasing the competition for markets. This could lead to some serious rethinking about prices and terms to potential customers.

John Hirsch explained this to me in a little more detail. He said, "Arabia and the United States have a common interest. The Arabs and other OPEC people have no other really profitable market for their product. The Eastern bloc and the Third World are not strong potential customers. The Third World is impoverished and the Eastern bloc trades in nonconvertible currencies such as the ruble, which won't buy anything except in the Soviet Union. So I don't think they have the alternative of telling us to go away."

Such a posture for the United States and the Western nations will require bold leadership. There is certainly a tremendous element of risk involved. The question that must be asked, however, is whether that risk is greater than the absolutely assured results which will come from doing nothing.

Clearly, the decisions made concerning these vital issues in the near future can well determine the ultimate future of Israel, the United States—and the whole world.

chapter 7

Jerusalem

Only a little more than a month had passed since the U.N. General Assembly, meeting in emergency session, had voted overwhelmingly to affirm the right of the Palestinians to establish a sovereign state. The same resolution had called for Israel to withdraw from the West Bank, Gaza, and East Jerusalem by November 15. The day after that vote, the Knesset passed a bill sponsored by Guela Cohen, whom *Time* magazine characterized as a "Zionist firebrand and opponent of the peace treaty." The bill had affirmed that all of united Jerusalem was the capital of Israel. It was largely a symbolic gesture, a way to strike back at the Arab assaults in the United Nations.

During this time I sat down with Prime Minister Begin and asked him to tell me about Jerusalem and the Knesset's vote:

"As you know, being a student of the Bible, more than 3,000 years ago, King David, when he united the Kingdoms of Judea and Israel, transferred the seat of his kingdom from Hebron, where he ruled for seven years, to Jerusalem, where he ruled for thirty-three years. He wanted to build the Temple on the mountain which in those days was called Moriah. And by legend, there Abraham was to make an offering of his own son, Isaac. But God told him that he was involved in too many wars and not he, himself, but Solomon, his son, would build the Temple. And so it happened. Solomon constructed the first Temple. Since then Jerusalem has been the capital of the Jewish state. That happened more than 3,000 years ago, which makes it one of the oldest capital cities in the world.

"So, we had to face a wrong done to a nation which is absolutely unprecedented. Every nation has its capital. And other nations recognize that capital, as they recognize the nation itself. The United States declared the city of Washington, D.C., to be its capital. Everybody recognizes that fact. The Russians said their capital city would be called Moscow. Then, during the Czar's period they transferred the capital to St. Petersburg. And everybody recognized St. Petersburg as the capital of Russia. After the Bolshevik Revolution, Lenin transferred the capital again to Moscow. And everyone began to recognize Moscow, once again, as the capital of the Soviet Union. Take a country like Luxembourg. Does anybody say to Luxembourg where its capital should be? The only capital in the world which is not being recognized as a capital is Jerusalem. Isn't it a real wrong? One of the most ancient capitals of all countries is not yet recognized by the United States. Although the Democratic platform (both 1976 and 1980) says that Jerusalem is the capital of Israel, and that the American Embassy should be transferred from Tel Aviv to Jerusalem. But it is not fulfilled."

"Mr. Begin, some are saying that there was no reason at all to pass this bill about Jerusalem being Israel's capital because nobody was talking about that—it was no problem."

"I am sorry, you make a mistake," Begin's face was quietly intense. "There was always a problem. We came to Camp David to make peace with Egypt, and a great statesman of the United States told me: 'The government of the United States does not recognize Jerusalem as the capital of Israel.' I had to answer, 'Whether you do recognize or don't recognize, Jerusalem is the capital of the State of Israel.' Lord Carrington of Great Britain said that Britain does not recognize Jerusalem as the capital of Israel. But people didn't pay attention to statements like his. They paid attention to the bill. Now what is the bill? The bill did not create any new situation, because we proclaimed that Jerusalem, in total, was the capital of Israel in 1967.

"After the end of the Six-Day War, we had liberated the eastern part of Jerusalem from Jordanian occupation. For nineteen years before that we couldn't go to the Western Wall to pray. That was the only time since the Temple had been destroyed by the Romans, the second Temple. Under all the other regimes we were free to go to the Western Wall. Under the Turks, and under previous conquerors, everybody let us go to pray. But the Jordanians didn't, in breach of the arms agreement. Then the Olive Mountain Cemetery, in which our greatest sages are buried for centuries, was completely desecrated. The monuments were destroyed and turned into floors of places which are unmentionable. I will not even use the names. And then all of our

synagogues were destroyed; only stone upon stone was left of
them. The Jewish Quarter, which was centuries old, was also
completely destroyed—leveled. This all happened under Jordanian
occupation for nineteen years.

"Under our jurisdiction, we reconsecrated the Olive Mountain
Cemetery and everyone has free access to the Holy Shrines. A
Christian can go to the Holy Sepulchre, or to Bethlehem—to the
Church of the Nativity—free and in absolute safety. A Muslim
goes to his mosque and prays freely in absolute safety. When
Sadat was here, he went to the El Aksa Mosque. Sadat went
there and prayed, of course, freely and in complete safety.
Everybody has free access to the holy shrines. This is exactly
what the law says.

"So there is no novelty in this bill. In fact, I also wrote in Camp
David, on the seventeenth of March, a letter to President Carter
stating these facts: since 1967 Jerusalem is one city indivisible—
the capital of Israel. However, I would like to add that it was not
a government-sponsored bill. I don't say that for any apologetic
reasons, but we in the government didn't find it necessary to
promulgate such a law because the law had already been
adopted in 1967, and because of my letter to President Carter,
which was published together in the same booklet with the Camp
David Agreement. But there was a private member of the
opposition who suggested this new law. Could anybody vote
against it? Imagine. If you were for Jerusalem being the capital
of Israel and one city, could you raise your hand against it? That
would be absurd, of course. And therefore not only the coalition,
the government supporters, but those of the opposition voted for
that bill. That was absolutely natural. Still, nothing new was
created. But it was useful. Because now everybody has to take a
stand to say what they think about Jerusalem. Is it the capital of
Israel or is it not? I asked that statesman in the United States,
when he said that his government does not recognize Jerusalem
as the capital of Israel, 'Tell me, if so, where is the capital of
Israel?' I couldn't get a reply. If Jerusalem is not the capital of
Israel, then where is our capital? In Petah Tikva? In Namat Gan?
In Tel Aviv? Where is our capital? Here in Jerusalem is the
government, the Parliament, the president, the Supreme Court.
Whoever says, either on behalf of a great power or of a small
country, we don't recognize Jerusalem as the captial of Israel,

my reply is always, 'Excuse me, sir, but we don't recognize your non-recognition.' "

Prime Minister Begin's words brought to mind some remarks Moshe Dayan had made about Jerusalem during his address at the Thirty-Fourth General Assembly of the United Nations (September 27, 1979). "Jerusalem," he said, "has known many foreign rulers during the course of its long history, but none of them regarded it as their capital. Only the Jewish people have always maintained it as the sole center of its national and spiritual life. For thousands of years Jews have prayed daily for their return to Jerusalem, and for the past century and a half Jerusalem has had a continuous and uninterrupted Jewish majority."

Jerusalem symbolizes all that Israel stands for and means in our world. Therefore it would be helpful to take an in-depth look at this peculiar city, to better understand the reasons for its special place in the hearts of virtually every Jew on the face of the earth.

During the long negotiations for the establishment of the Jewish National Home a friendship grew up between Dr. Chaim Weizmann, the Jewish statesman, and Lord Balfour, the British foreign secretary at that time. Balfour was unable to understand why the Jews were insisting that they would accept only Palestine as their permanent homeland. Turning one day to Dr. Weizmann, he asked for an explanation. "Well, Lord Balfour," replied Dr. Weizmann, "if I were to offer you Paris instead of London, would you accept?"

"But," answered Balfour in some surprise, "London is ours."

"Lord Balfour," said Weizmann, "Jerusalem was ours when London was a swamp."

"Jerusalem, this beautiful, golden city, is the heart and soul of the Jewish people. One cannot live without a heart and soul. If you want one single word to symbolize all of Jewish history, that word is Jerusalem." So writes the mayor of the city, Teddy Kollek.

What has been its history? It can be summed up in one word, troubled. Palestine, lying as it did between the rival empires of Egypt and Syria, both striving for dominance in the Middle East, was constantly tramped over by the opposing armies of north and south. To quote Mayor Kollek again, "Jerusalem has been coveted and conquered by a host of people. Canaanites, Jebusites, Babylonians, Assyrians, Persians, Romans, Byzantines, Mamelukes, Arabs, Crusaders, Ottomans, British, Jews."

Its origins are lost in the mists of antiquity, but evidence of human habitation which goes back 4,000 years has been found by the archaeologists. The biblical record first mentions Jerusalem in the book of Joshua (10:1). There we read that Adonizedek was king of Jerusalem and that he fought unsuccessfully against Joshua. The Israelites first occupied Jerusalem in the days of the judges (Judg. 1:8), but the Jebusites persisted there in the face of assaults by the tribes of Judah and Benjamin (Judg. 1:21). Finally, in 1049 B.C., David wrested the city once and for all from the Jebusites, making it his capital. From that time 3,000 years ago, Jerusalem has been the capital city of the Jewish people. The authors of that illuminating book *Jerusalem, Sacred City of Mankind*, Teddy Kollek and Moshe Pearlman, write, "The spiritual attachment of the Jews to Jerusalem has remained unbroken, it is a unique attachment. If you doubt that statement, try and find another relationship in history where a people, whether in actual physical possession of their capital city, or in temporary exile from it, have remained passionately attached to it, for three thousand years."

When the Jews were driven at various times from their land, wherever they found themselves, they faced towards Jerusalem when praying. Their synagogues were oriented towards the city, and when a Jew built himself a house he left part of a wall unfinished, to symbolize that it was only a temporary dwelling until he could return to his permanent home, Jerusalem.

Why is this the case? Compared with the great cities of Europe, Jerusalem is very small. It stands on no great river, as do London, Paris, or Rome. It has no port, no great industries, no mineral wealth, or adequate water supply (although the one main spring in Gihon gave in olden days a modest supply of water). Nor did the city stand on a great highway of the ancient world, or command a strategic crossroad. It was even off the main trade routes. Why then did it not remain merely an unimportant village, which, like so many others in the course of time, have vanished?

What accounts for its hold on the minds and hearts of

adherents of the world's three monotheistic faiths? It is surely the moral grandeur of the spiritual wisdom which the biblical prophets who spoke from Jerusalem gave to the world that has gained for the city its unique place in the minds and hearts of men. Which other of the world's cities can fairly claim that it was predicted that from her would go out the word of the Lord? A word which would change the moral standards of mankind?

Its spiritual stature is echoed in its physical situation, for it stands upon its hills high above the surrounding countryside. Coming to Jersualem is always spoken of among the Jews as "going up to Jerusalem." Those who leave her, having once lived in Israel, are considered ones that "go down," in more than just the physical sense.

Taking its history all in all, down the long ages of its existence, has any other city suffered as Jerusalem has suffered? This city, "beloved of God," says the Bible, has been tormented by man. At times it was conquered by violent assault, at other times brought to its surrendering knees by the horrors of starvation—sometimes leading to unspeakable suffering, as the prophet Jeremiah predicted—being reduced to the final degradation of cannibalism.

The kingdoms of Israel and Judah which King David had united were once again driven apart by his grandson Rehoboam, and after a three-hundred-year succession of kings, good and bad, came the final dispersion of the ten northern tribes, which had been taken captive to Assyria. Judah survived in the land but two hundred years more, until she was taken captive to Babylon. But wherever the Jews went they kept Jerusalem in their hearts and minds, and during their captivity in Babylon was heard David's passionate cry, "If I forget thee, O Jerusalem, may my right hand lose its cunning" (Ps. 137:5). Seventy years later, when Babylon had been overthrown by Persia, the tide turned. Cyrus, king of Persia, was one of history's most generous characters, who not only allowed the Jews to return to their beloved city, but even gave them back the precious gold and silver vessels which the ruthless Nebuchadnezzar had pillaged from the Temple. One of the captives, Nehemiah, who had risen to become the king of Persia's cupbearer, led his people back to their land, restored Jerusalem, and for the next three hundred and fifty years there followed a rare period of peace and prosperity for the city and its inhabitants, until their final dispersion by Rome in A.D. 70.

It was not until 1917, when under the British General Allenby Jerusalem was set free from the Muslim Turkish rule, that the long Diaspora of the Jews was over.

General Allenby's capture of Jerusalem fulfilled a twenty-five-hundred-year-old prophecy by the prophet Isaiah. This is what he had predicted. "As birds flying, so will the Lord of hosts defend Jerusalem; defending also he will deliver it, and passing over he will preserve it" (Isa. 31:5). With the prophecy in mind, compare what actually happened.

In 1917, in his campaign to oust the Turks from Palestine, General Allenby reached the gates of Jerusalem. Not the far-spreading city of today, but the tiny walled city of those days. If he shelled this city some holy place would inevitably be damaged, and then the Christian, Jewish, and Muslim world would be up in arms. What should he do? In his perplexity, the general dispatched a cable to the War Office in London, but the reply brought him little comfort. It merely said, "Use your own discretion." But that was just what he did not want to do. So, a second cable was sent, to King George V, who replied, "Make it a matter of prayer."

After that, Allenby hit upon the idea of printing leaflets which called on the Turks to surrender. He would send up a little open-cockpit biplane to drop them on the city. The order was duly executed but with no immediate or visible result. But next morning their effect was discovered in a most down-to-earth way. One of the British army cooks was facing what, to him, was a major disaster. He found that he had no eggs for the traditional British breakfast of bacon and eggs. Then, to his infinite relief, he heard the crowing of a cock, and with his native Cockney common sense and a traditional disregard for his aitches, he said to himself, "Where there's cocks, there's 'ens, and where there's 'ens, there's heggs." Sallying forth hurriedly, intending to go to the nearby village of Lifta, he missed his way, and found himself instead on the outskirts of Jerusalem. To his surprise he saw a group of Arabs carrying a white flag approaching him. In their midst was the Arab mayor of the city, who ceremoniously proceeded to offer him the keys of Jerusalem. Never having been initiated into the formalities of receiving the surrender of a city, he abruptly refused the keys, saying with some indignation, "I don't want no keys, I want heggs for me hofficers."

"As birds flying"—Isaiah could not use the word "airplanes," for neither he nor his hearers knew the word, so—"as birds flying shall the Lord of hosts defend Jerusalem." The little biplanes "defended" the city by those harmless but strangely potent leaflets. While defending they also "delivered" it, for the 400-year oppression of the city by the Ottoman power was now over, and the "passing over" of the planes certainly "preserved" it, for not a shot was fired, not a holy place was harmed. Incidentally, the motto of the Fourteenth Bomber Squadron which flew over the city of Jerusalem that day was "I spread my wings and keep my promise."

There is yet another prophecy which has been fulfilled in living memory. The twelfth verse of the twelfth chapter of Daniel runs like this, "Blessed [happy] is he that waiteth, and cometh to the thousand three hundred and five and thirty days." What, asked the students of prophecy, did these obscure words mean? The period mentioned, 1335 days, did not fit into any of those neat charts and graphs so beloved by those who investigate the prophecies in the hope of understanding what the future holds.

It remained a mystery until that day when General Allenby entered Jerusalem and set it free from times of the treading down of the Gentiles, an event which Jesus had predicted two thousand years before, and which Daniel had concealed in his prophecy hundreds of years before Christ.

The year when Jerusalem was set free from four hundred years of Turkish rule was 1917, which was the date stamped on the Turkish coins minted that year. And on the other side of the coins was the year 1335, according to the Turkish calendar.

Pulling back from these sorts of observations, we need briefly to examine Jerusalem's place in, and meaning for, the three monotheistic religions of mankind. What does the city mean to them? What place does it occupy in their thinking and in their faith?

Christianity. For Christians, Jerusalem is revered as the place in which the great final drama in the ministry of Jesus took place, His crucifixion and resurrection. It is a place of pilgrimage, but in no sense does it occupy a central position in the life of the

Christian. It is a place to which the pilgrim goes, but even in that case, he goes not so much to Jerusalem, as to the holy places he will find in and about the city.

Islam. In the Jewish Scriptures, the Christian's Old Testament, Jerusalem is mentioned more than 700 times, but it is not referred to once by name in the Koran, the holy book of Islam, though Muslims claim that a somewhat imprecise reference in that book refers to the city. To support their claims to the city, Muslims point to the fact that for thirteen years Mohammed and his followers turned their faces, when praying, to Jerusalem. However, this episode was of short duration, for after the Jews fell from favor, it was changed, and pious Muslims from that time on have prayed with their faces toward Mecca.

Jerusalem, for Islam, has only a derivative significance, gained from its place in Jewish and Christian thinking. Mohammed never actually set foot in the city. The whole Islamic structure and teaching concerning its importance to the Muslim rests on the somewhat flimsy foundation of a dream, during which Mohammed claimed to have ridden on his legendary horse to the Temple Mount in Jerusalem, to have stood upon the Rock of Sacrifice, Abraham's rock, and from there to have ascended for a heavenly visit.

For Muslims Mecca and Medina are their two holy cities. In this hierarchy Jerusalem ranks third. Whereas every pious Muslim dreams of making the pilgrimage to Mecca, a dream which, for multiple thousands each year becomes reality, Jerusalem is not a place of such pilgrimage, and the Islamic connection with Jerusalem did not commence until the seventh century A.D.

Judaism. The story of the Jews in Jerusalem began over three thousand years ago and has never stopped. Unlike the Christian and Islamic connections with the city, the Jewish people's link with Jerusalem has been historical, religious, cultural, physical, and fundamental. It has never been voluntarily broken, for any absence of Jews from the city has been the result of foreign persecution and eviction. For the Jews alone of all its residents, it has remained ever since. "Jerusalem was at once symbol, soul, and goal of the religious, national, cultural, and human strivings of the Jewish people, expressed regularly by facing Jerusalem in prayer three times a day. The site of continuous Jewish settlement, Jerusalem remained alive for the Jewish people." So affirms the historical and legal review of the Canada-Israel committee.

Professor R. G. Zvi Werblowsky writes of the matter in this way: "For the Jewish people . . . Jerusalem is not a city containing holy places or holy events. The city as such, is holy and has, for at least two and a half millennia, served as the symbol of the historic existence of a people hunted, humiliated, massacred, but never despairing of the promise of its ultimate restoration. Jerusalem and Zion have . . . become the local habitation and the name for the hope and meaning of Jewish existence, and of its continuity from the days when, according to the . . . biblical books, God spoke of a certain place that he would choose, to the days of the return which—however improbable it might seem— was never in doubt for the Jew."

chapter 8

Judea and Samaria

I asked Prime Minister Begin to speak to the controversial subject of the Israeli settlements in Judea and Samaria—what Israel's opponents call "the occupied territories." He began by sharing about his first meeting with President Carter.

"We were in the cabinet room and President Carter asked me a question. But, in that question, he made a statement that was very negative. He said the settlements were illegal. But I had prepared a counter question I wanted to pose to him. It was a prepared improvisation. One day Winston Churchill was interviewed in his study. He said, 'I'm preparing my improvisations for question time in the House of Commons—hard work!'

"So, I had asked our Israeli embassy in Washington to prepare a list of American cities that were named after cities in the Bible in Israel, like Bethlehem, Shiloh, Hebron, and Bethel. Then I showed President Carter my list—it was very long; the American people love the Bible—and I asked him if he could imagine that the governor of Pennsylvania would proclaim that anyone could live in the city of Bethlehem, Pennsylvania, except Jews. President Carter agreed that such a man, if he did such a thing, would be guilty of racism.

"Why? Because it was Bethlehem of Pennsylvania. Pennsylvania is in the United States and the United States is a free country. So, I pointed out that I was governor of the state in which the original Bethlehem, and the original Jericho, and the original Shiloh were located. Did he expect me, I asked, to say that everybody could live in those cities except Jews? Of course he didn't. It would be absurd. Jews must have the right to settle in these places as much as anyone else.

"This land we occupy is *Eretz Israel*, the land of Israel, since the days of the prophet Samuel, three thousand years ago. We had a downfall later, but even the Romans called us Judea until after the Bar-Kokhba revolt in the second century. Then, because the Jewish resistance had been so fierce and heroic, and because the Emperor Hadrian had suffered such severe casualties, he decided to try to delete all memory of the connection between that people and that land. The Romans had done it with Carthage, why not here? So he renamed the area *Syria et Palestina*, using the name of our ancient enemies, the Philistines.

"So the word Palestine came into all languages. Thus the preamble to the British Mandate after World War I used these words: 'recognition having been given to the historical connection between the Jewish people and Palestine.' So, in spite of Hadrian, nobody forgot that it was our land. Every intelligent person understands that Palestine is a misnomer for the land of Israel.

"So we have a right to live in Judea and Samaria, and we will live there. But that does not mean we want to evict even one Arab from his village or town. We never wanted to do that.

"And for us living there today there is an even more pressing need for these settlements. That is our national security. Without Jewish settlements in those hills, the PLO could easily hide in them and descend into the plain to kill our people whenever they liked."

Then I asked Mr. Begin if he was ever criticized for quoting the Bible on these matters, and, in general, how he regarded the Bible.

"When we face our various problems, we should always strive to live by the Bible. That is true for all of humanity. This is the book which has kept the Jewish people alive—that is my belief. And I am proud to quote the Bible in substantiation of our rights. If anyone brings it up, I tell them I plead guilty of quoting the Bible on matters of public policy, but I don't apologize.

"Ben-Gurion had a wonderful saying. He was my opponent, of course, but it was a wonderful saying when he addressed the British Royal Commission. He said, 'Some people say that the mandate is our Bible, but it is not. The Bible is our mandate.'

"And you know something? Every time you read the Bible, you find something new. Every Saturday night a group of sages gather in my home and we study the Bible together. And every time we find something new. The book which has been studied for thousands of years by great rabbis, professors, and sages still yields something new each time you study it. It's wonderful."

I asked him to talk about the idea of a Palestinian Arab state in Samaria and Judea (the West Bank).

"You know, there are twenty-one sovereign Arab states from
the Persian Gulf to the shores of the Atlantic Ocean. I would like
every man with a molecule of feeling of justice to ask himself,
should the Arab people have twenty-two states and the Jews
none?

"If the Arabs occupied twenty-two sovereign states, we would
be trapped on a narrow plain between the hills and the
Mediterranean. They would get up there in those hills with the
Soviet-made missiles they're already using, and they would
make a hostage of every child in Israel. They haven't abandoned
their plan to 'liquidate the Zionist entity' as they like to call us.
No nation in the world would agree to that.

"And I would like to remind the Free World nations who wish
us to agree to it anyway that the PLO is in alliance with the
Soviet Union. Judea and Samaria would be a Soviet base in no
time if we let them have a Palestinian state there. You can reach
Bethlehem in two and a half hours flying by jet from Odessa in
the southern Ukraine. It would be better than Afghanistan for
them. From Samaria they could move south, east, west—
wherever they liked. Is that what the Free World wants? A
Soviet base in the heart of the Middle East?

"That is why President Carter said he was opposed to a
Palestinian state. But some European countries are so thirsty for
oil and petrodollars that they would rather surrender. And it
would not be the first time they surrendered to pressure. It
happened in the thirties. And it brought disaster on the world.
Do we want to repeat that disaster?

"A Palestinian state is a mortal danger to Israel and a great
peril to the Free World. And we never agreed to a Palestinian
state at Camp David. What we agreed to was autonomy as a way
to solve the problem of the Palestinian Arabs. With autonomy
they can elect their own ministers of council to deal with daily
affairs and we shall not interfere at all. This would be a great
historic change for them. Under Turkish, British, and Jordanian
occupation they lived under the whip. The only thing we want to
retain is the matter of security. If we do not, the PLO will come
in.

"The PLO is a fact we must face. Only recently we uncovered
142 cells of the PLO. If we had not, they might have killed many
more people in Judea and Samaria and in the Gaza district. If

they were allowed to exist at will, peace would be murdered and we would have permanent bloodshed. No, it is out of the question. The Camp David agreement calls for security for Israel and autonomy for the Arab inhabitants. This agreement should be carried out by all of us. This is the great golden rule under international law: let us carry out our agreements."

I thanked the prime minister for his time. It had been a thoroughly informative half-hour, and I knew, after listening to Mr. Begin, that I wanted to fill myself in on the background of this thorny question about the territories that Israel has occupied since the 1967 war. The place to begin seemed to be at the United Nations in 1947.

All during 1947, the United Nations was facing and endeavoring to decide the grave issues involved in the Jewish-Arab conflict in Western Palestine. Finally, in November, they voted to repartition the land, dividing it between the Jews and Arabs. Although it would have meant a heartbreakingly small portion for the Jews, they accepted the proposal in the interests of peace. But the Arabs categorically refused the offer. Thereafter, tensions between Jews and Arabs became intense and often erupted in violence. Only the presence of British troops prevented all-out war.

In 1948, as the British were about to withdraw and dark clouds appeared on the horizon, Golda Meir risked her life in a last-minute effort to prevent the participation of Jordan in the coming war. Disguised as an Arab woman and accompanied by Ezra Danin, a brilliant orientalist and a long-time friend of the king, she drove from Haifa to Jordan's capital city, Amman, to plead with Abdullah, the king of Transjordan. On the three-hour journey, the car was stopped ten times, but each time, to the infinite relief of the two passengers sitting silently in the back seat, they were allowed to proceed.

At the conclusion of the interview, they tactfully reminded Abdullah that his only real friends were the Jews. To this he answered, "I know, I have no illusions. I believe with all my heart that divine providence has brought you back here, restoring you, a Semitic people who were exiled in Europe, and have shared in its progress, to the Semitic East which needs your knowledge and initiative. But," he added, "conditions are difficult."

At the door, Danin turned to Abdullah. "Your majesty," he said, "beware when you go to the mosque to worship and let people rush up to kiss your robe. Someday a man will shoot you like that." Danin's prophecy was fulfilled a few years later at the El Aksa Mosque, in Jerusalem.

On May 14, 1948, one day before the British troops withdrew, Israel made her declaration of statehood. The next day she was invaded by five Arab armies. For her part, Israel had done all that was possible to avoid the conflict. She had consented to partition against her own territorial interests, and, in her declaration of statehood read only hours before she was invaded, she had held out the hand of friendship to the Arab states surrounding her, whom she always spoke of as "neighbors." Now, she faced the long agony of fighting an unsought war against odds of something like forty to one, ill-equipped, with a tiny army of barely trained men.

Awakened from his much-needed sleep on the night of May 14, Israel's first prime minister, David Ben-Gurion, heard the heartwarming news that America had recognized the infant state of Israel. Three hours later, he was once more dragged from his slumbers to make a radio broadcast to America. Even as he spoke, the studio was shaken by the explosion of the first Egyptian bombs to fall on Tel Aviv—the start of Israel's War of Independence.

Casualties quickly mounted and Ben-Gurion reported, "We have one hundred and fifty casualties in a battalion of five hundred." The situation in upper Galilee was "dire" and the settlements feared that they would not be able to hold out. His concluding words were, "The south is open."

General Allenby, many years before, when faced with the prospect of having to shell the Holy City in order to dislodge the occupying Turks, had gone to all possible lengths to avoid damaging it. The Arabs felt no such scruples in spite of their claims concerning their reverence and love for Jerusalem. Now their shells tore the city apart, and after their capture of the Old City, the Jewish Quarter was systematically and wantonly destroyed. Fifty-three synagogues, including the great Hurva synagogue, known as "the glory of the Old City," were reduced to heaps of rubble. The cemetery most sacred in all the world to the Jews, on the slopes of the Mount of Olives, was desecrated, and thirty thousand of its gravestones were ripped up and either sold as building material or used to build the camp of the Arab Legion, including its latrines.

The United Nations tried to effect cease-fires on several occasions, but was generally rebuffed by the Arabs. Under threat of sanctions, periods of truce were enjoyed. By October 15, however, the war resumed with Israel launching a furious offensive to drive the Arabs back from their places of deep penetration. The war ended formally in July, 1949, when Syria—the last Arab nation to do so—signed an armistice agreement with Israel.

In 1950, King Abdullah illegally annexed Judea and Samaria, which he had invaded in 1948; this act was opposed even by the Arab League and recognized only by Great Britain and Pakistan. Abdullah renamed Judea and Samaria the West Bank and occupied it for nineteen years. He called it the West Bank because it extends from the west bank of the Jordan River into the heart of Israel's territory.

Why is this small area such a bone of contention? Why are its problems so acute that the superpowers are actively concerned to find their solution? Its history goes back some four thousand years, woven into the entire story of the Jews from the time of Abraham to the present day, a very long span of time. Let's summarize.

After a four-hundred-year exile in Egypt, the twelve tribes of Israel returned, thirty-seven hundred years ago, under General Joshua, to their promised homeland. Two and a half of the tribes did not complete the journey, but decided to settle east of the River Jordan. Meanwhile nine and a half tribes continued over the river and took possession of the land, and have remained there, representatively, ever since. It was from that part of the land, called Judea and Samaria, today's so-called West Bank, that their kings ruled, their law was administered, and their religion established.

But understanding why this area of Judea and Samaria is so dear to the Jews does not explain why it has become such a problem area. What then, is the problem? It is that the West Bank had, and still has, more Arab inhabitants than Jews. Today, there are roughly 700,000 Arabs in Judea and Samaria. In the much-criticized Israeli settlements in the West Bank, on the other hand, there are fewer than 15,000 Jews.

What historic connections have the Arabs with these territories? The Arabs and the Jews share a common father, Abraham. But the Jews are the descendants of his son Isaac and they have a clear and unbroken relationship with the land for four thousand years. The Arabs, on the other hand, descended from Abraham through Ishmael. In the Bible we read that Ishmael would "be a wild man, his hand against every man and every man's hand against him; and he shall dwell [over against] all his kinsmen" (Gen. 16:12). Later, after Abraham drove him and his mother out, he dwelt in the wilderness of Paran, and his mother took a wife for him from the land of Egypt (Gen. 21:21). The wilderness of Paran was in the Sinai, southwest of the Negev.

The Arabs took Palestine in A.D. 638 and held it thereafter for 400 years (638-1099). If, as the Palestinians insist, their claim to the land is equal to that of the Jews, why did they call their brief holding of the land a conquest? One does not conquer one's homeland, but returns to it, or repossesses it. Of the Arab connection with Palestine, their own eminent historian Professor Hitti, testifying to the Anglo-American Committee of Inquiry in 1946, said, "There is no such thing as Palestine in Arab history, absolutely not." Zuhair Mohsen, who, before his murder, was military operations chief of the PLO and head of its Syrian-backed terrorist Saiqa wing, said in 1977, "A Palestinian people does not exist. The establishment of a Palestinian State is just the name for continuing our struggle against Israel and for Arab unity . . . we all belong to the Arab people."

A great number of the inhabitants of the West Bank today are not indigenous to the region. Instead, they poured into Israel by the thousands from their own poverty-stricken lands when the Zionist redemption of the land commenced, when the early pioneers, fired by a passionate desire to reclaim their ancestral homeland, labored to drain the malarial swamps, to plant trees and to once again make the barren fields fertile. This was particularly the case during the period of the British Mandate, when large numbers of workers entered the country, lured by the prospect of work and wages.

During Jordan's occupation of Judea and Samaria, from 1948 to 1967, the Palestinians, who all had Jordanian nationality, demanded neither autonomy nor statehood, nor would Jordan have given either, because it recognized itself as a veritable Palestinian entity. Now, however, the West expects Israel to grant the Arab demands, and this in an area vital to her security. If the crux of the matter, according to the Arabs, is for Israel to withdraw to the pre-1967 borders, then *why*, when she *was* on those borders, did the Arabs attack her?

The Arabs and much of the Western world have repeatedly called for the creation of a Palestinian State, apparently failing to realize that one already exists. It came into being at the end of World War I, when the League of Nations granted Britain a mandate to superintend the affairs of the district of the now-defunct Ottoman Empire called Palestine. The League's Mandate to Britain incorporated the Balfour Declaration, thus reinforcing the idea that this area was to include a national home for the Jews. But, in 1921, the British partitioned this territory. They drew a line running north to south from the southern end of the Sea of Galilee, down the length of the Jordan River, through the Dead Sea, and thence onto Eilat at the northern tip of the Gulf of Aqaba. They named the territory to the east of this line Transjordan; the territory to the west was Palestine. Transjordan comprised about three-quarters of the original mandated territory, leaving only a quarter of Palestine as a homeland for the Jews. This meant, of course, that those districts lying east of the Jordan which had, in Bible times, belonged to the Israelite tribes of Gad, Reuben and the half-tribe of Manassah—some 17,000 square kilometers—fell under the sway of Transjordan's Arab government. The name "Transjordan" was changed to Jordan after the annexation of the West Bank in 1950.

Of the two million people living in Jordan today, nearly all are Palestinians, except perhaps for the Hashemite king, Hussein, because his dynasty was imported by the British from Arabia. So a Palestinian State on the West Bank of the river would be a second Palestinian State. Why then, was three-fourths of the land promised as the Jewish ancestral homeland? Very briefly, this is what happened.

In the carve-up of territories which followed World War I, the Peace Conference at San Remo, yielding to pressure from France, granted her control over Syria and Lebanon. Defying this decision, a so-called General Syrian Conference offered the country's throne to the Emir Feisal, the recognized leader of the

Arabs at that time. Installed in Damascus, Feisal set up his administration there, an act which was eventually countered by the French, who ordered Feisal out of the country in 1920.

In compensation, Britain offered Feisal the throne of Iraq, but this had been intended for Feisal's younger brother Abdullah Ibn-Hussein, who was thereupon left throneless. The enraged Abdullah emerged from his Arabian homeland in the Hejaz, in western Saudi Arabia, gathered a motley army of 1,500 Turkish ex-soldiers and Hejaz tribesmen, and entered eastern Palestine, announcing that he was on his way to Syria to drive out the French. His call for help to his fellow Muslims in Syria brought no response, and his continued presence in East Palestine was an embarrassment to the British. What could be done? There was a simple answer—cut off the major part of the territory promised to the Jews and give it to Abdullah for his kingdom, which he in turn dubbed Transjordan.

Before that, neither eastern nor western Palestine had ever been the sovereign national territory of the Arabs. Even when it was in Arab hands after the conquest in the seventh century, it was merely, like so many other places, an unimportant backwater province.

At any rate, when the dust settled from the War of Independence in 1950, Jordan was firmly in control of the West Bank. And, from it, terrorists easily gained access to Israeli-occupied land. In spite of the armistice agreements of 1949, Israel was under constant terrorist attack, especially from Gaza and the West Bank. In what follows, I will retrace, in greater detail, events I have already recounted in chapter one. We need to remind ourselves of these events here in some detail because they are important in helping us to understand the status of Judea and Samaria and the rest of the so-called "occupied territories."

A History of Survival

Reviewing the situation in 1956, the prime minister of Israel, Moshe Sharrett, presented this summary to the Knesset. "During the past five years, we have suffered 884 casualties from the operations of regular and irregular military bands, including 258 last year alone. . . ." These figures referred to civilian casualties inflicted by terrorists from Egypt and Jordan. In flagrant violation of the armistice agreement she had signed.

Egypt had continued to regard herself as still at war with Israel. And, in 1955, the Czechoslovakians, acting as Russia's agents, sold a significant amount of arms to Egypt. Israel had asked the United States, Britain, and France to keep the situation in balance by selling her military equipment. All three nations refused.

In the autumn of 1956, some particularly vicious murders of innocent civilians aroused Israeli indignation and by October the threat to the country's security became acute. In answer to the tripartite alliance between Egypt, Jordan, and Syria, it was decided that there would have to be an all-out offensive against Sinai and the Gaza Strip. Units of the Israel Defense Force, faced by three Egyptian divisions, and later reinforcements, nevertheless soon had practically the whole of the Sinai Peninsula in their hands. On the second day of the fighting, the governments of Britain and France issued an ultimatum demanding the withdrawal of the Israeli and Egyptian forces to a distance of ten miles from the Suez Canal. As Israel had had no intention of invading Egyptian soil, she complied.

Egypt, however, refused, whereupon France and Britain attacked Port Said in a disastrous effort to seize the Suez Canal. The political struggle lasted for four months, being finally resolved only when several maritime states guaranteed Israel's right of free navigation in the Strait of Tiran, her only exit to the Far East.

After the Sinai Campaign of 1956, the frontier between Egypt and Israel remained comparatively quiet, the center of terrorist attack having moved northward to Syria, although at the same time President Nasser of Egypt made no secret of his intentions to destroy Israel. Nasser had taken no part in the guerrilla activities of Syria, but now, on May 14, 1967, his chief of staff was sent to Syria to coordinate operations against Israel. Nasser's first step was to demand the withdrawal of the UN Emergency Force from the Egypt-Israel border, from the Gaza Strip, and from Sharm el-Sheikh, which commands the Tiran Strait. U Thant, the UN Secretary General, complied with Nasser's demand two days later.

Visiting his troops in Sinai, which now numbered 80,000 men, Nasser announced that the Strait of Tiran was now closed to Israeli shipping. Nasser stated, "The step we have taken means we must be ready for total war with Israel. . . . This is not an isolated act. . . . Our basic aim will be the destruction of Israel." The accusation that Israel started the 1967 war by making the first strike is answered by the fact that in international law, Egypt's behavior constituted an act of war.

At this point, King Hussein flew from Jordan to Cairo to sign a military pact with Egypt and placed the Jordanian army under Egyptian command. Israel now faced the tremendous odds against her; at least 270,000 troops, 1,400 tanks and overwhelming air superiority. The nearest Egyptian airbase was within a few minutes flying time of Tel Aviv, while no Egyptian target of vital importance was within similar range of Israel's air force. While the world held its breath in the certainty that Israel must be crushed, her destiny was suddenly and miraculously reversed. The Israelis launched a preemptive air attack during the Arab breakfast hour. The Egyptian air force was caught on the ground and within a matter of minutes hundreds of Egyptian planes had been destroyed and Israel was in command of the skies.

On this same day Jordan's air force was also smashed, but Jordan's entry into the war had given it an unexpected twist. Israel now had to fight on every front, with a vital battle being fought in and for Jerusalem. The Jordanians were driven back across the River Jordan in forty-eight hours, and although there would still be hard fighting ahead, the issue had been virtually decided in those first air strikes. The hardest fighting was in Jerusalem, where the Israelis had to attack the heavily fortified positions constructed during the nineteen years of Jordan's occupation of East Jerusalem. It meant fighting street by street, under constant sniper fire and ambushes. By June 7 the Israel Defense Forces (IDF) had achieved a position where the city would have fallen by siege, but the fear of a U.N. Security Council decision being taken to freeze the situation while the city was still divided spurred Israel to superhuman efforts and by the early afternoon the entire city of Jerusalem was under Israeli control.

The two thousand years of exile from their most sacred spot was over and young soldiers, hitherto avowedly secular, now battle-strained and near exhaustion, ran to stand weeping before the Western Wall, denied to their people for so many generations. The price of victory had been heartbreakingly heavy, and the miracle of what had been accomplished can only be understood in the words of Abba Eban, at that time Israel's foreign minister, "The nation which was supposed to have lost its youthful idealism and pioneering virtues now looked back to the old unifying visions. . . . Responsibility and sacrifice were no longer embarrassing words. It was a moment of special quality which would live on and on, deep in the heart and mind of Israel for generations to come. A new dimension had been added to the national memory and the exploration of it would take many years. The whole nation was convinced of a single stark certainty. The choice was to live or perish—to defend the national existence or to forfeit it for all time."

As a result of that lightning war, Israel had regained what had been taken from her by Jordan, Judea, and Samaria. Since then, Israel has been under constant international pressure to "return" this area to the Palestinians, who never owned it. It is as though a judge rules that the property stolen from the householder, when recovered by its owner, must be returned to the thief and his associates. Professor Werblowsky puts it like this: "The fact that East Jerusalem and the West Bank were conquered and occupied by Israel in 1967 is frequently and censoriously pointed out. That the same area was conquered and occupied by Jordan in 1948 is, oddly enough, mentioned much less often. Apparently nobody troubles to ask why the sanctity of the principle forbidding annexation of territories by military conquest should have begun only in 1967 and was, so it seems, not yet operative in 1948." Has international morality really sunk so low—or is it because the thief's family possesses two very potent weapons, oil and petrodollars?

How has the West Bank fared during the years of Israeli occupation since 1967? Living as she does in the Arab village of Bethany, on the West Bank, Joan McWhirter tells me her observations. "The village," she explains, "has an Arab mayor and town council, and a soldier is never seen, except when driving through in a lorry or jeep. Occasionally," Joan says, "you will find a jeep parked outside the local Arab men's coffee shop, while the soldiers are inside, drinking Coca-Cola and playing a game of cards with the locals. As an Arab neighbor put it to me, 'I don't trouble them—they don't trouble me. In twelve years, they have never knocked at my door.' "

There are restrictions, of course, and there *are* injustices—that is inevitable—but for law-abiding citizens, there are few restrictions, and most of these, such as roadblocks and searches of vehicles by military personnel, are the result of Arab terrorist activities and protect Arabs equally with Israelis.

It is a tragic and crippling fact that Israel spends over 40 percent of her national income on defense, situated as she is, with a population of only three and one-half million, in the midst of over twenty hostile Islamic nations whose total inhabitants number over a hundred million. In spite of this, much has been done in so short a time, that it has to be seen to be believed. Even in the occupied territories, which obviously do not have first claim on the hard-pressed social services, great improvements have been made.

The West Banker can now, for a nominal sum each month, get health insurance for himself, his wife, any number of children (families are usually large) and even, if necessary, for his parents. No Arab village mother is now more than three kilometers from a government clinic. What this means in the alleviation and prevention of suffering cannot be overestimated. Treatment in any of the nine government hospitals, including surgery, is available for a very small daily sum, and those who can prove their inability to pay are treated free, even to the extent of a costly open-heart operation in the great Hadassah hospitals, which have pioneered medicine in the Middle East.

Infant mortality has decreased greatly and life expectancy has increased. A higher proportion of Arab children are being educated than ever before. Israel's sharing of her agricultural know-how has increased Arab crops a hundred percent and more. The West Banker has his own law courts and municipalities, freely elected and administered under Jordanian law. An Arab worker in Israel gets equal pay for equal work. In 1948, there were 80,000 Arabs in Palestine; today, in the West Bank alone, there are 700,000. An Arab in Jordan when asked why he wanted to go to the West Bank for a visit replied, "Oh, I'm going for a holiday in the Zionist hell!"

This inevitably brings a question to mind, if the Arabs in Israel have such a bad time, as their propaganda states, why has the Arab population so greatly increased? In other occupied territories the subjugated people do not increase, but leave in large numbers.

And the future? What are the possibilities and impossibilities? One doubts that even the wisdom of Solomon could find an answer that would satisfy all the interested parties.

One of the saddest facts of history is that mankind never learns its lessons. The cost to the world of the policy of appeasement to Hitler was paid in twenty million lives. What is going to be the cost of the current, shameful, and all-but-universal bowing down before the god of Arab oil? How long is the Arab world to be permitted to hold the rest of us for ransom by its greedy, profit-making demands? Why does no nation call its bluff by pointing out that if the industrialized nations depend on the supply of oil, the Middle East depends also on the arms, technology, and food supplies they receive from the nations of the West?

Finally, we have looked at the West Bank in its relation to the Jews and the Arabs. What of its relation and value to the West? There are two contenders for total supremacy in the Middle East, Russia and the Islamic Arab powers. At the moment, a strong Israel is the chief obstacle to both their plans.

This does not alter the moral necessity to deal justly with the Palestinian question, but let it be remembered that for thirty years responsible Israeli leaders have been asking, time and time again, for responsible Palestinians to sit down with them, to find a mutually satisfactory solution, but every one of the fifty-three peace offers have been either ignored or rejected. There must also be justice for Israel.

The Golan Heights: A Special Story

We have focused almost entirely on the largest section of ground which the Israelis occupy—the West Bank. Much we have said about it also pertains to the much smaller Gaza Strip, except to say that the Gaza was under Egyptian control before 1967. One other "occupied territory" remains for us to discuss. That is called the Golan Heights, which stand on the border between Israel and Syria in the northeastern corner of Israel. To understand the Golan Heights, we need to dip back into recent history.

Israel's victory in the Six-Day War was universally looked upon as little short of miraculous, but a yet greater miracle lay in the future.

Yom Kippur, the Day of Atonement, is the most sacred day of the year for the Jewish people. The entire country comes to a standstill. There are no buses, no trains; the streets are empty of traffic; no telephones to ring; the radio and television are silent. The entire population gathers in the synagogues or in their homes. A great number also observe the twenty-six-hour fast.

Saturday, October 6, was the Day of Atonement in 1973. The day was being observed in traditional fashion. Perhaps in the synagogues there seemed to be more men than usual, and even many soldiers on frontier duty, unable to return home to observe the day, were keeping the fast.

Suddenly in Jerusalem the sirens wailed, and the men, abruptly summoned from the synagogues, rushed to their homes to change into uniform, and grab the emergency kit every Israeli man must keep in readiness. Some joined their units so quickly that they arrived still in civilian clothes.

The situation facing Israel on that day was infinitely more serious than that of the Six-Day War. The Arab armies were now better trained, largely by Russia, and had far more sophisticated weapons, in much greater supply. As a result, three out of every five Israeli jets were shot down in the first few days of the war. Casualties on the ground were also shockingly heavy.

The tank battle which developed in the Sinai has been described as even greater than the legendary Battle of El Alamein between Montgomery and Rommel in North Africa in World War II. Abba Eban reported to the United Nations on October 8, 1973, "Egypt attacked with 3,000 tanks, 2,000 heavy guns, 1,000 aircraft and 600,000 men."

A comparison with the German-Russian conflict in 1941 makes clear what Israel was facing. The Germans attacked Russia along a two hundred-mile front with 1,000 tanks. Now on the Golan Heights, Syria had 1,200 tanks along a twenty-mile stretch of country. It takes a visit to the Golan Heights to bring home the realization of how vital they are to the defense of the Jordan Valley. During my first trip to Israel, I visited a kibbutz which stands on the eastern shore of the Lake of Galilee, immediately below the frowning cliffs of the Golan. One would only have to stroll through the grounds to notice peculiar marks on the trunks of the eucalyptus trees, planted by the founders of the settlement. Those marks are not from weathering, but they have been caused by Syrian sniper bullets from the Golan Heights. There is never safety there, whether working in the field or looking after livestock. For years, children of the kibbutz have been unable to sleep at night in their homes; because of this, they are taken to underground shelters to spend the nights.

Leaving Ein Gev, I drove up the winding road to the Heights. Getting out of the car, I walked to the very edge of the cliffs and found myself looking straight down onto the fertile fields and the fish ponds of Ein Gev—then I understood.

Meanwhile, in October, 1973, the world stood aside, either passively watching or in some cases actively hindering Israel by obstructing the delivery of aid to her. The American airlift on behalf of Israel did not get started until the war was ten days old and the Israeli army was almost at the bottom of the ammunition barrel. The delay was, in the main, caused through the refusal, by Britain and her NATO allies, to give the United States refueling facilities for her planes. Mercifully, in the end, Portugal allowed American transport planes to use her bases in the Azores, and the supplies which saved Israel started to roll. In her autobiography, Golda Meir—Israel's prime minister at this crucial time—tells how, at an international socialist conference, she expressed her sorrowful amazement that lifelong colleagues could have so betrayed their fellows in Israel. As she asked how was it that no voice had been raised in Israel's behalf, a man behind her on the platform said quietly, "How could they, their throats were choked with oil?"

The World Council of Churches sent two million dollars in aid to Jordan and an even larger sum to the Palestinians. Not a dollar was sent to Israel, though strong criticism from the churches in Israel finally stung the WCC into sending some medical equipment to the Israelis. In his book, *Israel: A Secret Documentary*, Lance Lambert puts it like this: "Egypt and Syria should have beaten Israel, but they were inexplicably stopped. . . . One Egyptian tank commander said later, 'I was only half an hour's drive from the Mitla Pass, and there was nothing to stop me.' But he stopped. . . . When the Syrians were first advancing, the Israelis had only two tanks and ten men at the Golan headquarters. . . . Wave after wave of tanks bore down on them. Then, when they came to within one mile of the Golan headquarters, they stopped. The commander put it very humorously. He said 'They saw the Lake of Galilee; they liked the view, and they stopped.' " Others attribute the Israeli victory against overpowering odds to the intensive prayer made at the time by those who stood with Israel.

The net result of all this, for our purposes, was that Israel maintained the possession of the Golan Heights she had gained initially in 1967. Israeli Defense Force units had, in fact, pushed back the Syrian offensive and had come within artillery range of Damascus. They did not, however, fire on the city. They pulled back to the line they had established in the war of 1967. This line commences in the north around the eastern slopes of Mount Hermon and continues south from there through Al-Kuneitra and thence onto the Jordanian frontier. The people of Ein Gev could continue to be largely free from the terrorist marksmen on the Golan Heights who had harassed them steadily between 1947 and 1967.

Questions and Answers

It has now, according to the West, become self-evident that the PLO is the sole legitimate representative of the Palestinians. Is it reasonable to expect Israel to hand over territory vital to her very existence to an organization which is Soviet-controlled and openly dedicated to her destruction? If she is forced back to indefensible borders, which at one point would mean that there would be only eight miles between the border and the sea, what then?

1. What is the legal status of the areas that came under Israeli administration?

The undetermined nature of the status of Judea and Samaria was expressed by Secretary of State Cyrus Vance during a press conference in Washington, D.C., on July 28, 1977, when he said, "There is, I think, an open question as to who has legal rights to the West Bank."

William O'Brien, Professor of Government at Georgetown University in Washington, D.C., writes concerning Judea-Samaria:

The West Bank was not and is not clearly the sovereign territory of Jordan, from whom Israel took it in a war of self-defense in 1967. The West Bank is an integral part of the Palestine mandate within which a Jewish national home was to be created. In this sense the territory must be considered today to be unallocated territory.

The former legal adviser to the U.S. State Department, Professor Stephen M. Schwebel, takes the question a step further. In the May, 1970, issue of the *American Journal of International Law*, he wrote: "Where the prior holder of territory had seized that territory in the lawful exercise of self-defense has, against that prior holder, better title. . . . As between Israel, acting defensively in 1948 and 1967, on the one hand, and her Arab neighbors, acting aggressively in 1948 and 1967, on the other, Israel has better title in the territory of what was Palestine, including the whole of Jerusalem, than do Jordan and Egypt. . . ."

2. Do Israelis have the right to establish and maintain settlements in these areas?

The charge of illegality in regard to the founding of settlements is constantly leveled against Israel. The instrument of international law cited in support of the charge is the Fourth Geneva Red Cross Convention of 1949 on the Protection of Civilians in Time of War, Article 49. This forbids an occupying power to transfer parts of its civilian population to the occupied territory in question. However, since the prior legitimate sovereign in these areas was the British Mandate and not Jordan or any other Arab power, the applicability of the Fourth Geneva Convention to Judea-Samaria is highly questionable. The Mandate explicitly charged Britain with the duty to encourage "close settlement by Jews on the land."

Dr. Eugene V. Rostow, Professor of Law and Public Affairs at Yale University and former undersecretary of state (1966-69) has pointed out that:

> Under the mandate, Jewish settlement was contemplated and permitted in the entire area of the mandate. That is, the area now known as the West Bank was available to *all* Palestinians—Muslim, Christian, Druze and Jewish alike. . . .

So, since Jordan was never the legitimate sovereign in Judea-Samaria or Egypt in the Gaza district, the provisions of the Fourth Geneva Convention, which were designed to safeguard

legitimate sovereign rights with regard to the transfer of
civilians to the occupied territories, do not apply with respect to
these areas.

Although, strictly speaking, Israel need not consider herself
restricted by these provisions, she has nevertheless scrupulously
adhered to the humanitarian provisions of the convention. In the
Washington Star of November 26, 1978, Professor O'Brien
summed up the issue in these words:

> The fact is that, while not strictly bound by the traditional
> international law of belligerent occupation, Israel has
> maintained an occupation on the West Bank that is fully
> consonant with the principles of international law and
> natural justice. The settlements on the West Bank are not
> "illegal." The manner in which the lands for the settlements
> have been acquired is violative neither of international law
> nor of human rights.

3. Are such settlements an obstacle to peace?

The Arabs insist that the settlements are an obstacle to peace,
but the facts of recent history do not bear them out. When Jordan
invaded Judea-Samaria in 1949, all the Jewish villages of the
area were wiped out and, for nineteen years, no Jew was
permitted to live there.

Did this bring peace? On the contrary, not only did the Arab
States refuse to make peace with Israel, they persistently
endeavored to destroy her. The absence of settlements brought
no peace. Half a million Arabs live free and unmolested among
three million Jews. Why then must Jews be denied the right to
live among the Arabs?

William Safire, writing in *The New York Times* in 1979, said
this:

> Sovereignty—who owns the land—is the key. Jordan claims
> it, the PLO claims it, and Israel, through its continued
> settlement policy, asserts its own claims. The moment
> Israel gives up its right to settle, it gives up that claim to
> sovereignty. If Israel were to admit it is not at least part
> owner, an independent Palestinian state would be born
> which—in this decade at least—would be an intolerable
> threat to Israel's security.

In demanding that Israel surrender her right to create settlements, she is being asked to grant her enemies veto powers over her elementary rights, which, as she knows from experience, can only result in the total loss of those rights.

chapter 9

The Past

George Santayana wrote, "Those who do not remember the past are condemned to relive it." Unfortunately, those who would jeopardize the security of the state of Israel know very little of its past. Jewish history is not studied widely. Most people are familiar with their own nation's history and with a smattering of world history—the Greeks, the Romans, and the Europeans usually. Because of the Bible, however, many more people than would otherwise be the case are somewhat familiar with the ancient roots of the Jewish people. Because our focus is upon a matter that vitally involves modern Jews, we need to build a bridge between them and their ancient ancestors.

We will begin our survey, then, in the fourth century before Christ, when Alexander's Macedonians replaced the Persians as rulers of the eastern Mediterranean region.

On Alexander's death his three generals divided his eastern kingdom among them. Judea, Samaria, and Galilee went first to Ptolemy Soter, who reigned in Egypt. But the Ptolemies in turn ceded the territory to the Seleucids, the most powerful of Alexander's successors. The Seleucid capital was Antioch of Syria. The appalling excesses of the Seleucid king, Antiochus Epiphanes, provoked the noble Jewish family of Hasmon into open revolt. The revolt was successful and the Maccabeans, as they are better known, from the Hebrew word for a hammer, reigned for a hundred years of comparative peace, until Jewish rule was shattered by the Roman legions under Pompey in 63 B.C.

Twelve thousand Jews were massacred in Jerusalem. The priests serving at the altar of the Temple were killed at their posts, and the Holy Land passed under Roman rule. Pagan Rome, "the iron hand which threshed the world in blood," was constantly at odds with the religious fervor of the Jews, and finally, in A.D. 66, the flame of Jewish rebellion flared once more and the Zealots captured Jerusalem and held it, against the might of Rome, astonishingly, for four years. This, of course, was a situation not to be tolerated, and in A.D. 70, Rome dispatched Titus to recapture the city.

With frightful thoroughness he did the job, and a forest of crosses, each with its gruesome burden, rose upon the hills around Jerusalem. The Temple was destroyed and as the flames consumed its glory, many of the priests leapt from its walls to a fiery death rather than witness its destruction. The majority of the remaining inhabitants were driven into that second exile, the Diaspora, which was to last for almost two thousand years of persecution and suffering, culminating in the most appalling crime of history, the cold-blooded murder of six million Jewish men, women, and children in the concentration camps of Nazi Germany.

Large numbers of Jewish sages and scholars from Babylon, which corresponds roughly to modern Iraq, made their way to the Iberian Peninsula during the early medieval period, initiating a Golden Age of the Jews. Ultimately the Jewish communities in Spain rose to positions of wealth and power, and under the tolerant rule of the Moors (Arab Spanish Muslims) the Jews found one of the happiest and most fruitful periods in all their history. Jewish culture produced works of genius, and one of their most valuable contributions to medieval civilization was the liaison they formed between the Arabs and the Christians. Their translations of Arabic and Greek writings were partly responsible for bringing to Europe the outstanding work of the Arabs in mathematics and astronomy.

The brightest star in the firmament of the Jews in Spain was Maimonides, or Moses ben Maimon, the great Jewish writer, philosopher, and physician, who was born in Córdoba in 1135. When, in 1148 southern Spain was invaded by Berber princes from North Africa, Maimonides and his family fled, finally finding refuge in Cairo. There his gifts brought him to the attention of the Sultan of Egypt, the great Saladin, who appointed him to be his court physician.

The reputation earned for him by his writings led to his being made rabbi of Cairo. All but one of his books were in Arabic. His most widely known work was his intriguingly titled *Guide to the Perplexed*. His influence was considerable and is said to have affected Spinoza's thinking.

The Jews of Spain became known as Sephardim, from the medieval Hebrew name for Spain, *S'farad*. For a considerable time the Sephardim were the cultural elite of Jewry. But, in the fifteenth century, the Christians of northern Spain began to defeat and drive out the Arab invaders and the Jews fell on evil times. Terrible persecutions broke out and, to save their lives, great numbers of Jews ostensibly converted, while secretly retaining their Jewish faith—they were called Marranos. This availed them little and many died at the stake and on the rack, hunted down by the Inquisition. In 1492 the Jews were finally expelled from Spain by royal edict and once again commenced their wanderings into many lands, largely to the Mediterranean countries and those of North Africa.

Ashkenazi was the designation given to the Jews of eastern Europe, from the Hebrew name for German lands, *Ashk'naz*. During the last three centuries the Ashkenazi have become both numerically the largest section of world Jewry and also the most creative. Between 1881 and 1945, among the early Jewish settlers who came to America, only a few were Sephardim, while three million were Ashkenazi. The Holocaust took a terrible toll of those who remained in Europe when 5,872,000 Ashkenazi died in the concentration camps.

The time is the end of the eighteenth century, and the first crack in the walls of the Jewish ghettos has appeared with a call in the French National Assembly that the Jews should be granted full rights. In Rome the ghetto had opened, and even in Germany there were signs of improvement. The joy of the Jews was great, for up to this time they had been treated like pariahs. The Jewish response can be seen in the words of one of their manifestos: "Oh, what a rapturous idea to call a spot, a place, a nook one's own upon this lovely earth." This reaction can be better understood when one reads the description by Ludwig Borne of their position. They enjoyed, as he put it, "the loving care of the authorities: they were forbidden to leave their street on Sundays, so that the drunks should not molest them; they were not permitted to marry before the age of twenty-five, so that their offspring should be strong and healthy; on holidays they could leave their homes only at six in the evening, so that great heat should not cause them any harm; the public gardens and promenades outside the city were closed to them and they had to walk in the fields—to awaken their interest in agriculture; if a Jew crossed the street and a Christian citizen shouted, 'Pay your respect, Jud,' the Jew had to remove his hat, no doubt the intention of this wise measure being to strengthen the feelings of love and respect between the Christians and Jews."

But a beginning had been made and a tide which no man could turn back had started to flow. British and French statesmen slowly began to think in terms of a Jewish homeland; associations were formed, literature was published and the dream which had lain dormant in the Jewish soul for century upon century began to awaken and become reality. In the 1890s the term Zionism appeared for the first time, though the basic idea of the return to Zion had never left the Jewish people. All through the millennia of the Diaspora, had not the Passover meal ended with the words of longing which were also a prayer, "Next year in Jerusalem"?

At this point, in 1897, Theodor Herzl appeared on the scene, and proceeded to give reality to his own challenging words, "If you will it, it is no dream." Born in 1860, his parents were well-to-do, assimilated Jews who providentially gave him an education which fitted him for his destined role. Had he received a traditional, religious education he could have become a great rabbinical leader, but would never have gone to a secular high school or to a university. His language would have been only Yiddish, instead of the four languages in which he was fluent—Hungarian, French, German, and English.

Familiarity with the political thought and nationalism of Europe, legal knowledge, awareness of the problems of economy, initiation to international diplomacy in all its intricacy—all this would have been denied him. As Raphael Patai, the renowned Jewish writer, says, "Without being himself a product of assimilation, he would never have acquired that polish and charm which, coupled with his innate personal magnetism, were primary prerequisites for any man, let alone a young middle-class Jewish intellectual, to be received and listened to by the monarchs and masters of the great powers of his day." Again, had not the Jews been granted emancipation by those same powers only a few years previously, the best education would have been of little use.

In his later school days Herzl had experienced some anti-Semitism, but it had not affected him very deeply. He studied but did not practice law. His strong ambition to be accepted as a writer and playwright finally took him into journalism. In 1891 he was appointed as the French correspondent of a German newspaper and his years in Paris proved to be the turning point of his life. Here he met rich and influential Jews and gradually clarified and formulated his own ideas, which tended to be, at times, somewhat fantastic. His moods alternated sharply between the hope of realizing his dreams for the Jewish people and disgust at their indifference. His times of despair were confined to his diary alone; to the outside world he showed only confidence.

To read of the almost total opposition and derision that he encountered from his fellow Jews is to get a measure of the man's stature, of the iron will that drove him on once the idea of a national home for his dispossessed people had taken hold of him. Speaking to close friends years later of those early struggles he said: "I am not better nor more clever than any of you. But I remain undaunted and that is why the leadership belongs to me."

During his stay in Paris something occurred which finally made a Zionist of Herzl. It was the notorious trial of the Jewish French army officer, Captain Dreyfus, who had been brought to trial on false charges, and sentenced to the terrible French penal settlement on Devil's Island. Years later Dreyfus's name was cleared. Reporting the trial for his paper, Herzl was profoundly shocked when he heard the mob outside the courtroom shouting "Death to the Jews." It was his first experience of naked anti-Semitism and convinced him that only in their own homeland could the Jews find safety from this evil, ugly thing.

Herzl became totally possessed by his vision and for the next eight years he traveled ceaselessly to seek help from the crowned heads of Europe; to establish the First Jewish Congress in Basel, Switzerland, in 1897; and to lay the foundation of the Jewish State. His encounter with the great banking family of Rothschild, who afterwards gave so generously to help Israel, was unproductive.

Theodor Herzl was a man of striking appearance, handsome and with a regal dignity of bearing that made a lasting impression on those who came in contact with him. His titanic efforts in great part made possible the modern State of Israel. Writing of the First Zionist Congress, he confided these words to his diary: "If I were to sum up the Congress in a word—which I shall take care not to publish—it would be this: at Basel I founded the Jewish State. If I said this out loud today I would be greeted by universal laughter. In five years, perhaps, and certainly in fifty years, everyone will perceive it."

Herzl gave himself for, and to, his people without stint, spending his great gifts with prodigal generosity until his tragically early death at the age of forty-four. His remains were ultimately brought to Jerusalem for burial. He lies on Mount Herzl, overlooking the spreading modern city he never saw, but which owes its existence in no small measure to his labors.

Herzl's viewpoint was essentially political; his eyes were fixed on the vision of an established, ordered state. However, another leaven was working in the Jewish thought and consciousness of those days, and men and women were quietly making their way from their own countries back to Zion, possessed by a strong urge to work in the soil, something their people had not done for many hundreds of years, to redeem the land of their fathers. They encountered innumerable difficulties; the hazards to health of an unfamiliar climate, unfamiliar and often insufficient food, the rampant malaria which took a heavy toll of their strength, and in many cases of their lives, the hostility of the Arabs, and the opposition of the Turkish officials.

Many of these early pioneers were reluctantly forced to return home, but many remained and gradually conquered their environment, starting what has perhaps made the greatest of all contributions to Israel's life—the kibbutz. These communities were founded on and have maintained a pure socialist ideal of communal ownership and effort, where the individual works for the community and receives in return the provision of his needs.

There has often been criticism of certain aspects of the kibbutz system, especially in the early days, but experience has brought modification and, interestingly, a very high proportion of Israel's leaders are the products of the kibbutz way of life. In agriculture and now in light industry their contribution to the well-being of the State of Israel has been incalculable.

By 1904 Herzl was gone, but his work continued, carried forward by, among many others, the outstanding Jewish scientist Dr. Chaim Weizmann, who had made a significant contribution to the British war effort in World War I. He worked tirelessly on Israel's behalf and became her first president. Hoping to establish good relations with the Arabs, Dr. Weizmann undertook a long and difficult journey, on foot and by camel through inhospitable country, to meet the Emir Feisal. He was warmly received and the two men established a good relationship. The Emir declared, "We are working together for a reformed and revived Near East and our two movements complement one another. The Jewish movement is national and not imperialist, and there is room in Syria for us both." He reiterated that the Arabs looked with the deepest sympathy on the Zionist movement and that they found its proposals moderate and proper. The Arabs, he said, would do their best to help them through.

It was surprising, in the light of later events, that the initial Arab reaction to the Balfour Declaration was not unmitigatedly hostile and Weizmann announced that if there had been misunderstandings between Jews and Arabs, it was now a thing of the past. Signing an agreement with Weizmann on January 3, 1919, Feisal renounced any claim to Palestine, which should, he stated, be the territory of the Jews. While making this declaration he covered his position by stating that this was contingent on the Arabs achieving the Arab State they aspired to. This did not happen, due to the continuing British domination of Iraq, and of the French in Syria, and under pressure, Feisal retreated from his pro-Zionist stand.

Abba Eban, who through much of the life of the State of Israel has held high office, writing of the period of the giving and implementing of the Balfour Declaration, says: "In later years, when many complex problems crowded in, it became the fashion to say that Zionists in the early Weizmann era suffered from two illusions: they convinced themselves, without reason, that a 'National Home' inevitably meant a sovereign state; and they failed to grasp the ominous consequences of Arab opposition. In each case the judgment is too harsh. When the British tutelage began, Zionists had a very clear conception of what it was meant to achieve. The authors of the Balfour Declaration and the Mandate envisaged that an autonomous, distinctive Jewish society would evolve until it was strong enough to establish an independent government. It was also believed, not unreasonably, that since Arab nationalism was going to win lavish gains in the main center of Arabism, it would accommodate itself to an independent Jewish neighbor. The British Royal Commission in 1937, having examined the documents, stated clearly that the plan was for the Mandate to be succeeded by Jewish statehood, and if the Arabs 'secured their big Arab State outside Palestine, they would concede little Palestine to the Jews.' The slogan was 'Arabia for the Arabs, Judea for the Jews!' "

According to Abba Eban, the Arabs were prepared to recognize the difference between the purely Arab lands and Palestine, about which at that time they were willing to compromise, in view of its long historical connection with the Jewish people.

The period of British mandatory rule was an ugly period. It had been entered upon with high hopes by the Jewish community—hopes that slowly passed into bitter, frustrating disappointment. The British administration proved to be biased in the Arabs' favor, which is hard to understand in light of the fact that the Arabs hoped for a Nazi victory. The Grand Mufti of Jerusalem, the notorious Haj Amin el Husseini, having liquidated some three thousand of his fellow Arabs who were not prepared to toe his particular line, finally fled to the welcoming arms of Nazi Germany, to spend the remaining war years in propaganda efforts on behalf of Hitler.

Nowhere was the British attitude toward the Jews more clearly reflected than in the horrors and frustrations to which they subjected European Jews when they attempted to emigrate to Israel. The first ships began to arrive, in defiance of British restrictions, in 1934. But this prewar movement was sporadic. After the war and the nightmare of the death camps, emigration from Europe to Palestine-Israel began in earnest. By December, 1946, 23,000 Jewish survivors had smuggled their way into Israel. Many others, of course, had tried and failed. Great numbers of them had been captured by British police and interned on Cyprus.

Then, in 1947, the Jewish underground bought an old four-thousand-ton steamer in America, *The President Warfield*. It was renamed *Exodus* and arrived in southern France at Sete in July of that year and took on 4,500 Jewish refugees who wanted to get to Palestine. British authorities managed to prevent the French pilot from going aboard to take the ship out of port. So, the Jews defiantly weighed anchor and set sail without a pilot.

Incredibly they got out to sea and made it across the Mediterranean and were within twenty-two miles of the coast of Israel when they were intercepted by British destroyers. They ordered the *Exodus* to stop its engines and prepare for towing. When she refused, the British came up alongside and, without warning, opened fire on her bridge with machine guns. Two of the destroyers rammed the old ship and a boarding party stormed the wheelhouse. The Jews counterattacked and retook the wheelhouse. Three of the British boarding party were taken prisoner and the rest were thrown overboard.

The British rammed her again and sent another boarding party. In addition they lobbed in gas bombs to subdue the refugees. The explosions killed two of them. The second boarding party was also counterattacked and thirty British sailors and marines were taken prisoner.

Finally, however, the British overwhelmed the refugees and towed the *Exodus* into Haifa. Thereupon, they were transferred to three deportation ships. The British wanted to "teach the Jews a lesson" and decided to return them to Europe rather than to an internment camp in Cyprus. No European country, however, would receive them, and, as a final cruelty, the surviving refugees were delivered back to camps in Germany.

The Jews in Palestine retaliated against the British for their cruelty. They attacked British installations, sabotaged oil pipelines, and murdered British soldiers. A radar station on Mount Carmel was destroyed and a British transport sunk.

In 1948 the British resigned from their mandatory rule and left the country to its own bloody and bitter devices. Unfortunately though, fortified positions, arms, and vehicles were often handed over to the Arabs in the confident expectation that the coming conflict would certainly end in defeat for the Jews.

It was at this point that Harry Truman figured importantly in the story. He was under enormous pressure to lend his nation's support to one or the other side in the conflict between the Arabs and the Jews in Palestine. His foreign policy advisors urged him to be cautious about backing Israel. And Truman was inclined to take their advice, except for one thing: his old friend Eddie Jacobson. He and Eddie had been in business together in a haberdashery back in Kansas City. The business had failed, but they had remained good friends.

At a critical moment, March 13, 1948, Jacobson went to Washington to see Truman. Truman had already suffered some embarrassment over the matter and was feeling pretty hostile about it. He told Jacobson so in no uncertain words. In fact he had never spoken so strongly to his friend. Jacobson was taken aback, but he regained his composure. Then he noticed the bust of Andrew Jackson that Truman kept in his office.

"Harry," tears streamed down Jacobson's cheeks, "all your life Andrew Jackson has been your hero. You probably know more about him than most history professors. You were always reading about him.

"Well, Harry, I have a hero too. I've read a lot about him, and I agree with what you've said about him—that he's a true gentleman and a great statesman. You know who I mean—Chaim Weizmann. And now you're refusing to see him. But every time I think of the homeless Jews, homeless for thousands of years, and I think about Dr. Weizmann, I start crying. I can't help it. He's an old man, and he's spent his whole life working for a homeland for the Jews, and now he's sick, and he's in New York and he wants to see you. And every time I think about it I can't help crying."

Truman said . . . , "Eddie, I ought to throw you out of here, but you know good and well I can't stand to see you crying."

Jacobson smiled, continued weeping, and said, "Thank you, Mr. President," and he left.

"After he was gone," Truman reports, "I picked up the phone and called the State Department, and I told them I was going to see Weizmann. Well, you should have heard the carrying-on. The first thing they said—they said Israel wasn't even a country yet and didn't have a flag or anything. They said if Weizmann comes to the White House, what are we going to use for a flag?

"And I said, 'Look here; he's staying at the Waldorf-Astoria hotel in New York, and every time some foreign dignitary is staying there, they put something out. You find out what it is, and we'll use it. And I want you to call me right back.' "

On March 18, Chaim Weizmann came to the White House, but no flag was necessary. He came in through the east gate, and the fact of his visit was not known until later.

In any case, only eleven minutes after Israel became a state in May, its existence was officially recognized by the

United States.

A year later, the Chief Rabbi of Israel came to see the President, and told him, "God put you in your mother's womb so that you could be the instrument to bring about the rebirth of Israel after two thousand years."

At that, great tears started rolling down Harry Truman's cheeks. (Merle Miller, *Plain Speaking* [New York: Berkley, 1974], pp. 234-36.)

Author Mike Evans with Prime Minister Menachem Begin.

Sir Moses Montefiore's Windmill and Museum.

The Jerusalem Symphony Orchestra conducted by Gary Bertini.

The arch at the Ramban Synagogue in the reconstructed Jewish Quarter of Jerusalem's Old City.

(Photo courtesy of Consulate General of Israel in New York.)

View of Jerusalem, showing section of the green belt, a planned landscaped area of native flora around the Old City.

Mishkenot Sha'ananim, an artists' quarter, Jerusalem.

(Photo courtesy of Consulate General of Israel in New York.)

Air view of Masada, ancient Jewish fortress.

One of Israel's most beautiful national parks, Gan Hashlosha (Garden of the Five).

Flocks of tourists enjoy the healthful benefits of the Dead Sea area.

(Photo courtesy of Consulate General of Israel in New York.)

Young Israelis hike into Nahal David, a nature preserve near Ein Gedi.

(Photo courtesy of Consulate General of Israel in New York.)

Swimming by the Roman aqueduct at Caesarea on the shores of the Mediterranean Sea.

(Photo courtesy of Consulate General of Israel in New York.)

Swimming at Ein Avdat in the Negev.

(Photo courtesy of Consulate General of Israel in New York.)

(Photo courtesy of Consulate General of Israel in New York.)

Desecration of the Jewish Torah Scrolls at the Tomb of the Jewish Patriarchs (Cave of Machpela), Hebron—October 3, 1976.

Burnt out bus resulting from Arab terrorist action which killed 34 on March 11, 1978, near Tel Aviv.

(Photo courtesy of Consulate General of Israel in New York.)

Two artists, an Arab and a Jew, have joined forces to create a successful art gallery in the reconstructed Jewish Quarter.

The bibliobus brings books weekly to a recently built neighborhood in Israel's capital city.

Remains of bus destroyed by Arab terrorist bomb in Jerusalem. The incident killed six people, including two teen-age girls.

Over five million trees a year are planted in Israel, covering thousands of barren acres.

View of the city of Jerusalem from the Mount of Olives.

Harvest time in the Negev Desert.

Rows of gladioluses grow in the fields of the Negev.

Arab women shopping in West or "New" Jerusalem.

The Catholic Hospice of Notre Dame was shelled by Jordanian troops at point-blank range from the Old City Wall (at right) in 1948 and again in 1967.

The Catholic Hospice of Notre Dame after repairs carried out in conjunction with Israeli authorities.

(Photo courtesy of Consulate General of Israel in New York.)

Children in Israel regularly participate in the planting of trees, one of the most important methods of protecting the environment.

Panoramic view of the Old City of Jerusalem.

(Photo courtesy of Consulate General of Israel in New York.)

A Jerusalem synagogue rebuilt after 1967 and reconsecrated.

A Jerusalem synagogue desecrated by Jordan.

Jews and Arabs in Old Jerusalem.

Jews and Christians in Jerusalem.

The divided city of Jerusalem (1948-1967).

The residents of Jerusalem's Old City will enjoy better services, such as sewage, thanks to efforts by the Israelis to improve the ancient site.

Children's house in Kibbutz Gvat damaged by Soviet "Frog"—a ground-to-ground missile used by Arab terrorists.

The Western Wall, Jerusalem.

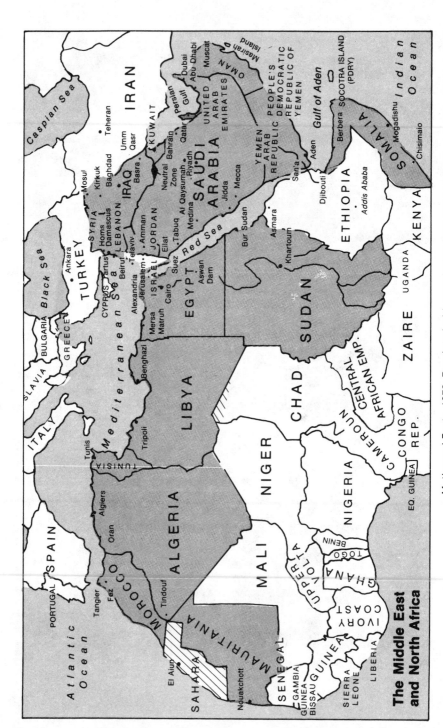

The Middle East and North Africa

Myths and Facts, 1978. Reprinted with permission from "Near East Report," Washington, D.C.

chapter 10

Holy Land

Let us examine what life has been like for the inhabitants of
the Holy Land under the regimes of Christianity, Judaism, and
Islam.

First, what was the condition of the Jews during the nineteen
years of the Jordanian occupation of East Jerusalem? To understand this question it is necessary to know something of the basic
thinking of Islam concerning minority people. In Islamic terms,
all minority people living under their jurisdiction are regarded
as *dhimmi*, that is, "protected" people. What in actual practice
did this term *dhimmi* mean? Many interested parties have tried
to show that Arabs and Jews have lived together in Arab
countries in peace and harmony, with very little trouble. There is
some small measure of truth here, but it is a very small measure
indeed. What in reality was the "protection" worth? For all
practical purposes, it meant that the "protected" people were
treated as second-class citizens.

The edicts which referred to such people began with the re-
assuring words "In the Name of Allah, the All-Merciful, the
Compassionate." They then went on to list all the prohibitions
which were to govern the lives of "protected" people under
Islamic laws. Some of these rules stipulated that a Jew must not
raise his voice in the presence of a Muslim; if he was riding any
beast and met a Muslim, he must dismount; when walking he
must cross to the other side of the street; distinctive clothing
which would mark him out as a Jew had to be worn; he was not
allowed to bear arms, to buy property, or to build a house which
was higher than Muslim buildings.

When a Jewish community became long-established under
Islamic rule, many of these harsh laws were relaxed, particularly as the Jews gradually rose to positions of wealth and some
authority, so making considerable contributions to many Muslim
countries; but the heavy taxes they were forced to pay were never

remitted, nor were they ever safe from sudden outbreaks of religious fanaticism which would end, all too often, in a pogrom.

With this background it is easier to understand the conditions which prevailed in East Jerusalem during the Jordanian occupation. According to the terms of the armistice agreement made at the end of the 1948 war, Jews were to be allowed to visit the Western Wall, or Wailing Wall, to pray. As the only remaining vestige of their Temple buildings, it was of paramount holiness and importance to them. The agreement was not honored and for nineteen years the Jews were denied all access to the Wall. Under Jordanian-Arab rule even their fellow Arabs who were Israeli citizens were denied access to East Jerusalem, and were also not allowed to go to the El Aksa Mosque on the Temple Mount to pray.

From 1948 until 1967 no voice was raised in the United Nations to protest the Jordanian destruction of the Jewish Quarter, the vandalizing of Jewish graves, or the exclusion of Jews and Israeli Arabs from the occupied sector. On the other hand, since the reunification of the city under Israel, Communist and Third World governments have passed a series of resolutions condemning Israeli building, urban development, and archaeological work in the eastern part of Jerusalem.

Under Jordanian occupation, East Jerusalem degenerated into a provincial town. All available resources were put into building up Amman, the capital of Jordan. Not surprisingly, enterprising Arabs left Jerusalem for Amman and the oil states. It is a quite common cause of complaint against Israel that under Israeli rule large numbers of Arabs had to leave the Old City. The reverse is the truth. They left under Jordan; they have prospered under Israel. Unfortunately, this exodus of Old City Arabs left the door open to more aggressive newcomers from Hebron, a notoriously fanatical Muslim stronghold, and to terrorist elements.

The "Eye Witness Reports on Jerusalem" of 1972 contained this comment: "Jordan deliberately neglected the city. Its leaders constantly complained that it was treated like a 'village,' suppressed its political freedom . . . and excluded all Jews, not only Israelis. The economic prosperity which the Arabs in Israel now enjoy has revolutionized Arab society. They now get national assistance, old age pensions and social security at the same rate as Israelis."

Under Jordanian rule, they felt that Jerusalem was neglected and that Amman was favored over Jerusalem, as indeed it
was. The Jordanian government rejected the idea of establishing its capital in Jerusalem after it had annexed the West
Bank and incorporated it in the Hashemite Kingdom. Instances
of Jordanian neglect—and disrespect—for Jerusalem were
numerous. To cite one such example contrary to expectation
and hope, the Jordanian government rejected a plea to establish an Arab university in Jerusalem and instead, they built it
in Amman.

When the Hospital of the Order of St. John of Jerusalem was
about to be built, the Jordanians tried to persuade the order to
build it in Jordan's capital. Only after the order threatened not to
build its hospital at all did it get the necessary permission to
build in Jerusalem. No industry was started in Jerusalem. The
largest single enterprise in Jordan-controlled Jerusalem, outside
of hotels, was a cigarette factory that employed twelve people.
Nothing was done to improve Jerusalem.

Recently, a plan for Jerusalem was voiced by Yasir Arafat. He
said, "We will fight until the Arab flag flutters over Jerusalem . . . the battle is long and arduous. . . . The Americans
can give the Israelis F-15s but, in one of their planes, the U.S.
Ambassador will flee from Jerusalem, because the Palestinian
forces, the Syrian forces, and the Iraqi forces will reach
Jerusalem." It is, however, doubtful whether the Arabs of East
Jerusalem really want Arafat's solution. The desire is to remain
in Jerusalem and preserve the Arab character of their section.
The PLO would jeopardize their plans. Today they have economic prosperity and employment, without which they cannot
remain. This is based on cooperation with the Jewish economy,
and the terrorism which would result from the advent of the
PLO would be disastrous for the Muslim community. They have
only to look at Lebanon and other parts of the Muslim world to
realize that the PLO does not, and would not, serve their real
interests.

Many Arabs have a very real fear that should the PLO gain
control of the West Bank and East Jerusalem they would be in
danger. Those who did not agree with their way of doing things
would suffer.

"Never," writes Albert Memmi, a political theorist and writer born in Tunisia, "except perhaps for two or three eras with very clear boundaries in time, such as the Andalusian period . . . have the Jews lived in the Arab countries otherwise than as diminished people in an exposed position, periodically overcome and massacred so that they would be acutely conscious of their position." He goes on to make this startling statement. "If we leave out the crematoria and the murders committed in Russia, from Kishinev to Stalin, the sum total of the Jewish victims of the Christian world is probably no greater than the total number of victims of the successive pogroms, both big and small, perpetrated in the Moslem countries."

Jews under the Arabs

What is the present situation in the Arab lands for their Jewish minorities? Syria in 1948 had a Jewish population of 45,000. Today the Jews in Syria number 5,000. The Arab equivalent of the western ghetto was called a *mellah*. The Jews of Damascus were not permitted to leave the *mellah*, and even before the Six-Day War their situation had been one of constant terror, subject to night arrest, interrogation, imprisonment, and torture. After the war the situation became worse. Before 1976, no Jew was permitted to leave the country, to sell immovable property, to work in a bank or for the government, to have a telephone or a driver's license, or to leave his property to his heirs. There were numerous tales of the murder and torture of those Jews who were caught trying to leave, which answers the question so often asked, why don't they get out of such countries?

The next chapter in this story opens in Iraq. Here, in 1948 the Jewish community numbered 25,000. In 1979 it numbered 5,000 and today there are 300 Jews in Iraq. It is said that no Jewish community since Hitler has suffered such persecution as the twenty-seven-hundred-year-old community in Iraq. Following the vicious anti-Jewish riots and pogroms of 1941 and 1947, most Iraqi Jews fled to Israel in 1951. In 1963, with the rise of competing Ba'ath factions in Iraq, things went from bad to worse. No Jewish property might be sold, all Jews were forced to carry yellow identity cards, and all freedom of movement was restricted. Even their synagogues and schools were sequestered, but that was not the worst that happened. Following the Six-Day War, Jewish bank accounts were frozen. Jews were placed under house arrest for long periods, their telephones were cut, they were dismissed from public posts, and their businesses were closed down. All emigration was forbidden.

A charge that there was a local Jewish spy ring was trumped up, and in 1969, nineteen Jews were hanged in the public squares of Baghdad, while others were tortured to death. Baghdad Radio called upon the Iraqis to "come and enjoy the feast" and a crowd of some 500,000 men, women, and children danced and paraded past the scaffold while they rhythmically chanted "death to Israel" and "death to all traitors" in front of the bodies of the Jews hanging from the scaffolds. When this barbaric behavior brought a shocked worldwide protest, President Bakr dismissed it as "the barking of dogs."

From 1970 to 1972 another eighteen Jews were hanged and the Jews were forced to house Palestinians and to raise money for terrorist groups including the murderous Al Fatah. As the Ba'ath party machinery increased, Jews began to disappear, their property being seized by officials who covered this misdeeds by posting signs on the Jewish houses saying that the "Jewish occupants have fled the country." As a result of international pressure following the hanging of the Jews, the Iraqi authorities quietly allowed the majority of the remaining 2,500 Jews to leave the country in the early 1970s. More than two dozen Iraqi Jews still cannot be accounted for and the most of the 300 who remain are too old to leave. The value of Jewish community property in Iraq is estimated at over $200 million in apartments, schools, hospitals, and fields. This tiny community is being pressured to turn over these holdings to the government without compensation.

In the light of such facts it is somewhat odd that the PLO should invite Jews to leave Israel and return to the Arab countries they have left. In spite of the fact that almost every Arab country has declared Islam to be its state religion, the PLO continues to state that Jews may return to those countries to enjoy "every right."

An ironic situation developed in Iraq recently, when the government of that country invited all former Iraqi Jews to return "home." Their invitation was taken up by only one Jew, Yusuf Navi. This did not prevent the Iraqi officials from informing Western reporters in Baghdad that "a trickle of Iraqi Jews" were returning. Mr. Navi then became known as "Mr.

Trickle." However, after a year in Iraq the "trickle" dried up completely, as Mr. Navi decided to re-emigrate to Israel.

Now we turn to Libya, where in 1948 there were some 40,000 Jews. As far as is known, none remain today. In 1945, hundreds of Jews were destroyed in a savage pogrom during which they were hurled from rooftops, beaten to death, and burned in their shops. The same melancholy story as that of the Arab lands we have already looked at has to be told concerning Libya. By 1967, the Jewish population had dwindled to 4,500 and as a result of the brutal pogroms which followed the Six-Day War, there was an almost total exodus. Muammar Qadaffi's regime then proceeded to confiscate all Jewish property and canceled all debts owed to Jews. Jewish claims for compensation, amounting to millions of dollars, were of course refused. Any homeless Jews were herded into special camps, and today the ancient Jewish community in Libya has virtually been obliterated.

Lebanon alone, of all the Arab nations, has treated the Jews with some tolerance. But of a population of 20,000 in 1948, today fewer than 300 remain. In 1976 there was a mass emigration of the Jewish community, who feared the growing Syrian presence in Lebanon, which might make emigration impossible. During the fighting in Beirut many Jewish homes, businesses, and synagogues were damaged.

The story in Yemen varies from the usual pattern somewhat. Practically the entire population of 54,000 was taken to Israel in that amazing airlift known as Operation Magic Carpet. The Jews in Yemen had lived in that Muslim country for centuries, mostly in hard conditions, desperately poor and usually treated as second-class citizens. They were skilled silversmiths, creators of the beautiful Yemenite jewelry. Of their music it has been said that it is probably the nearest we can get to the music of King David, "the sweet singer of Israel." The Yemenites were helped to endure the poverty and hardship of their lives by the hope that in His own good time God would once again restore His people to their land of Israel. Then, mysteriously and wonderfully, across that arid land, the "grapevine" brought the rumor that the unbelievable had come to pass—the State of Israel had been born. Spontaneously, the scattered Jews all over Yemen started to dispose of any property they possessed and to begin the long, hard desert trek to the Port of Aden, then under British control.

They remarked among themselves, "Had not the Scriptures told us that God would bear His people on eagles' wings?" And here, before their very eyes, were the "eagles." A small, fine-boned people, they were so emaciated by the rigors of the march, weighing on the average a mere sixty pounds, that many more could be carried on each flight than was normally possible. The magnificent airlift, in which 50,000 Jews from Yemen were brought from Aden to Israel, was a superb operation, a saga which will live as long as Jewish history is preserved. In 1976, traveling in a remote district, an American diplomat discovered some 1,000 Jews were still living there. Although the Imams, the Muslim clergy, had always treated the Jews in North Yemen as infidels and imposed the usual restrictive Muslim laws on the community, it appeared that the group was secure and free to emigrate.

There are some unusual features of the situation in Tunisia, where in 1948 there was a Jewish population of 110,000, which by 1978 had shrunk to 2,000. When during the 1967 war in Israel the Jews in Tunisia were attacked and their synagogues and shops were burnt, the outbreak was denounced by the government and President Habib Bourguiba promised compensation and apologized to the chief rabbi. No one was prevented from leaving, though the government did appeal to the 20,000 remaining Jews to stay. Many of them emigrated to France. The rioters who had attacked the American and British embassies and looted Jewish property were tried and convicted, as were two youths, who received sentences of fifteen years for burning the Great Synagogue.

King Hassan of Morocco has tried to protect the Jews in his kingdom, but the 1948 population of 300,000 had nevertheless dwindled to only 18,000 by 1978. The perniciously forged *Protocols of the Elders of Zion* was published in Morocco in 1967, however many Moroccan Jews living in Europe still feel free to visit their relatives who are living in a country that is one of the more tolerant environments for those Jews who live in the Arab world. In spite of this there has been a virtual disappearance of the Jewish middle class, and the younger Jews are eager to emigrate.

A French organization endeavoring to trace 6,000 missing people, including Jews, who had disappeared, reported that in

Algeria there are some 600 Jews living in forced labor camps, where the conditions are subhuman. Most of Algeria's 150,000 Jews left with the French in 1962, leaving only about 500 in the country.

The Egyptian story follows the usual pattern, in the main, though since President Sadat came to power, conditions have improved. A population which numbered 75,000 in 1948 had decreased until it numbered a mere 300 in 1979. There was the usual confiscation of homes and property during the 1967 war with Israel, and all of the 2,500 Jews were forced to register. Six hundred men, the heads of families, were imprisoned near Cairo, while 200 were taken to Alexandria's Al Baraga jail. Some were tortured, some were beaten, and the majority were crammed into stifling, overcrowded cells. Now, these have become the first Jews in the Arab world who have been able to establish official contact with the State of Israel. An Egyptian-born Israeli rabbi has volunteered to live in Cairo in order to be able to minister to the tiny community of 300 who are too old to emigrate.

Christians under the Arabs

How then do the Arabs treat their Christian minorities? Writing in the London *Observer* in 1977, Patrick Searle said, "Secular nationalism throughout the Arab world has lost ground to a militant revival of Islamic orthodoxy, making all minorities tremble." Returning to Jerusalem, we find that under Jordanian rule the Christians were also subject to repressive laws. Their church schools were compelled to give equal time to the teaching of the Bible and the Koran and Christians could not buy land in East Jerusalem.

It does not seem to be generally recognized in the West that the Arab has no more love or tolerance for the Christian than he has for the Jew, which is summed up in their saying, "Today we will deal with the Saturday people; tomorrow with the Sunday people."

Lebanon has provided and is still providing a tragic illustration of Islam's attitude toward Christians. An estimated 20,000 Christians have died in the two-year civil war in that troubled country. A proclamation of protest was issued by the Lebanese Maronite Bishops in 1975, against "the abuse of the sacredness of churches and places of worship, desecration of Holy Places, firing at monasteries, hospitals and ambulances, . . . attacks on ecclesiastics, as well as monks and nuns. . . ."

Another minority Christian community which has been subject to persecution at times has been the Coptic community in Egypt. The churches, shops, and houses they own have been burned by Muslim fanatics. Shawky F. Katas, president of the American Coptic Association, said in 1976 that the position of the Copts in Egypt had not improved. The Copts claim to be the oldest of all the Christian communities. In Egypt they represent 10 to 15 percent of the population, but this was Mrs. Katas's report: "Job discrimination is at all levels. The Christians are denied leadership positions. No Christian is a college dean, a police commissioner, a city manager, or a province governor. There are two Christian Egyptian ambassadors out of more than 120 ambassadors. Christian college students are exposed to harassment by Muslim students. Muslim professors give lower grades to Christian students than they deserve so that they will be deprived of college assistances and consequently they cannot have scholarships to study abroad or to continue their graduate studies in Egypt. The percentage of Christians who are awarded scholarships to study abroad dropped from thirty percent in the fourth and fifth decades of this century to 2.5 percent in the 1970s" *(Christian Science Monitor*, December 9, 1976).

In Libya, more than 4,000 Christians were forced to leave behind their property, money, and belongings. Later 25,000 more were expelled. The Libyan government proclaimed that its purpose was "to avenge the past. . . . The feeling of holy revenge runs in our veins."

Arabs under the Jews

How do the Jews treat their Arab minorities? First, let's look at the condition of the Arabs under Jewish rule in the Holy City.

Jerusalem, in Israel's hands, is a free and open city—for Arabs, Christians, and Jews alike. Each may worship according to his own beliefs, without hindrance.

There is also freedom of the press. Here is the testimony of a Jordanian journalist on this point. He said, "Had I written half of the things I write now against the government I would have been thrown into jail [under Jordanian administration]. Being a journalist now, under Israel, is so much easier." Under Jordanian rule, the editor of the leading Arabic newspaper in Jerusalem spent two years in prison for daring to criticize Jordan's government.

There is also freedom to travel. A Jerusalem Arab is free to go, and to come back when he wishes to do so. One hundred fifty thousand Arabs come every year to Jerusalem from Jordan, Egypt, Kuwait, and Libya—everywhere in the Arab world, in fact, even from countries that are at war with Israel—and they are welcome, because Israel's policy is to make the Holy Places accessible to all.

In 1967, during that amazing Six-Day War, the Israelis recaptured the entire city, setting it free from Muslim rule. Within four days from the end of the war, General Dayan handed back the Temple Mount to the Muslim Council, an act which elicited comment from *The Guardian* newspaper, in London, a by-no-means pro-Israel organ. It wrote, "To hand the Temple Mount back to the Muslims, in the moment of victory and Jewish Liberation from centuries of discrimination, exclusion and massacre, was a brave act."

One solution which was pressed for by several Catholic, Arab, and Muslim States to the problem of Jerusalem has been the suggestion to make it an international city. This is unacceptable to both Jews and Arabs, to the latter because the Temple Mount, they affirm, cannot be ruled by infidels, that is, by a non-Muslim state. Apart from any question of religion, internationalization does not work, as has been proved in such cities as Danzig and Trieste. Neither could the United Nations, in view of its past record with regard to Israel, be trusted to be impartial.

A solution to the knotty question favored by Mayor Kollek advocates a system of boroughs, moulded on the boroughs of London, each borough to have its own budget, and a considerable degree of independence.

Every effort is made in the city to allow the Arabs to live their lives in their own way. The city's population of 330,000 is divided into about 260,000 Jews (they have been a majority since 1840), about 90,000 Muslim Arabs, and 15,000 Christians. The pattern has been much the same for the last hundred years or so. In those days the square kilometer of the Old City had a Greek Quarter, an Armenian Quarter, a Latin Quarter, with several other little groups of Christians, a large Muslim Quarter and an even larger

Jewish Quarter, as it has today. There was little social contact and no intermarriage, but relations were reasonably good. The basic idea was that each person felt himself superior to everyone else.

Arab schools with Arab curriculums are maintained by the city. During their last three years the pupils can either take a course which will qualify them for university acceptance in an Arab country or an alternative course for an Israeli university. Special efforts are being made to encourage the study of Arabic for Jewish young people and the Arab children are learning Hebrew.

Israel has built vocational schools and hopes to build more, in an effort to give Arab youngsters the chance of improving their prospects, and with them, their self-respect. The Rotary Club Fund provides scholarships for both Jewish and Arab youngsters of talent.

Unfortunately, most of whatever Israel does for the Arabs has to be done unilaterally, for although Mayor Kollek has repeatedly urged the Jerusalem Arabs to share actively in municipal affairs they have not, for the most part, done so. It is not hard to understand the reluctance of the Arab leadership to hold political office, or to take part openly in the city's elected government. To do so would subject them to the danger of punishment by the PLO. However, there *are* some high municipal offices held by Arabs, and well over 20 percent of the city's employees are Arab.

The Supreme Muslim Council, a self-appointed body, is the authority for Muslims under a non-Muslim rule. Though not officially recognized, Israel deals with its leaders in day-to-day affairs.

There is a free flow of people and goods across the River Jordan. This is made possible by the help of the Chamber of Commerce of East Jerusalem. In these ways contacts of all kinds are maintained with the Arab community of the city. Arab lawyers, judges, doctors, dentists and pharmacists practice without having to pass Israeli qualifying exams. Corporations and other businesses operate without the necessary licensing and registration required by Israeli law.

The social welfare program has been extended to East Jerusalem, which had not before had such a service. Electricity and roads have been brought to outlying districts for the first time. Part of the sewage system of the Old City goes back to Roman times, and it has cost a great deal of public money to enable it to deal with the large quantities of water now provided.

To sum up the Arab attitude, the mayor writes: "Despite all our efforts, it is obvious that the Arabs in Jerusalem still do not accept being included within Israel's frontiers. But then it must not be forgotten that they complained about occupation by the Turks, the British and the 'Jordanian Bedouins' as they called them when they were in control. They called it 'occupation' even then!"

So far, we have dealt only with the situation as it affects Jerusalem, but now we must consider the wider perspective of the Israeli treatment of Arabs in the territories she has occupied since the 1967 war. It is necessary at this juncture to point out that there are two classes of Arabs in Israel, those who have availed themselves of the offer of Israeli citizenship and those in the occupied territories who have Jordanian passports. The first category will be referred to as Israeli Arabs, the others as West Bankers, or as those from Gaza.

The 600,000 Israeli Arabs enjoy a higher standard of living than their fellows in most Arab countries. Israeli Arabs sit in Israel's Knesset, where both Arabic and Hebrew are the official languages, and they have the right to vote. The Arab population has increased only threefold in the last thirty years, but today there are fifteen times as many Israeli Arab students as in 1948, with some 700 Arab educational institutions educating 170,000 students. Every child under fourteen years of age, both Arab and Jew, must go to school.

There is a gap between the Jews and Arabs of Israel, caused in great part by the long-continued state of war between their respective countries, but it is a gap which is more psychological and social than legal or economic. Israeli Arabs have belonged to the Israel Federation of Labor (Histadrut) since 1960, and are given equal pay for equal work. The number of Israeli Arabs in white-collar jobs outnumbers the 110,000 day-laborers. In 1978, the "Country Reports on Human Rights Practices" was issued by the State Department and reported that the "average per capita income among Arabs in Israel is probably higher than in any of the surrounding countries, and is, in fact higher than that of

Jewish Israelis of Sephardic origin."

Despite his antigovernment views, in 1975, in a free election, an Arab communist was elected mayor of Nazareth. The free elections carried out under Israeli rule have given the Arabs of the territories the first free and secret balloting they have ever experienced. The elections in the West Bank are conducted in conformity with Jordanian law, with two important exceptions. Two groups, which under Jordanian rule had no voting rights in municipal elections, have been granted them under Israeli rule. The two groups are women and non-landowners. In 1978 the U.S. State Department also reported, "Israel permitted Arab nationalists outspokenly hostile to Israel to run for office in the second West Bank election and honored the results of those elections."

All Israeli citizens have to do compulsory military service, with the exception of the Israeli Arabs, a distinction made to avoid a conflict of conscience for her Arab citizens, but there are some Arab volunteers. At their own request, compulsory military service does apply to the Druze and Circassian communities. During both the 1967 and 1973 wars there was no disloyalty or sabotage behind Israel's lines and Arabs voluntarily did essential jobs, gave money, and donated blood to the war effort.

Most military occupiers in history have drawn up military blueprints, and appointed district officers and "collaborationist" local councils to administer the plan, but this has not been Israel's way. Aware that such an imposed administration would only lead to considerable resistance, Israel followed a policy of "non-presence and non-interference." She has endeavored to provide a decent life for the people of the territories, the military administration being charged with responsibility for their welfare. Welfare assistance has been given to the families of dead Jordanian soldiers and even to the families of Al Fatah terrorists. It was realized that here was an opportunity to prove that the Arabs had nothing to fear from their Jewish neighbors.

The charge of torture and imprisonment without trial is one of the most frequent of those brought against Israel.

The State Department's human rights report has stated, "We know of no evidence to support allegations that Israel follows a consistent practice or policy of using torture during investigations." The operative word here is *policy*. That there are isolated incidents of torture in the treatment of prisoners no one in Israel has ever denied, but that is a very different thing from a deliberate policy of the use of torture. According to the State Department, "Israel is a full-fledged parliamentary democracy with extremely high standards of justice and human rights." When an incident of brutality is brought to light, the individuals concerned are tried and sentenced.

Almost all the 2,500 Arab prisoners held in Israeli jails were captured during terrorist missions against Israel, or were found in possession of arms and sabotage plans. Several groups of Arab prisoners have recently been released as a gesture to President Sadat. Every prisoner held under administrative detention, of whom there are about twenty, has the right of appeal. The International Red Cross is free to inspect Israel's prisons at any time it wishes to do so.

In 1979, the American Bar Association's U.N. Committee took the trouble, unlike some other so-called "investigators," to come to Israel and see conditions for themselves. Their chairman, Leo Nevas, who is also vice-chairman of the United Nations Association of America, after a tour of Israeli prisons and interviews with Arab prisoners commented, "If you ask me, the Israelis are more indulgent over many issues concerned with the rights of the individual than a number of democratic Western countries I could name. And that is without taking into account the situation of war and terrorism that Israel has to deal with and the rest do not." It has been discovered that in some cases, fellow prisoners acting as a "court of inquiry" have tortured their countrymen in an attempt to discover in what way and to what extent they had given information to the police.

The charge has been leveled against Israel that under her administration the West Bank and Gaza have suffered economically. The reverse is the truth, as any observant visitor to the territories can see for himself, as he notices the amount of building which is going on, in spite of the appallingly high cost of building materials. Until very recently there was very little unemployment and such things as private cars, refrigerators, and televisions, unknown not so long ago, are now common. Thanks to Israel's policy of open bridges over the River Jordan, West Bank agricultural produce flows freely across the river, increasing its prosperity. Some 65,000 West Bank and Gaza

Strip Arabs are employed all over Israel and they enjoy the benefits which the Israel Labour Federation has achieved for Israeli citizens.

The accusation has been brought that the Israeli occupation of the West Bank has divided families. During the 1967 war thousands of Arabs fled to neighboring Arab countries. Those who remained suffered no harm, but those who heeded Arab propaganda telling them to leave were absent when, following the war, a census of the West Bank was taken, and so they did not receive identity cards entitling them to return permanently. In spite of this, by 1976, family reunions totaled over 44,000. Some hard cases inevitably occur in such a situation. The West Bank is not sealed off from Jordan and the Arab world. There is a constant flow across bridges over the Jordan, and in 1977 more than a million visitors from Arab countries came to see their relatives in the territories.

Concerning Arab women in the territories, the State Department's human rights document remarks, "Changes are taking place due to . . . exposure to education, to a basically egalitarian attitude toward women by Israelis. The average annual rate of growth of female enrollment in primary and secondary schools in the occupied territories during 1968-1977 has been 6.3 percent, and in 1977 females comprised 43 percent of the total student body. . . . The younger generation of women is growing up with different expectations about their status. . . . Women who work in Israel proper or for Israeli firms receive the benefits of Israeli labor laws and practices."

Anti-Semitic prejudice could not go much further than it did in the matter of the condemnation of Israeli health care on the West Bank. The resolution condemning Israel was pushed through the World Health Organization (WHO) by Arab and Third World delegates in May, 1975. The firsthand report of Dr. A. Bellerieve, the special representative of the director-general of the WHO, was ignored when he said that he "saw nothing that would suggest that standards of medical care had declined . . . in some areas there were manifest improvements." In 1976, an informal experts' group from WHO visited Israel "to conduct an investigation of health conditions in the occupied territories. When the group produced a report that reflected favorably on Israel's administration, the report was rejected by the WHO

Assembly on political grounds, without reference to the merits of the report," said Dr. Bellerieve.

Christians under the Jews

There remains a third community in Jerusalem, and throughout Israel, which must be looked at—the Christians. Under Israel, Christians administer the Christian Holy Places. In this connection, Teddy Kollek, Jerusalem's mayor, has remarked, "Israel is a tolerant enclave in an intolerant part of the world."

Jerusalem holds about 15,000 Christians, of whom the majority belong to the Greek, Latin, Anglican, Armenian, Ethiopian, Coptic, and various other denominations, of whom, all told, there are over thirty in the city.

The facts point overwhelmingly to one conclusion. The Jewish people truly care for the land for the highest ideals of democracy and fairness. Their administration of the land has been benign beyond what anybody might reasonably expect under the circumstances. The same cannot be said for Jordan, and it is ludicrous to imagine that such things would constitute high priorities under a PLO administration.

chapter 11

Jihad

Despite the coverage of the Islamic world by the media, the West and the rest of the non-Muslim world is largely ignorant of Islam. The average person fails to realize that Islam is more than a religion but an all-embracing system—a code and pattern of life, including political, economic, and legal matters.

The strenuous character of Islam's intolerance of other religions came clearly into focus for me when I talked with the famous Bible smuggler Brother Andrew. He told me that of all the nations in the world into which he has smuggled Bibles—and among them are the Soviet Union and China—he had never encountered more difficulties than he faced in Saudi Arabia and several other Islamic nations.

What is the source of this unbending hostility and isolation? It stems, in some measure, from the humiliation Muslims have felt in reaction to the ascendancy of the West—of Christendom. There was a day, long ago, when their civilization shown brightly while Europe sat in darkness. In those days Jews probably fared somewhat better under Islamic jurisdiction than under Christian rulers—as in Spain. Still, as we noted in an earlier chapter, Muslim tolerance was based on the concept that Jews and Christians in their society were *dhimmi*—protected ones—in every sense inferior to themselves.

So, while it was one thing for Jews to exist in Muslim culture, it was quite another thing for them to take dominion over territory that had previously been in Muslim hands. Then, for the Jews to have humiliated the Arabs by defeating them in war has added to Arab resentment. And we in the West have failed to realize how deep has been their sense of outrage and shame over the success and even the existence of Zionism. Nor should we overlook the usefulness of Israel as a catalyst to give the Arabs and the wider family of Islam some sense of unity. It has been virtually impossible for them to unite on any positive basis. Israel, however, arouses such deeply felt emotions in them that, in order to destroy that nation, they would let down their distrust of one another for a short while in order to work together.

Commenting along these lines, Gil Carl Alroy writes, "To acquiesce in the loss of Muslim land to non-Muslims is tantamount to heresy. To struggle with the enemies of Islam is religious duty. The waging of war ruthlessly on any *dhimmis* endangering Muslim overlordship is a categorical injunction. Even a presumption to equality elicits stern reprisal" (*The Middle East Uncovered*, p. 58). He goes on to remind us of how the Muslim Ottomans waged genocide against the Christian Armenians around the turn of this century because they were suspected of cooperating with hostile foreign powers. And the Christian Greek population of Turkey fared quite as badly on the same grounds during World War I.

Bernard Lewis, a noted authority on Islamic matters, wrote, "The emergence of Israel in 1948—or rather, the failure of the Arab armies to prevent it—was a climactic event in the history of the Middle East, comparable in many ways to the landing of the Greeks in Izmir in 1919. It was bad enough to be dominated by the Franks [Europeans and Americans]—but they were after all, the invincible masters of the world, who, on both occasions, had just defeated their enemies in a great war. It was a very different matter, and an intolerable humiliation, to submit to the Greeks or the Jews—to local *dhimmis* whom Muslims had long been accustomed to despise as inferiors. The Franks, moreover, would sooner or later go back whence they came. The Greek great idea . . . of a revived Byzantine Empire, and the Zionist idea of a revived Jewish state, were clearly intended to be permanent. The same sense of outrage colours the Kemalist [Turkish] reaction against the Greeks, and the Arab reaction against Israel. Some of the difference in the subsequent development of Turkey and the Arab states may be ascribed to the fact that the Turks won their war, whereas the Arabs lost theirs" (*The Middle East and the West*, p. 126).

Let us, then, look a bit more deeply into the religion that has shaped and defined Arab culture for over thirteen centuries. It is a fierce and powerful force that has altered the course of the entire world's history.

Articulated by a nearly illiterate camel driver named Muhammad, it took the name *Islam*—submission to God.

At first confined to the tribal societies of Arabia, Islam's flickering light soon roared into a voracious, consuming flame that swept in all directions across the known world, from southern Spain to northern India. By the fourteenth century, the crescent force had cut a swath across Java, Sumatra, and the Malay Peninsula and farther east to the Moluccas, the Sulu Archipelago, and parts of the Philippines.

With the rise of the Mongols and the Turks, the fire of Islam seemed to die down and lie dormant through four centuries of the Dark Ages, extending through the imperialism of the nineteenth century and into the twentieth century's era of world conflict. But beneath the ashes of the burned-out mantle of world domination once worn so defiantly, the red-hot coals of Islamic passion continued to smolder.

At the first sign of weakness by the colonial powers, those coals began to stir, and ultimately found the fuel of new life in the falling timbers of ruined empires. Soon the fires were burning again, coloring the skies over the Middle East with an eerie glow, and casting long shadows of uncertainty across virtually every continent on the globe.

Zbigniew Brzezinski, President Carter's advisor on foreign policy, viewed the resurgence of Islamic political influence with concern and alarm. He said, "An arc of crisis stretches along the shores of the Indian Ocean, with fragile social and political structures in a region of vital importance to us threatened by fragmentation. The resulting political chaos could well be filled by elements hostile to our values and sympathetic to our adversaries."

Brzezinski's arc of crisis extends from Iran to Southeast Asia, taking in Afghanistan, the Persian Gulf States, Pakistan, Bangladesh, the Yemens, and Somalia, which are all Islamic states. But the area of potential crisis is much more widespread, stretching from Morocco to Egypt and including much of North Africa. It involves Turkey and the six Muslim states of the Soviet Union. It reaches as far as Indonesia and the Philippines. It covers the forty-four states of the Muslim world, and the Islamic Union which has sizeable minority populations in the West—a million in Great Britain and two million in France.

Overall, Islam represents a coming change in the world's bal-

ance of power. At the United Nations or any great world conference, almost one-fourth of the delegates are likely to be Muslims.
And the foremost leaders of this Islamic force come from the
twenty-two Arab nations!

The Israeli victories in the wars of 1948, 1956, and 1967, as we
have seen, were not so much military as religious defeats to the
Muslims. Subjugation by the vastly superior Western powers
involved no great shame. But defeat by a handful of Jews was an
intolerable humiliation of Islam. And they were ready to avenge
that shame by fighting Israel again in 1973, on a "carpet of blood,"
if necessary. The initial successes in the war were hailed as great
triumphs. And when the Americans prevented the Israeli army
from destroying the Egyptian Third Army, which the Israelis
had surrounded and cut off, they were laying the foundation not
only for the myth of Arab near-victory in the Yom Kippur War,
but for the resurgence of Islam as a world force.

Not since the fierce warrior "tribes of believers"—the followers
of the prophet Muhammad—swept out of the desert in the seventh
century to establish an empire which occupied much of the world
and threatened the rest of it has Islam felt so strong and confident.

Muhammad

To understand Islam it is necessary to know something about
its origin and founder, what it claims to be and what it proves
itself to be. Islam was founded by Muhammad, who was born
about A.D. 570 in Mecca. His father died before Muhammad's
birth, and his mother when he was six. After the death of his
grandfather two years later, Muhammad was raised by his uncle,
Abu Talib, and grew up working as a shepherd and camel driver.

Traveling with the trade caravans, the young Muhammad was
exposed to the religious and philosophical debates of the Middle
East at that time, and became familiar with the teachings of both
Judaism and Christianity. Apparently these teachings made him
dissatisfied with the traditional Arab polytheistic religion, with
its many tribal gods.

At age twenty-five, Muhammad married a wealthy widow
for whom he had worked as a camel driver, and began to spend
time alone in the desert to contemplate and pray. One of these
periods of meditation lasted six months, and climaxed with the
appearance of the angel Gabriel, who commanded the seeker to

"proclaim."

Then came a period of revelation. Over a period of some twenty-three years, Gabriel dictated the 114 suras, or chapters, of Islam's Koran, or holy scriptures, which are about the same length as the New Testament. According to Islamic teaching, the Koran is the final and unchangeable revelation of the divine will, superseding all previous revelations, such as the Old and New Testaments.

In the meantime, the prophet of the world's newest religion set out to win his first converts. His first believer was his wife, Khadijah. But his insistent belief in a single God posed a threat to the people of Mecca, whose commercial prosperity depended on those who came to venerate the 360 idols which surrounded the holy "Black Stone" in the Ka'ba. The Meccans, particularly the merchants, opposed and persecuted Muhammad and his followers, and an attempt was even made on his life.

On June 20, A.D. 622, the prophet fled to the city which became known as Medina, some 200 miles to the northwest. This night of the flight, or *Hegira*, is considered the most important date in Islamic history and marks the beginning of the Muhammadan Era.

The natives of Medina were more receptive to the teachings of the prophet, and he soon had built a base of religious authority and political power. The Jews who inhabited Medina and the surrounding area refused to accept the new religion, claiming it had twisted the teachings and Holy Scriptures of Judaism. Muhammad accused them of falsifying the scripture. Failing to convert them, he eliminated the danger they represented by slaughter and banishment. It is from this time that we can readily trace the Arab-Jew/Israeli conflict. If it was all right for Muhammad to kill Jews, then certainly Qadaffi, Sadat, and Arafat could justify killing Jews as a holy cause!

When he had a strong enough force—some traditional sources say 10,000 men—Muhammad marched against Mecca. It was essential for his prestige that he capture the traditional sanctuary of his own tribe—and take vengeance for his earlier humiliation at their hands. His forces defeated the city's defenders and seized the Ka'ba. It was to become the holy place of Allah, and Mecca the holy city of the Muslims, the spiritual center of Islam.

Muhammad began unifying the Arabian tribes into a new civilization. He called on them to wage a *jihad*, or holy war, against all dissenters. To those who would accept Islam peaceably, Muhammad sent his blessing. To those who rejected him, he sent word that "I, last of the prophets, am sent with a sword! The sword is the key to heaven and hell; all who draw it in the name of faith will be rewarded." He taught that all who died fighting the infidel would go to paradise, a conviction still deeply rooted in Muslim thinking.

By the time of his death, most of Arabia had come under Islamic control, and Muhammad had turned his thoughts and set his objectives toward Persia and the world. His methods of rising to power have been emulated by many later Islamic rulers. He used religious power for his own political ends, considering that the ends justified the means. Militarily, he was ruthless, using terror—even massacre—if need be. Politically he was an opportunist, seeking alliances where he could find them. He was remarkably aggressive and impatient. And he had the unshakable belief that he had been called by Allah.

Twenty-five years after his death, Muhammad's followers had captured and "converted" Persia, Syria, Palestine, and Egypt.

In less than seventy-five years they had taken North Africa and had entered Europe through Spain. Charles Martel defeated the Muslim forces at the Battle of Tours in A.D. 732, stemming the tide of onrushing Islamic expansionism. Islam had become the dominant power of the Mediterranean world. Its realm of influence stretched from the Atlantic Ocean to the borders of China, encompassing the territories of all the great empires of past history.

Some 350 years later, the Christian Crusaders of Europe set out on their valiant and foolhardy missions to recover the holy places of Christendom from Muslim control. Eight principal crusades were launched between 1095 and 1272, but in the end the relentless Muslim martial pressure was too much, and Islam continued to control Palestine.

The Turks, Mongols, and Tartars came next, and although more successful militarily, they soon submitted to the religion of Islam and became its staunch defenders. So whether by defeat or conversion, Islam's enemies were vanquished and the spirit of Muhammad was triumphant.

Interestingly enough, even through long years of little or no political dominance, Islam has continued to control many sites of great historical and religious significance to both Judaism and Christianity. No place on earth is more sacred to the Jewish people than the site of the Temple. Yet a Muslim mosque and the famed Dome of the Rock have stood in that place for centuries.

Another site revered by Jews is the cave of Machpelah at Hebron, where Abraham and four other patriarchs are buried. It, too, is covered by a mosque.

For Christians, the place of Jesus' death is all important— Calvary, Golgotha, the place of the skull. Yet today, a Muslim cemetery occupies the top of Mount Calvary, shut away behind fences, steel gates, chains, and locks. At the base of the hill is a bustling, noisy, dirty Arab bus station.

But let us examine more closely what the Koran teaches, what the requirements are to become a Muslim, and what Muslims believe.

Islamic law

The Koran, which means *The Reading*, consists of the 114 suras which contain Muhammad's revelation. They are not arranged topically or in the order in which they were set down, but according to their length—the shortest first and the longest last. In Islamic life, the ideal is to know all 77,639 words of the Koran by heart. Sometimes boys of ten or twelve are able to recite it all. At Cairo's Al Azhar University, every incoming freshman is required to commit the Koran to memory—the oral exam takes three days.

The fundamental doctrines of Islam, which are accepted by all the various Muslim sects, are based on the Koran. They include:

The belief in one God, Allah, who rules the world.

The belief in angels who do Allah's bidding.

The belief in the major and minor prophets. Among the major prophets, Muhammad listed Adam, Noah, Abraham, Moses, and Jesus—and of course, himself, the final prophet. He taught that every country had a national, or local prophet.

The strong belief in the Day of Judgment. True believers were to be rewarded in paradise, a "garden of delight." Unbelievers would suffer the tortures of the Seven Terrible Hells.

The belief in determinism. Muslims believe nothing in the world happens unless Allah so wills it.

The Koran also teaches the concept of *jihad*—holy war. The scriptural statements include: "Make war upon those who believe not . . . even if they be People of the Book (that is, Christians and Jews). Make war on them until idolatry is no more and Allah's religion reigns supreme."

Islamic scholars have developed a comprehensive policy toward *jihad*, based on the Koran's teachings. They say it is unlawful to give up *jihad* and adopt peace unless the purpose of giving up is for preparation, whenever there is something weak among Muslims and their opponents are strong.

Further, war is the basis of the relationship between Muslims and their opponents unless there are justifiable reasons for peace. Muslims are free to break their covenants with enemies if they are uneasy lest the enemies should betray them. *Jihad* will never end—it will last to the Day of Judgment.

To become a Muslim, one must profess belief in the unity of God and apostleship of Muhammad. Then he is expected to follow and obey the "Five Pillars of the Faith." These tenets include:

1. Confessing with heart and lips the *shahada*—"There is no god but Allah and Muhammad in His messenger."
2. Saying five daily prayers while bowing in the direction of Mecca. The worshiper is to pray standing, bowing down, prostrating, and sitting. Prayers are to be offered in the morning before sunrise, just after midday, late afternoon, at sunset, and at night.
3. Muslims are to fast twenty-eight consecutive days every year during the month of Ramadan. A fasting person cannot eat or drink, smoke, or engage in sex from dawn until sunset, although he can do these things during the night.
4. Every adult who is physically and financially able is to make a pilgrimage, or *hajji*, to Mecca at least once in his life.
5. Islam requires that every believer give a portion of his earnings to charity. Omar II said, "Prayer carries us halfway to God, fasting brings us to the door of His palace, almsgiving lets us in."

In addition to the Koran and the basic tenets of the Islamic faith, the followers of Muhammad have developed a complex, all-embracing code of ethics, morality, and religious duties. These teachings explain in great detail even the smallest matters of conduct.

One of Muhammad's written works contained a code of behavior that was said to be "a rigorous, minute, specific codification of the way to behave in every conceivable circumstance, from defecation to urination, to sexual intercourse, to eating, to cleaning the teeth."

The conception of law in Islam is authoritarian to the last degree. The law forbids frivolous pleasures, singing and playing of musical instruments of any kind, gambling, the use of liquor, slander, lying, meanness, coarseness, intrigue, treachery, calumny, disloyalty in friendship, disavowal of kinship, ill nature, arrogance, boasting, sly scheming, haughtiness, insult and obscenity, spite and envy, inconstancy, aggressiveness, and tyranny.

Whatever else it may or may not be, Islam as practiced in the world is violence, militancy, and deadly treachery—always to outsiders, and often to those within its own fold. Assassination is an accepted means of political expression. Between 1948 and 1979, twenty-five heads of state and prime ministers were murdered together with another twenty ex-prime ministers. Numerous unsuccessful murder attempts were made on other leaders, including fourteen known attempts to kill King Hussein of Jordan. In the same thirty-year period there were twenty-two inter-Muslim wars and civil wars, and on thirty-two occasions between 1958 and 1979, Muslim states broke off relations with other Muslim states—apart from the mass Arab repudiation of Egypt in 1979.

Since 1948, numerous attempted or successful revolutions have taken place in Islamic countries, including twelve in Iran, seven in Egypt, seven in the Sudan, five in Saudi Arabia, six in Jordan, and three in Algeria. These facts certainly bear out the statement of an Arab leader in 1926 who declared, "The Islamic religion is based on the pursuit of domination and power and strength and might."

Nor are religious and political schisms within Islam a recent or modern development. The first breach in the unity of Islam came

shortly after Muhammad's death when disputes arose over his
successors. The first three caliphs, Abu-Bakr, Omar, and Osman,
were elected almost unanimously. But when Osman was assassinated and Ali succeeded him, part of the faithful refused to
recognize his authority. The result was a battle which ultimately
divided the Muslims into two groups, the Shi'ite conservatives
who supported Ali, and the more liberal Sunnites who opposed
him.

Today about 25 percent of the Muslim world are Shi'ites, who
believe that soon an *imam*, an all-powerful spiritual guide of the
line of Ali, will appear and expound the law and lead them into a
greater Islam. The majority of the world's 750 million Muslims
are Sunnites.

Now let us examine some of the problems posed by militant
religious orthodoxy in some of the main Islamic countries:

Egypt—Few people understood the bold step President Sadat
took when he began the peace initiatives with Israel. This was
certainly out-and-out consorting with unbelievers in the eyes of
all other Muslims. He was therefore guilty of a crime against
Allah, against the Koran, and against every tenet of Islam. He
was making peace with a country still regarded as an enemy by
Muslims.

Since the beginning of the century Egypt has been thought of
as one Muslim nation which has come to pragmatic terms with
its religion, but this is not now the case. Militant undercover
groups incited by Libyan, Iraqi, Syrian, Saudi, and PLO agitators will not rest until revolution comes and Sadat is overthrown.

Egypt is a powder keg waiting for an Islamic fuse to detonate it.

Pakistan—This nation on the subcontinent of India was formed
to be a refuge for middle-class Muslims who could not live under
the more dynamic Hindus, who were greatly in the majority. But
the division of the nation into two widely divergent groups, sepa-
rated by a thousand miles of hostile Indian territory, was doomed
to failure. East and West Pakistan began to seek separate roads
of self-interest, and the more aggressive West Pakistan began to
dominate.

The people of the east broke away to form their own nation,
which they called Bangladesh. The revolt was horribly expensive

in terms of human life, as the Pakistani forces embarked on what was called a course of genocide. In nine months two million people were killed, and the war crushed the economies of both Islamic states, as well as India. In fact, the war has been called "easily the greatest human disaster in modern times."

In 1977, President Bhutto's government was overthrown from within by the army, and direct power fell to Gen. Muhammad Zia al-Huq. Despite appeals by practically every leader in the world for clemency for Bhutto, he was executed by Zia. More than any other single incident in modern times, Zia's treatment of Bhutto shows the uncompromising and merciless nature of Islamic law.

Saudi Arabia—As the guardian of most of the holiest places of Islam, Saudi Arabia is the key Muslim country. Owner of 30 percent of the world's oil reserves and wealthy beyond calculation, it is Islam's principal financier, providing money for development in fifty or more countries.

Much of the Islamic world looks to Saudi for political guidance, but its feudal leaders are in no position to provide it. Despite their wealth they are desperately insecure, since they face dangers from Communist expansion and from the PLO, which constantly tries to force its leaders to take a more active role in the fight against Israel.

While Saudi Arabia covers an immense area, one-fourth the size of the United States, it has a population of only eight million, many of them desert dwellers who could never fit into an army. Saudi's power does not lie in its military potential but in the Islamic example it sets to the Muslim world and in the terrorism and propaganda it finances. Saudi Arabia does not engage in terrorism itself, but pays large sums of money to the PLO.

Iran—Of all Islamic states, Iran provides the most striking example of the use of the dagger of Islam in modern times. Islam came into being by force when a revolution installed Reza Khan as monarch. In 1925 he proclaimed himself Shah, and ruled the country for sixteen years with a heavy hand.

His son, Muhammad Reza, had a great dream—to create a modern industrial Muslim capital in the ancient sands of Persia. He did almost everything wrong. A catalog of his mistakes would fill pages, but his greatest failing seems to have been that he forgot he ruled an Islamic country. His second greatest mistake was to cancel the eighty-million-dollar annual subsidy paid to the mullahs to spend on mosques, scholarships, and travel.

Khomeini saw that Iranian Muslims were reacting violently to the pace and pressures of modernization. He understood how to appeal to the revolutionary nature of the people, and continually incited them to bring about change and a return to orthodoxy. The rest is history.

Returning to Iran soon after the Shah left, Khomeini said, "I will devote the remaining one or two years of my life to reshaping Iran in the image of Muhammad . . . the purge of every vestige of Western culture from the land. . . . What the nation wants is an Islamic republic. Not just a republic, not a democratic republic, not a democratic Islamic republic. Just an Islamic republic."

Turkey—When Kemal Ataturk brought the first Turkish republic into being in 1923 and made it a secular state, he denounced Islam as "the rules and theories of an immoral Arab sheikh" and banned the pilgrimage to Mecca. By its support of the U.N. action in Korea, its admission to NATO, and its leadership in concluding the Baghdad Treaty, Turkey was firmly committed to the West.

In the 1970s, Turkey suffered tremendous problems as its people began rebelling against the lack of religious leadership. Ataturk had failed to kill Islam—and it struggled free and gave birth to a National Survival Party, whose leader depicts the West—Christian and Jew alike—as the common enemy of the Muslim countries.

Escalation of political violence has reached a dangerous peak and it raises serious doubts about the nation's future. The murders of university professors, schoolteachers, judges, and army officers are part of a campaign of terror. Almost certainly the dagger of Islam will next be drawn in Turkey.

Algeria—This nation differs from other Arab Muslim countries in that it has found a way of using the best the West can offer while remaining genuinely Islamic. The Algerian leaders have always insisted that their one-party constitution is a modern version of the Islamic society inspired by tribal conditions, then adapted to city life and directed by Allah's will. The nation's new president, Benjedid Chadly, will keep Algeria firmly socialist, centrally run and anti-Israel, supporting such "liberation movements" as the PLO.

Tunisia—While not one of the important Islamic countries in prestige, military power, or militancy, since 1977 Tunisia has become a likely victim of Islamic republicanism. The change has been dramatic. Once an island of stability and progress in an ocean of Islamic-world unrest, a constant state of threat and chaos now exists. Riots broke out in Tunisia in January, 1977, as young demonstrators, provoked by Muslim agitators from Libya, Saudi Arabia, Iraq, and Algeria, moved in to continue stirring trouble and bring down President Bourguiba, long detested as too moderate to be a Muslim leader. One of his gravest "crimes" is that he has tolerated Christian and Jewish minorities. It is likely that the president will be one of the next Islamic leaders to fall.

Lebanon—This country has suffered more grievously than any other Middle Eastern nation in recent years, yet Lebanon was often presented as an example of the idea where followers of the two great world faiths could live in balanced numbers and share the responsibility of government. The system worked well enough and any conflict was easily controlled. The population totaled about two million people, who adhered variously to seventeen different sects and religions.

The presence of the Muslim Palestinians, as we noted earlier in our discussion of the PLO, changed all this. Before 1970, Lebanon had about 200,000 Palestinian refugees; by 1975, the figure was between 400,000 and 450,000. The Lebanese had no idea that the Palestinians would become a problem. The plan was to assimilate them, and with U.N. help, good homes and settlements were built. But Egyptian and Syrian agents incited the Palestinians to destroy these homes. By keeping the people in squalid camps, they could more effectively exploit them. What has happened since is familiar to us from our earlier investigation of the PLO.

Restoration of a truly free Lebanon will happen only when the president is able to reestablish his authority over the whole country with a new nonsectarian army. This will allow the Syrian and U.N. peace-keeping troops to withdraw, but it is doubtful whether the Muslim leaders will for long tolerate the Christian part of the population.

Libya—Libya's radical policies contribute heavily to Middle East instabilities. Tension between Libya and Egypt has grown steadily. Egyptian army units have been transferred from the Suez to the Libyan border. Traffic has been severely curtailed.

Libya has organized, financed, and trained a force of 7,000 volunteers, mostly Palestinians, Tunisians, Egyptians, and other Africans, armed by Libya and trained by Cuban, East German, and Soviet instructors in the arts of subversion, assassination, and sabotage. Their objective is the overthrow of pro-Western regimes, particularly in Egypt, Sudan, and Tunisia.

In the past year, Libya has done the following: attempted to assassinate Sadat; incited religious riots in Algeria; sent two hundred Libyan-trained Tunisians to raid the phosphate mines of Gafsa in Tunisia in an attempt to take control of the area; burned down the U.S. Embassy in December, the French Embassy in its Benghazi consulate in February, and bombed the British Embassy in June; tried to save Idi Amin's regime in Uganda; sent Libyan-trained African tribesmen to overthrow the republic of Chad; armed the Muslim underground in the Philippines; sent financial aid and arms to various terrorist organizations in Europe; financed the acquisition of Soviet bombs by Ethiopia; liquidated political rivals in Europe and various Middle East countries; and contributed to the Shah's downfall by providing financial assistance and arms shipments to Khomeini's forces. Like the PLO, Libya openly advocates the destruction of the state of Israel and the elimination of the Zionist entities. The most recent action by Libya resulted in a breaking of diplomatic relations with Saudi Arabia in an argument over American radar planes to monitor the Iranian/Iraqi crisis.

The Associated Press now reports that Libya is buying medium-range missiles that are capable of delivering nuclear warheads to any target in the Middle East or Southern Europe. The West German manufacturer of these missiles denies these reports, but Moroccan sources state that the reports are true.

Of all the Islamic nations, Libya appears to be the most militant and dedicated to the principles of *jihad*.

chapter 12

Future Tellers

I climbed to the top of the hill and looked out over the valley below. A few miles to the north I could see the city of Nazareth, its white-walled buildings glistening in the bright sunlight. Farther beyond, and to the east, was Tiberias, on the shore of the Sea of Galilee. Some eighteen miles to the northwest was the Mediterranean and the beautiful, modern port city of Haifa.

I was at Megiddo, and the great plain that stretched out before me is the site where the Battle of Armageddon will take place, according to many scholars. Countless bloody battles have been fought here. And for centuries various prophets have warned that here would take place the final conflict between the forces of good and evil.

Napoleon is reported to have stood upon the hill of Megiddo to survey the great battlefield. Gazing in awe at the huge expanse of the Plain of Jezreel, which extends from the Mediterranean to the Jordan, he exclaimed, "All the armies of the world could maneuver for battle here."

As I looked down into what the Old Testament prophet Joel called the "valley of Jehoshaphat," I found myself wondering how long it would be until this scenic, tranquil spot would be filled with the men and machines of death and war.

It seems inevitable. When the Jews reestablished their nation in Palestine in 1948, they immediately were embroiled in a controversy that has never ended over the ownership of the land. The Middle East conflict has become a sore that never heals, a pit of white-hot coals that can burst into roaring flames at any second. And it is a fire which could well draw in and involve all the nations of the world.

As I made my way down from the hill of Megiddo, I remembered tuning in an English-language "news" broadcast from Radio Amman, the voice of Jordan, Israel's neighbor to the East. It seemed strange to sit in my Jerusalem hotel room and hear

what amounted to a propaganda barrage calling for the reduction—even the destruction—of the Jewish state. Among other
things, the broadcast reported that Jordan's King Hussein and
the vice-premier of China had met to discuss "the Palestinian
problem and Arab legitimate rights." The cultured voice of the
lady newscaster calmly asserted that the Chinese official had
"reaffirmed his country's support to the Arab effort to liberate
the occupied territories and achieve a just and durable peace in
the Middle East."

The radio news report continued: "The World Islamic Conference decided to expand the Arab boycott to Israel to apply
throughout the Islamic world . . . the thirty-nine Islamic countries also decided to try to bar Israel from every United Nations
General Assembly meeting. Other key points in the declaration
pledged Islamic countries to continue the struggle against
the Camp David Accords in order to force the accords' eventual
collapse. The declaration condemns the United States for supporting Israeli aggressive practices against the holy Islamic
places in the Palestinian and Arab-occupied land. It also asks all
countries to prevent Jewish immigration to the occupied Palestinian and Arab territories."

The so-called "news" broadcast continued its verbal attack
against Israel by reporting that the Saudi foreign minister had
said that the Muslim nations were being forced to consider "El
Jihad, the Holy War," as the only means to liberate the occupied
Arab land.

The program also reported: "Israeli forces and their Lebanese
right-wing allies shelled the civilian areas in South Lebanon
today for the fourth consecutive day. The indiscriminate shelling
[hit] the city of Tyre and the refugee camp. . . . A United Nations
spokesman in Beirut said ten villages which lie within the area
policed by the United Nations south of Tyre were also shelled.
Two civilians were wounded in today's shelling, which continued
for seven hours. A total of eight civilians were reported killed in
the previous three days of bombardment that included the shelling of Tyre by Israeli missile boats and helicopter gunships on
Thursday."

An item later in the report quoted an official from Kuwait as
saying, "The main obstacles to a just and comprehensive Middle
East peace is Israel's intransigence and refusal to withdraw

from the occupied Arab territories, as well as its denial of the Palestinian people's legitimate rights."

The preceding quotes were taken from just one broadcast from a single Arab radio station. These kinds of provocative reports fill the Arab airwaves constantly to ensure that the climate for peace remains nonexistent.

Although broadcasting to Arabs, the government-controlled stations may be sure that the people of Israel are getting their message. And they are determined to defend their land to the death, if need be. They will never give up.

I remember talking with several Orthodox Jews in Tel Aviv who bitterly denounced the constant Arab harangue about lost territory. One man told me, "The Arabs have twenty-one states already, but that is not enough for them. We have this little country, no bigger than your state of Vermont or New Jersey, and the Arabs want us to partition it in order to build up another state which has no history and no roots. They want it, obviously, as a springboard for our liquidation."

A few weeks later I talked with a prominent Israeli government official. He said, "I have a very deep conviction that we are reliving the 1930s. The whole world has moved back fifty years. We are viewing the rise of a new Nazism or fascism. In the 1930s the strength and the might of Nazi Germany was its steel and coal. Now we have the Arabs with their oil. But their thrust is anti-Semitic now, just as it was then. And the attitude of the Western democracies is one of appeasement now, as it was then.

"It was a fashionable intellectual mood in the West to appease the Nazis and say, 'What do you know, they are making the trains run on time . . . and basically we need to make sure that we have steel and coal for our economy, so we mustn't rock the boat. If they want to gobble up Czechoslovakia, why make a fuss?' "

He told me about finding a dusty and forgotten book in a library which contained the speeches of a Mr. Henlein, who was the leader of the German Nationalist Movement during the 1930s. He said, "Those speeches are identical—almost word for word—with those of Yasir Arafat today. The idea of concocting a pseudo-nationalist movement like that Hitler used against Czechoslovakia is being copied now by the Russians in the form of the PLO. Henlein, in his day, said that democratic Czechoslovakia was oppressing Germans, just as the PLO says Israel is oppressing the Arab peoples.

"Chamberlain was willing to sacrifice Czechoslovakia to avoid confrontation, and America just didn't want to get involved. So an entire nation was lost to the Nazis without interference. Well, Israel is just trying to get across to the world today that the message from Jerusalem is 'We're not Czechoslovakia.' We will not permit a sellout. In our struggle, things are going to turn out rather differently."

How will things turn out? Many Israelis take comfort in the words of the Hebrew prophets. Did they actually have anything to say about what is happening in Israel now—and what will take place next? Do the New Testament prophetic Scriptures shed any light on these matters?

Prophetic Detail

We've already seen that virtually all of the significant historical events in the story of the Jewish people were foretold by the prophets hundreds of years before they actually came to pass. If all these prophecies proved to be accurate, can we not expect other prophetic passages to unveil the future of Israel and the world and help to prepare us for what will come?

The Old Testament, accepted by the Jews as the Word of God, has sixteen books which deal with prophecy, in addition to the Psalms. Christians, of course, accept the Old Testament Scriptures and the New Testament writings, which also contain numerous prophetic passages. The parables of the Gospels often deal with prophecy, as do certain of the Epistles (especially First and Second Thessalonians, Romans 8, and 1 Corinthians 15) and the Revelation.

For hundreds of years, Jewish and Christian Bible scholars have studied the scriptural prophecies. Many agree that there is one inescapable conclusion: the Middle East crisis will continue to escalate until it threatens the peace of the whole world. The problem will eventually involve all the nations of the earth, and will bring them to the precipice—to Armageddon—to what many now predict will be a thermonuclear holocaust.

In recent years, those who have compared biblical prophecy with current world events have become convinced that the "last days" spoken of by the prophets are upon us now. The end of the present age and the dawn of a new era is actually within view.

Their warning is echoed by secular world leaders. On June 8, 1978, Alexander Solzhenitsyn, Soviet exile and modern-day prophet to the West, stood to accept an honorary doctorate from Harvard University. He said, "The fight for our planet, physical and spiritual, a fight of cosmic proportions, is not a vague matter of the future; it has already started. The forces of evil have begun their decisive offensive. You can feel their pressure. . . ."

Newsweek recently reported the comments of the Saudi ambassador, Ali Alireza, as he met with a group of dignitaries in Washington, D.C., to honor the departing Pakistani envoy. He stunned his guests by sounding an alarm about Soviet designs in the Red Sea, the Arabian Peninsula, and the Persian Gulf. He said, "Our friends do not seem to realize that a crisis of historic magnitude is close at hand for the Western world, and for those who share its values in our entire area."

The Pakistani envoy, Yaqub Khan, agreed. "I fear that historians will look back at 1978 as a watershed year, when the balance of power shifted against the Western world."

To understand what is happening and what is yet to come, it is helpful to examine the writings of the prophets. The Old Testament prophecies of Daniel and Ezekiel, and the New Testament's Revelation, are especially important.

In his excellent book *Israel's Final Holocaust*, Dr. Jack Van Impe notes that skeptics dislike the prophet Daniel because his outline of the future is too accurate. Daniel's first recorded prophecy was actually the interpretation of a dream which came to Nebuchadnezzar, the powerful king of the Babylonian Empire. According to the late Dr. H.A. Ironside, this interpretation, which has come to be known as the A B C of Prophecy, "contains the most complete, and yet the most simple, prophetic picture that we have in all the word of God."

History already has proved the accuracy of much that Daniel foretold as world events have fulfilled what he said would come to pass. It appears that the stage is set for the remainder of the prophecy to develop.

Briefly, the dream of Nebuchadnezzar was of an image of a man. His head was gold, his breast and arms were of silver, his midsection and thighs were brass, his legs were iron, and his feet were part iron and part clay. As the king watched, a great stone crashed down upon the image, smashing it so completely that the wind blew away the pieces. Then the stone became a great mountain that filled the whole earth (see Dan. 2:31-35).

Daniel's interpretation of the dream was simple, yet profound. He said the head of gold represented Nebuchadnezzar, whose power in the Babylonian Empire was absolute. Many scholars now see relationships between Daniel's interpretation and later events. Their beliefs are summarized as follows. The silver breast and arms of the image represented the Medo-Persian Empire which would come after the fall of Babylon. The Grecian Empire, headed by Alexander the Great, was symbolized by the belly and thighs of brass. The legs of iron were the Roman Empire, while the feet, part iron and part clay, foretold the revival of the Roman Empire in the last days. The ten toes represent the ten leaders of the coming European federation. The stone represents an all-powerful divine force that will ultimately destroy all earthly kingdoms and be recognized as supreme. This, it is believed, refers to the coming kingdom of the Messiah which will be established upon His return to earth.

The Luxembourg Agreement—December 1-20, 1980

The Belgian daily newspaper *Le Soir* reported on December 27 that the European Common Market had devised a detailed list of options for its Middle East activities, including the internationalization of Jerusalem, the withdrawal of Israel from "contested" territories, and the new international peace-keeping force.

The Belgian newspaper said that the options were approved as "starting points" by the nine market heads of government at the Luxembourg Summit meeting held from December 1 to December 20, 1980.

According to the report, the plan calls for the following:

1. The withdrawal of Israel jurisdiction over all the territories taken in the 1967 war—areas in Jordan, Gaza, East Jerusalem, and the Golan Heights. The withdrawal would be carried out over a two-year period with "temporary security points" as the last areas are turned over by Israel. The United Nations would supervise the withdrawal in conjunction with a mixed commission of Israelis, Jordanians, and Palestinians. Alternatively, it could be supervised by the United Nations or Jordan, or supervised by the United Nations, local mayors, and notables.

2. During the withdrawal, relations between Israel and its Arab neighbors would be normalized under procedures similar to those used in the Camp David Accords.

3. Most Israeli settlements in the administered areas, including East Jerusalem, that are considered illegal, would be dismantled. However, Israel would be allowed to keep some of them as "foreign enclaves" in Arab lands. (This is a reference to settlements existing before 1948.)

4. Palestinians would be given an independent state, perhaps with some links to Jordan and Israel. There are, in fact, three options: an independent Palestinian state; an independent Palestinian state federated with Jordan; an independent Palestinian state federated with Jordan and Israel. The nature will be determined by a referendum supervised by an advisory council. All Palestinians will be entitled to participate in the referendum with special weight given to the residents of Judea, Samaria, and Gaza.

5. Demilitarized zones would be set up on both sides of the border. This will be patrolled by a U.N. Force that would guarantee Israel's security. The European nations are prepared to participate in this force.

6. Jerusalem would become an international city with Jewish, Muslim, and Christian control over their own religious sites. The rest of the city would be run by a communal authority.
   The options available for the future of Jerusalem are:
   (a) Internationalization.
   (b) Division of the city with responsibility for holy places in the hands of the respective religions.
   (c) Division and internationalization of the Old City.
   (d) If the city is redivided, the possibility of joint administration would be considered.

7. Palestinian refugees would be allowed to return to the new Palestinian state but the report added that European leaders doubt that many would choose to return to Israel.

The Scriptures give us reason to believe that out of the Common Market a man of sin will come forth. In light of strange things that are happening in the Common Market today, it is wise for us to be alert to developments that could be a fulfillment of biblical prophecy.

Some forty years after Nebuchadnezzar's dream, Daniel had a vision which was a confirmation and extension of his first interpretation of the future. The vision consisted of the appearance of four beasts, which he saw as representing major world empires. Daniel saw a lion with eagle's wings, a bear with three ribs in its mouth, a leopard with four wings and four heads, and a strange ten-horned beast, "dreadful and terrible, and strong exceedingly" (Dan. 7:1-7).

Many Bible scholars hold that the lion represents the Babylonian Empire headed by Nebuchadnezzar. From their perspective, the bear was the Medo-Persian Empire that followed, and the ribs in the bear's mouth were to indicate the three major conquests of that empire. Alexander the Great's Grecian Empire was represented by the leopard, the four heads indicating the division of the empire between four generals upon Alexander's death in his early thirties.

According to this system of interpretation, the beast with ten horns was the symbol of the coming Roman Empire. Daniel noted that after a time another little horn grew upon the beast and plucked up three of the other horns by the roots. With eyes like a man and a mouth speaking great things, the little horn portrayed a powerful leader who would come in the end time. Near the end of his life, Daniel began praying about returning to Jerusalem. He may well have remembered the prophecy of Jeremiah that had specified that the captivity of the Jews in Babylon would last seventy years. As that period of time came to an end, he began confessing his own sins and the sins of his people, crying out to God for forgiveness.

During his prayer, the angel Gabriel appeared to Daniel and revealed a timetable of coming events that would especially affect Israel. The angelic message, referred to as the vision of seventy weeks, may well be the backbone of prophecy. This mathematical revelation gave the Jews the exact time at which to expect the coming of their Messiah. It also foretold His death, the destruction of Jerusalem, the rise of the antichrist, and the establishment of the Messiah's coming kingdom on earth.

The prophecy said that seventy weeks of trouble were coming upon the Jewish people. These "weeks" were not units of days, but of years. These 490 years would cover a series of events that would determine the eternal destiny of the Jews. From a definite starting point—when the order was given to rebuild Jerusalem—a period of 483 years would elapse before Messiah would come—and be rejected (see Dan. 9:24-26).

Interestingly enough, the Bible gives the precise date when Artaxerxes, king of Persia, granted the request of Nehemiah and decreed that Jerusalem and its Temple should be rebuilt. The Bible says, "And it came to pass in the month of Nisan, in the twentieth year of Artaxerxes the king" (Neh. 2:1).

Since the king had taken the throne in 465 B.C., his twentieth year would have been 445B.C. The month was Nisan, and Jewish custom is to date events on the first of the month unless a specific day is mentioned. Translating the date given to our calendar, the king's decree to rebuild Jerusalem was issued on March 14, 445 B.C.

Precisely 483 years after that decree, the Messiah came riding into Jerusalem as had been prophesied:

Rejoice greatly, O daughter of Zion; shout, O daughter of Jerusalem: behold, thy King cometh unto thee: he is just, and having salvation; lowly, and riding upon an ass, and upon a colt the foal of an ass. (Zech. 9:9)

Daniel's extraordinary prophecy went on to say that the Messiah would be "cut off," which is an idiom for being killed. After that, an army would march in and destroy Jerusalem and the Temple which had been rebuilt by the returned Babylonian exiles.

Since the destruction of Jerusalem and the Temple were carried out by Titus of Rome in A.D. 70, the Messiah had to appear before then. Hal Lindsey, in his best-selling book *The Late Great Planet Earth*, observes: "There was only one person who was taken seriously as the Messiah before A.D. 70. We have the logical candidate for that role in the carpenter from Nazareth."

But what happened to the last "week," the last seven years covered by Daniel's vision of seventy weeks? These events are yet to come. The end of the age will be highlighted by the return of the Messiah and the resurrection of the dead:

For the Lord himself shall descend from heaven with a shout, with the voice of the archangel, and with the trump of God: and the dead in Messiah shall rise first: Then we which are alive and remain shall be caught up together with them in the clouds, to meet the Lord in the air: and so shall we ever be with the Lord. Wherefore comfort one another with these words. (1 Thess. 4:16-18, author's paraphrase)

Then the seventieth week begins—the last seven years of time on earth before the Millennium, the establishment of the Kingdom of God on earth for a thousand-year reign of peace. But the seven years are to be the most awful time in the history of the world since time began.

The prophet Jeremiah said:

Alas! for that day is great, so that none is like it: it is even the time of Jacob's trouble. (Jer. 30:7)

Messiah said:

For then shall be great tribulation, such as was not since the beginning of the world to this time, no, nor ever shall be. (Matt. 24:21)

The prophet Daniel declared:

There shall be a time of trouble, such as never was since there was a nation even to that same time. (Dan. 12:1)

As this fearsome era begins, the "dreadful and terrible, and strong exceedingly" ten-horned beast that Daniel had prophesied about earlier appears on the scene in the form of a revived Roman Empire. Out of this ten-nation European federation will emerge a powerful political leader whose magnetic charm and personal appeal will win the confidence and loyalty of the world.

This immensely powerful leader, whom the Bible identified as the antichrist, will offer solutions to the perplexing problems and international crises that threaten the very existence of the world. Daniel predicts that he will sign a seven-year peace treaty with Israel. "And he shall confirm the covenant with many for one week" (Dan. 9:27).

At first everything will appear to be going well. The centuries of armed tension will be relieved by the peace imposed by the power of antichrist. Israel will be able to turn its full attention to the development of the country and its resources, and will prosper as never before. Some arrangement will even have permitted the rebuilding of the Temple in Jerusalem and the resumption of sacrifices and oblations.

Just when peace seems to have come for Israel, it will be taken from her. After three and a half years, the antichrist will break his treaty with Israel. He will go to the Temple and "cause the sacifice and the oblation to cease" and bring about the "abomination of desolation" by proclaiming himself to be God.

Now the prophetic narrative of the last days is picked up by the prophet Ezekiel. The credibility of Ezekiel is already well established by his foretelling the scattering and return of Israel some twenty-five centuries before the fact. His vision of the valley of dry bones is one of the most vivid and moving passages in all of the Bible (see Ezek. 37:1-10).

Ezekiel relates how he was taken to a vast cemetery, a great valley full of bones. After long exposure to the sun and wind, the skeletons had become dry, bleached, and disconnected. As he viewed this grisly sight, the Lord asked him if the bones could live. He simply replied, "O Lord God, thou knowest."

He was then given the responsibility of prophesying over the bones, promising them that they would receive flesh, breath, and life. As he obeyed the Lord, there was a great shaking and a loud noise as the bones came together, were covered with flesh, and received the breath of life, then stood to their feet and became a great army.

The prophet said the Lord showed him that the bones represented Israel. Their dry and disconnected condition represented the dispersion of the Jews around the globe, and their hopeless despair at ever becoming a nation united again.

So Ezekiel proclaimed the message God had given him, and his words helped keep a glimmer of hope alive in the hearts of the Jewish people across the centuries from their "boneyards" in every nation of the world. In the midst of incredible persecution and suffering, the promise of God offered something to hold on to: "For I will take you from among the heathen, and gather you out of all countries, and will bring you into your own land" (Ezek. 36:24).

And again, the words of the Lord in Ezekiel's prophecy were

like a bright light cutting through the gloom and darkness of the
Jewish ghettos and death camps:

> Behold, O my people, I will open your graves, and cause you
> to come up out of your graves, and bring you into the land of
> Israel. And ye shall know that I am the Lord, when I have
> opened your graves, O my people, and brought you up out of
> your graves, And shall put my spirit in you, and ye shall
> live, and I shall place you in your own land. (Ezek. 37:12-14)

The establishment of the new nation of Israel in 1948, and the
subsequent emigration of Jews from more than one hundred
nations to populate the Jewish state, brought obvious and un-
deniable fulfillment of this part of Ezekiel's prophecy.

I remember talking about the importance of the prophecies
with Benjamin Netanyahu, the Israeli scholar who is the head of
the Jonathan Institute. He said, "The truth of the matter, Mike,
is that if it had not been for the prophetic promises about
returning to our homeland, the Jewish people would not have
survived. There is something about reading the statements of the
prophets in the original Hebrew language—the powerful impact
of those words bores deep into your heart and is implanted into
your mind. There is absolutely no question but that those ancient
prophetic promises kept hope alive in the hearts of Jewish people
and sustained us over the generations when we had nothing else
to cling to."

With the survival of the Jewish people and the rebirth of Israel
as a nation in the Promised Land, Ezekiel's track record as a
prophet is totally convincing. He speaks in specific detail about
coming events which will bring the world to the awesome edge of
Armageddon.

In Ezekiel 38 and 39, the prophet gives a detailed account of a
great military offensive which will be launched against Israel by
Russia and a confederation of Arab and European countries.
Ezekiel identifies the participants in the invading force with
names such as Gog, Magog, Meshech, Tubal, Gomer, Togarmah,
and such familiar appellations as Persia, Ethiopia, and Libya.

A great many biblical scholars are convinced that the evidence
clearly identifies Magog as modern Russia, and Meshech and
Tubal as the Soviet cities of Moscow and Tobolsk. Gomer refers

to Eastern Germany and Slovakia, Togarmah is Southern Russia and Turkey, Persia is modern Iran (and may include Iraq), and Ethiopia and Libya include the black descendants of Cush and the North African Arabs.

This is the force that will arm itself and march against Israel. Russia will lead the invasion at a time when war is not expected. Having made a treaty with the antichrist, the emerging world leader, Israel will have been lulled into a false sense of security as a result of the three and a half years of peace and prosperity she has enjoyed. Ezekiel says Russia will resolve to "go up to the land of unwalled villages; I will go to them that are at rest, and dwell safely, all of them dwelling without walls, and having neither bars nor gates, to take a spoil, and to take a prey . . . upon the people that are gathered out of the nations . . ." (38:11-12).

Reinforcing the words of Ezekiel, Daniel declared:

And at the time of the end shall the king of the south [Arab and African confederacy] push at him: and the king of the north [Russia and confederates] shall come against him like a whirlwind, with chariots, and with horsemen, and with many ships; and he shall enter into the countries, and shall overflow and pass over. (Dan. 11:40)

Russia's attack on Israel, though seemingly unstoppable, will be her greatest military blunder. The brief battle will undoubtedly be one of the most destructive in history. Ezekiel says that when Russia's hordes have invaded Israel "as a cloud to cover the land," there will come a great shaking, with earth-splitting explosions, mountains toppling, and a deadly rain of hail and fire. The vision is strongly suggestive of nuclear warfare. Whatever it is, the prophet says that the defeat of the northern invaders will make it clear to the Jews that God has protected them.

Ezekiel says that only one-sixth of Russia's great army will escape death in the battle. So many will die that it will take Israel seven months to bury all the bodies left behind, and the burning of the weapons will go on for seven years.

With the destruction of the Arab and Russian forces, only two great spheres of power will remain to fight the climactic battle of Armageddon. The combined forces of Western civilization under the leadership of the Roman dictator, antichrist, will face the vast hordes of the Orient, probably united behind the Red Chinese war machine.

The attack by Russia will give the antichrist the excuse for full occupation of Israel under the pretense of protection. With forty-two months remaining in the last prophetic "week," the antichrist will suddenly begin asserting his power and trying to gain control of the world. His first challenge is the massive Oriental army marching toward the Middle East. "But tidings out of the east and out of the north shall trouble him: therefore he shall go forth with great fury to destroy, and utterly to make away many" (Dan. 11:44). The Bible says the casualties of this confrontation will total one-third of the remaining world population. John wrote in Revelation:

> And the number of the army of the horsemen were two hundred thousand thousand: and I heard the number of them. And thus I saw the horses in the vision . . . and the heads of the horses were as the heads of lions; and out of their mouths issued fire and smoke and brimstone. By these three was a third part of men killed, by the fire, and by the smoke, and by the brimstone. (Rev. 9:16-18)

This description certainly could be of an all-out nuclear attack, with the "horses" being motorized tanks or mobile-based missiles. The victory in this confrontation would give antichrist control—at least temporarily—of the entire world.

At this point he will break his treaty with Israel, and refuse to allow further sacrifices or rituals at the Temple. Instead, antichrist will commit the "abomination of desolation" by desecrating the holy of holies by using it as a platform to declare himself to be God and demanding the worship of all mankind.

He will also assume total economic control, requiring his mark on the hand or forehead in order for any person to transact any business. The penalty for opposing him will be death.

The Revelation tells us that as the world moves toward Armageddon, a great Jewish revival will break out. But at the same time, the antichrist will accuse the Jews of causing every problem and ill on the earth. He will issue a call to all the armies of the world to come to the Middle East to destroy the Jews and stamp them out forever. And having heard that Messiah was soon to return to set up His kingdom on earth, his strategy will be to try to defeat the Messiah with military power. As Dr. Van Impe writes, "Armageddon will demonstrate man at the height of his pride and folly. Convinced of the power of their weaponry and deceived by a leader energized by Satan, the armies of earth will march to their doom, expecting to destroy the Christ they have rejected."

So here it is, the last great conflict. The battle lines are drawn throughout Israel, with the vortex centered in the Valley of Megiddo. According to Zechariah, terrible fighting will center around the city of Jerusalem (12:2; 14:1). Isaiah speaks of frightful carnage taking place south of Jerusalem (63:1-4). And the Apostle John predicts that so many people will be slaughtered in the conflict that blood will stand up to the horses' bridles for a total distance of 200 miles northward and southward of Jerusalem (Rev. 14:20).

In addition to the indescribable slaughter in the Middle East, there will be a worldwide shock wave that will race around the globe and destroy all the cities of the nations. The biblical record isn't clear as to whether the destruction will come from a natural force like an earthquake or from some super weapon. But in an instant, all the great cities—Paris, London, Tokyo, New York—will be gone (see Rev. 16:19).

As the battle reaches its awful climax it appears that all life on earth will be destroyed—at that moment Messiah returns to save man from self-extinction. Jesus prophesied:

Except those days should be shortened, there should no flesh be saved: but for the elect's sake those days shall be shortened. . . . and they shall see the Son of man coming in the clouds of heaven with power and great glory. (Matt. 24:22, 30)

John reported:

And I saw heaven opened, and behold a white horse; and he that sat on him was called Faithful and True. . . . And I saw the beast, and the kings of the earth, and their armies, gathered together to make war against him that sat on the horse, and against his army. And the beast was taken, and with him the false prophet that wrought miracles before him. . . . These both were cast alive into a lake of fire burning with brimstone. And the remnant were slain with the sword of him that sat upon the horse. (Rev. 19:11, 19-21)

Only with the coming of the Messiah of Israel will lasting peace come to the Middle East—and to the world. Daniel declares, ". . . the God of heaven [shall] set up a kingdom, which shall never be destroyed" (2:44). When the governments of men have finally fallen, God will set up His Kingdom, and the long-awaited Millennium will begin. The word "millennium" means "one thousand years," and in biblical interpretation, this refers to that period of time when there will be total peace among people and nations. Jerusalem will at last become a city of peace and the capital of the world.

Isaiah described this glorious time which is coming by saying:

And they shall beat their swords into plowshares, and their spears into pruninghooks; nation shall not lift up sword against nation, neither shall they learn war any more. (Isa. 2:4)

How Near Are We Now?

Where are we now in the countdown to the beginning of the last chapter in the history of mankind? What events must yet take place to trigger the ticking of God's prophetic clock?

Bible scholars say there is nothing to delay the return of Messiah for those who serve him. It could take place at any moment, and no one can say for sure when it will be. Jesus said:

But of that day and hour knoweth no man, no not the angels of heaven, but my Father only. (Matt. 24:36)

He warned:

Be ye therefore ready also: for the Son of man cometh at an hour when ye think not. (Luke 12:40)

However, there are certain events that are to serve as a sign or forewarning that the last days are upon us and the final act of Israel's great historical drama has begun. The prophets have outlined three specific conditions that would certainly have to be met for the end of time to come, and all of them center upon

Israel. So Israel is greatly significant as a sign of the time.

First, the Jewish nation would be reborn in the land of Palestine. Second, the Jews would repossess old Jerusalem and the sacred sites. And third, they would rebuild their ancient Temple of worship upon its historic site. The years 1948 and 1967 saw the realization of the first two conditions. There remains but one more event to completely set the stage for Israel's part in the final performance of mankind. This is to rebuild the Temple.

According to the Law of Moses, the only place the Jewish Temple can be built is upon Mount Moriah, where the first two temples were erected. There is one major obstacle to building the Temple there—the third holiest place of the Muslim faith, the Dome of the Rock, is squarely in the middle of the old Temple site. And it is no newcomer, having been there for thirteen centuries. Razing that structure to make room for the Temple would cause no little consternation to Muslims around the world.

Obstacle or no obstacle, prophecy demands that the Temple be rebuilt. Daniel spoke of the prince who will make a covenant with the Jewish people and guarantee them religious freedom to make sacrifices and oblations. These can only be done in the Temple. The prophet also predicted that after three and a half years, the Temple would be desecrated by this prince, the antichrist, who would invade the inner sanctum and proclaim himself God. So it is a certainty that ultimately the Temple will be rebuilt.

Shortly after the recapture of Old Jerusalem in 1967, a reporter interviewed a famous Israeli historian, Israel Eldad. He asked, "Do your people intend to rebuild the Temple?"

Eldad said, "From the time that King David first conquered Jerusalem until Solomon built the Temple, just one generation passed. So will it be with us."

"What about the Dome of the Rock which now stands on the Temple site?" asked the reporter.

"It is, of course, an open question," said Eldad. "Who knows, maybe there will be an earthquake."

At some point after the rebuilding of the Temple, Israel will sign a treaty with a world leader who will be in a position to guarantee peace, security, and religious freedom. The minute this pact is made, God will start the prophetic clock on the last "week," the last seven years, beginning the period of biblical history previously noted as the Tribulation.

How could such a thing happen? The perilous position of our planet has leaders of the world talking about a new world government that will guarantee peace at any price. With global powers spending a billion dollars a day on arms, with a population crisis and a raw materials crisis, leaders are ready to look anywhere for possible solutions.

And the world grows more dangerous every day. More than $370 billion a year is being spent on armaments. Sen. Mark Hatfield of Oregon has computed the amount of destructive weapons in the world and announced that there is enough firepower stockpiled in nuclear bombs, rockets, and ammunition to equal fifteen tons of dynamite per person on the face of the earth.

A Princeton University professor published a work on the arms race entitled "Thinking about the Unthinkable." It said: "The only way to solve the problem is maybe some form of world government." Five nuclear arms experts from Harvard University and the Massachusetts Institute of Technology warned: "A very nasty kind of world government may be the only way to keep the world from blowing itself up in a nuclear war."

The desire for global peace might well lead to the rise of a single governing force headed by a politician of inordinate appeal and power. The hope for self-preservation might force the most unyielding antagonists to compromise and accept even distasteful solutions that promised new hope for survival. The great historian Arnold Toynbee wrote: "One of the most conspicuous marks of a disintegrating society is when it purchases reprieve by submitting to forcible, political unification."

History bears record that one of the Roman Empire's greatest strengths was the *Pax Romana*, the Roman peace. Again and again, Rome's legions were able to secure large regions without a struggle, with only token resistance. The provincials willingly turned to Rome for law and order, peace and security, freedom from war.

And it will happen again. Many students of prophecy feel there is no doubt that the Roman Empire will be reestablished in the form of a ten-nation confederacy which will spawn a religious and political leader who will rule the world. Hal Lindsey writes, "We believe that the Common Market and the trend toward the unification of Europe may well be the beginning of the ten-nation confederacy predicted by both Daniel and the Book of Revelation."

The leader who comes out of the new Roman Empire will assert his world ambitions by taking on the most troubling problem of his—or any other—age, the Middle East crisis. He will devise and impose a solution which will be accepted. And peace will result—for three and a half years. Then the cataclysmic events which will climax at Armageddon will begin. As the Bible says, "When they shall say, Peace and safety; then sudden destruction cometh upon them, as travail upon a woman with child; and they shall not escape" (1 Thess. 5:3).

We've examined in considerable detail the fate of Israel in the ending days of time. But what about the Arab states? Do the prophets have anything to say about their role in the final act of history's drama? What is to be their end?

A careful examination of the prophetic writings provides some startling specific information about several of the Arab nations, including Lebanon, Jordan, Egypt, Syria, and Iraq.

In Ezek. 47:13-48:29, the boundaries of the territory which the nation of Israel will occupy during the Messianic Kingdom are specifically defined. The passage also spells out how the land is to be divided among the people. But the significance of the passage comes when these boundaries are traced on the map of the Middle East. They include all of modern-day Lebanon. From this we can only deduce that the day will come when Israel will possess and occupy all of Lebanon.

The fate of Jordan is foretold by no less than four Old Testament prophets, who see only utter and total destruction for the land and its people. Referring to Edom, the ancient name for what is now Jordan, the prophet Isaiah declared:

> For Jehovah hath a day of vengeance, a year of recompense for the cause of Zion. And the streams of Edom shall be turned into pitch, and the dust thereof into brimstone, and the land thereof shall become burning pitch. It shall not be quenched night nor day; the smoke thereof shall go up forever; from generation to generation it shall lie waste; none shall pass through it for ever and ever. (Isa. 34:8-10, ASV)

Jeremiah paints the same awful picture. He says:

> Edom shall be a desolation: everyone that goeth by it shall

be astonished, and shall hiss at all the plagues thereof. (Jer. 49:17).

Obadiah, who denounced Edom because of her sin in turning the Jews over to the Babylonians and predicted the future of Edom, grimly declared:

Israel will be a fire that sets the dry fields of Edom aflame. There will be no survivors, for the Lord has spoken. (verse 18, TLB)

Ezekiel confirms that the destruction of Edom will come at the hands of Israel. He writes:

Thus saith the Lord God; I will also stretch out mine hand upon Edom, and will cut off man and beast from it; and I will make it desolate. . . . And I will lay my vengeance upon Edom by the hand of my people Israel: and they shall do Edom according to mine anger and according to my fury; and they shall know my vengeance, saith the Lord God. (Ezek. 25:13-14)

The complete story of Egypt's future is related by the prophet Isaiah. In the first ten verses of chapter 19, Isaiah described how God would punish Egypt for her sins through civil war, destruction, and famine. Then he asserted that the leaders of Egypt would lead the nation astray—"And they have caused Egypt to err in every work thereof, as a drunken man staggereth in his vomit" (verse 14). History shows that the dictatorships of King Farouk, Nasser, and Sadat have on four occasions plunged the Egyptians into disastrous war with Israel.

The prophet then states that the day will come when the Hebrew language will be spoken in some parts of Egypt (verse 18), and that the Egyptians will worship the God of Israel. "And the Egyptians shall know the Lord in that day, and shall do sacrifice and oblation; yea, they shall vow a vow unto the Lord, and perform it" (verse 21). After Egypt is greatly subdued by oppressors, such as the antichrist and his cohorts, God will save the Egyptians from the domination of their enemies. This will result in the entire nation undergoing a spiritual conversion, the people offering sacrifices to Jehovah.

Isaiah goes on to relate how Assyria (present-day Syria and Iraq) will enter into a peaceful relationship with both Israel and

Egypt. He seems to describe an economic unity between Egypt and Iraq which is dependent upon a highway between the nations. This ancient roadway, known as the Via Maris, was closed when Israel became a state in 1948 because the Egyptians and Syrians both closed their borders.

The Living Bible quotes Isaiah's vivid description this way:

> In that day Egypt and Iraq [Assyria] will be connected by a highway, and the Egyptians and the Iraqi will move freely back and forth between their lands, and they shall worship the same God. And Israel will be their ally; the three will be together, and Israel will be a blessing to them. For the Lord will bless Egypt and Iraq because of their friendship with Israel. He will say, "Blessed be Egypt, my people; blessed be Iraq, the land I have made; blessed be Israel, my inheritance." (Isa. 19:23-25)

Before those happy days can come, Israel must endure the Tribulation. And all signs seem to indicate that time is running out. Current conditions in Israel seem to offer every imaginable cause for alarm and despair.

The economic situation is perhaps the most obvious indicator. The inflation rate reached nearly 130 percent by the end of 1980, and government economists openly predicted bankruptcy for the nation within two years. Foreign reserves are, of course, in danger of being completely wiped out. The danger of this situation is underscored by the historical fact that out of the last thirty nations that have suffered chronic inflation, twenty-eight have ultimately challenged their democratic society.

The loss of buying power resulting from inflation has led to an increasing wave of strikes and sanctions by workers all over the country. Add to this the burden of short supply, with the water shortage reaching a first-class crisis stage, particularly in the agricultural areas which must be irrigated to survive. Also, electricity is rationed, power being cut off all over the country from time to time.

Immorality is an alarming and ever-increasing problem. Crime is reaching epidemic proportions, the abuse of drugs is virtually out of control, and prostitution (with its accompanying diseases) has become so overwhelmingly prevalent that even United Nations "peace-keeping" troops are complaining.

In the face of these problems, it has been reported that one-sixth of the entire national population of Israeli sabras—that is, native-born citizens—have fled to the United States.

All the while, the Soviets continue to maneuver ever closer to Israel, spreading their power base in preparation to strike. On February 9, 1981, The Associated Press released an article entitled, "U.S., USSR on Collision Course." The former U.S. ambassador to Moscow, Thomas Watson, says that unless the United States and the Soviet Union change their collision course, there's bound to be an explosion down the line somewhere.

I believe that Israel is the key to America's survival, and that the future is certain, but no one knows the timetable. There's no way we could tell for sure when the prophetic clock will chime. But there's one thing that most Bible scholars agree on, and that is that God is a merciful God, and a great time of refreshing can come for the nations of America and Israel, if we stand for that which is right. I believe God will bless our land in a very special way. But on the other hand, if we find ourselves in the lineup of those who are undermining Israel's survival and cursing her, we will learn what it means to fall into the hands of an angry God.

chapter 13

Lovers of Israel

By now you are fully aware that I have not come to this subject as a disinterested analyst. I have written this book to inform you and to awaken you to what I believe is a summons from God to all who will hear it.

During the Nazi takeover of Germany, the church remained largely silent. Indeed, the pastors who spoke out against Hitler's evil were regularly imprisoned or pressed into the army to serve on the Russian front. But most of the people in the churches quietly acquiesced because Hitler was not pouring out his wrath on them, just on the Jews. It was a scandal and a shame that must not be repeated. One evening, I had the pleasure of entertaining three Jewish men. All of them had gone through the holocaust. One had been imprisoned for over six-and-a-half years and suffered unmercifully. His body was covered with scars from the terrible beatings. The two others, Sam and Rachmiel, suffered greatly during that period of time. Let me mention something Rachmiel Frydland told me. This beloved man lived like an animal in the woods, sleeping in a hole, and tying ropes around his clothes to keep them together. He was literally kicked out of the church he was baptized in. The pastor of the church told him, "I'm sorry, but I must obey the laws of the land because the government is ordained by God, and the government of Germany requests that all Jews are not to be members of Christian Churches; therefore you must find some other place to worship."

We must not remain silent. I believe the handwriting is on the wall, and that now is the time to become keenly aware of the strong wind that is blowing, because if it is not brought under control, it could turn into an uncontrollable demonic hurricane in years to come.

We must remember the examples of men and women like Dietrich Bonhoeffer, Corrie ten Boom, Martin Niemöller, Andreas Szeptycki, Father Marie-Benoit, and Pastor Vergara.

"I pray for the defeat of my country. Only in defeat can we atone for the terrible crimes we have committed. . . ." Dietrich Bonhoeffer, a German Protestant pastor, uttered those words in Geneva in 1941. He had been in America before the war and could have remained there in safety, but he chose to go back to Germany to bear witness to the truth among his people. He worked hard against the Nazi regime and, in 1944, he was hanged by the SS. In the thirties he had written *The Cost of Discipleship*, in which he inveighed against what he called "cheap grace." He had in mind the way in which preachers too often invite people to come to Christ because He will lift their burdens and heal their wounds. Too seldom, said Bonhoeffer, were any of Jesus' sterner words mentioned to the members of the parish. They were hardly aware that He called men to deny themselves and to take up their crosses and follow Him.

Corrie ten Boom's story is widely known today because of her book *The Hiding Place*. Corrie lived with her sister and father above their little watchmaker's shop in Haarlem, the Netherlands. When they saw the plight of their Jewish neighbors, there was no question in their minds as to what they ought to do. They turned the *Beje* (the name of their building) into a hiding place for Jews. They loved the Jews because of their Christian faith. Their Dutch Reformed pastors had long emphasized that *both* the Old and the New Testaments were the Word of God. Eventually Corrie and her family were caught by the Germans and imprisoned. Her elderly father died soon, but Corrie and Betsy went on to the horrors of Ravensbruck. There, however, they encountered Jesus in a new depth and dimension. Betsy perished, but Corrie survived and has spent the remaining years of her life traveling around the world with the message of God's love and forgiveness.

Martin Niemöller was a scholar and theologian who pastored a congregation in Berlin-Dahlem. At first he had favored the national renaissance that seemed to be coming about under Hitler. But then, in time, the Nazi program became clearer. It had amalgamated the many sects and denominations of German Protestants into a single national church. At first that seemed all right, until the Nazis insisted that all the churches embrace the "Aryan paragraph" into their creeds. It spoke of the racial supremacy of the Aryans and the inferiority of the Semites. That created a schism in the church in which about 9000 pastors joined together in the Confessional Church, so named because of its emphasis on confessing the true faith unembellished by the Aryan paragraph. Niemöller was an important leader in the Confessional Church. At first he remained aloof from the plight of the Jews, but, as Nazi methods grew harsher, he changed. Finally, on May 27, 1936, he and the other leaders of the Confessional Church submitted a memorandum to Hitler: "When blood, race, nationality, and honor are regarded as eternal values, the First Commandment obliges the Christian to reject this evaluation. . . . Anti-Semitism of the Nazi world-view forces one to hate the Jews, while Christianity directs one to love one's neighbor."

Niemöller and a number of other leaders of the Confessional Church were arrested forthwith. After his prison term, Nazi doctors recommended that he undergo a period of "convalescence" in a concentration camp. He was sent first to Sachsenhausen and, in turn, to Dachau. But he survived the war and resumed preaching. In one of his first sermons he declared, "Nobody wants to take responsibility for the guilt . . . but instead points to his neighbor. Yet the guilt exists, there is no doubt about it. Even if there were no other guilt than that of six million clay urns, the ashes of burnt Jews from all over Europe. And this guilt weighs heavily on the German people and on the German name and on all of Christendom. These things happened in our world and in our name. . . . I regard myself as guilty as any SS man." So little had been done, in fact, to really help the Jews that Niemöller concluded, "We let God wait ten years."

Metropolitan Andreas Szeptycki, archbishop of Lwow, was the leader of the Ukrainian Greek Catholic Church in Galicia. By the time the Germans drove through his land on their way to Stalingrad, he was seventy years old. But he worked with all his might to oppose their atrocities. He preached many sermons and issued written pronouncements to his flocks. He warned them that any who shed innocent blood would invoke God's wrath against themselves and make themselves outcasts by disregarding the sanctity of life. After the massacre at Rohatyn, he wrote a scathing letter to Heinrich Himmler.

Szeptycki's protests didn't have any dramatic effects either on the Germans or their Ukrainian collaborators. But they apparently did among the peasants, workers, clergy, and a number of the intelligentsia. Nor did the Metropolitan content himself with words. He also harbored Jewish children and adults, Rabbi Dr. David Kahane among them. He also put out the word to the monasteries and nunneries in his jurisdiction, who concealed 150 Jews, mostly children. The old man survived the war by only a few months. The Vatican approved a petition from Archbishop Ivan Buchko to have Szeptycki beatified.

In France, a Capuchin priest, Father Marie-Benoit, transformed a monastery in Marseilles into a rescue agency for Jews. It produced forged papers of all kinds and set up procedures for smuggling Jews into Switzerland and Spain. After the Germans occupied Marseilles, Benoit searched desperately to find new routes to safety for the Jews. Italy was his only chance and, soon, large numbers of Jews were escaping from France into the Riviera and Haute-Savoie. Ribbentrop, Hitler's foreign minister, complained to Mussolini about this, and Mussolini appointed a Commissioner for Jewish Affairs, Guido Lospinoso, who located his headquarters in Nice on the Riviera (at that time under Italian occupation).

Benoit was not intimidated, however. He got in touch with Angelo Donati, an Italian Jewish financier. Together they paid a call on Mussolini's new commissioner in Nice. None of the participants ever reported what happened at that meeting. We only know that, afterwards, Lospinoso did nothing to obstruct the flow of Jews.

Conditions were forever changing, and the resourceful Benoit was forever coming up with new programs and methods for rescuing Jews from all over southern Europe. He later transferred his work to Italy and, finally, in early 1945, had to disappear from sight in order to avoid arrest by the Gestapo.

After the war France bestowed many honors on the priest, as did many of those he helped rescue. His favorite was the simple appellation, "Father of the Jews."

One of the less-renowned protectors of Israel was a simple Protestant clergyman in Germany named Vergara. After the massive roundup of Jews in July, 1942, Vergara had the pluck to show up at a concentration camp near his home. He demanded to see the officer in charge and presented him with a forged document ordering the release of the Jewish children in the camp into Vergara's care. It worked and the little man with ruffled gray hair and protruding cheekbones escorted seventy children away from the camp. The Gestapo learned what had happened, but too late to get the children back. They had been secreted away in the homes of various Protestant and Catholic families in the area with the help of two local priests. However, the Gestapo did get their hands on Vergara's son-in-law, whom they killed. They also tortured his wife and deported his son. Undaunted, the little pastor emerged from hiding later on and resumed his rescue work.

Such were the men and women who took the gospel seriously in the face of the Nazi horror. Surely they are the ones whom we want to emulate—as the dark shadows of totalitarianism and anti-Semitism are cast further and further over our world.

We have a chance now to stand with Israel at a time when they have almost no friends in the international arena. And surely we ought to do it because God bids us to do so. God has forever promised that blessing will follow obedience, just as cursing follows disobedience.

We learn a sobering lesson from Great Britain. It was at or near the height of her imperial power in 1917 when the Balfour Declaration was issued. But steadily after that, British policy moved in favor of Arab interests and against Jewish interests. We will not completely trace the record here. One illustration will suffice. In 1948, the British were still patrolling Jerusalem, supposedly in the interests of peace. It was not atypical, however, when, one day, a British sergeant major of the Highland Light Infantry arrested four Haganah (prototype of the Israeli Defense Force) men and, instead of hauling them off for trial or imprisonment, simply delivered them into the hands of a bloodthirsty Arab mob in the Muslim Quarter. The mob mutilated and hacked the men to death.

What we want to connect with this betrayal of Israel—which happened in higher echelons as well—is the way in which the British Empire declined rapidly and drastically between 1925 and 1975. Once it could be said that the sun never set on the British Empire, but no longer. Today Britain is beset with enormous problems and a seriously declining economy. I want to suggest that this is because the Bible says that God will bless those who bless Abraham's children and curse those who curse his children (Gen. 12:3).

Early in 1948, Golda Meir traveled to the United States. At this critical moment, only a few months before the British withdrawal, Israel needed enormous sums of money—at least thirty million dollars—to equip itself with tanks, artillery, and some aircraft. The American Jewish community had grown weary of appeals for help from Palestine. The regular fund-raiser had come back to Tel Aviv to report that they could only expect to receive five million dollars from across the Atlantic in the next few months. So it was that Golda was dispatched on her vital errand.

She arrived in New York in the dead of winter with only a spring dress on her back and her purse—with ten dollars in it—in her hand. A customs agent asked her how she planned to get by, and she replied, "I have family here."

Her arrival coincided with a meeting of the leaders of the Council of Jewish Federations in Chicago. They were just about to gather there from all over the country. Friends in New York urged her not to go. Many in the council were indifferent or even hostile to her kind of Zionist thinking. Besides, most of them were heavily committed to raising support for hospitals and other Jewish charitable causes. Foreign appeals had to wait for what was left, if anything.

Nevertheless, Golda went to Chicago and got a place on the speaking schedule. Two days later, she stood trembling before a podium, without notes, and began to speak.

"You must believe me," she said, "when I tell you that I have not come to the United States solely to prevent seven hundred thousand Jews from being wiped off the face of the earth. During these last years, the Jewish people have lost six million of their kind, and it would be presumptuous indeed of us to remind the Jews of the world that seven hundred thousand Jews are in danger. That is not the question. If, however, these seven hundred thousand Jews survive, then the Jews of the world will survive with them, and their freedom will be forever assured. But if they did not," she said, "then there is little doubt that for centuries there will be no Jewish people, there will be no Jewish nation, and all our hopes will be smashed."

In a few months, she told her audience, "a Jewish state will exist in Palestine. We shall fight for its birth. That is natural. We shall pay for it with our blood. That is normal. The best among us will fall, that is certain. But what is equally certain is that our morale will not waver no matter how numerous our invaders may be."

Yet, she warned, those invaders would come with cannon and armor. Against those weapons, "sooner or later our courage will have no meaning, for we will have ceased to exist," she said.

She had come, she announced, to ask the Jews of America for twenty-five to thirty million dollars to buy the heavy arms they would need to face the invaders' cannons. "My friends," she said in making her plea, "we live in a very brief present. When I tell you we need this money immediately, it does not mean next month, or in two months. It means right now. . . .

"It is not to you," she concluded, "to decide whether we shall continue our struggle or not. We shall fight. The Jewish community of Palestine will never hang out the white flag before the Mufti of Jerusalem . . . but you can decide one thing—whether the victory will be ours or the Mufti's."

A hush had fallen on her audience, and for an instant Golda thought she had failed. Then the entire assembly of men and women rose in a deafening wave of applause. While its echoes still rang through the dining room, the first volunteers scrambled to the platform with their pledges.

Before coffee was served Golda had been promised over a million dollars. They were made available immediately in cash, a fact without precedent. Men began to telephone their bankers and secure personal loans against their own names for the sums they estimated they would be able to raise later in their communities. By the time that incredible afternoon was over, Golda was able to telegraph Ben-Gurion her conviction that she would be able to raise the twenty-five "Stephans"—twenty-five million dollars, in the code they had chosen (using the name of American Zionist leader Rabbi Stephen S. Wise). (Collins and LaPierre, *O Jerusalem!*, p. 164)

The time has come for us to rise to our feet in like manner. We cannot expect our government to take the lead and do this for us. Our nation was created to be ruled by the people. It is our individual responsibility to become informed, committed, and prayerful. We cannot sit back and wait. As Edmund Burke put it so articulately, "The only thing necessary for evil to prevail is for good men to do nothing." The nations of the West, even the United States, are in serious danger of casting in their lot with the crumbled civilizations of the past which have put their feet, each in turn, on the neck of Israel. It is time for us who call ourselves Lovers of Israel, to take the lead by doing the right thing—by refusing to stand idly by in this season of Israel's peril. Praying and believing together, we will be able to break through Satan's barriers and deal with the demonic forces that are trying to hold back the revival God has promised for the House of Israel. If you don't believe that this is a spiritual battle, you need only to listen to a few of the following statements.

This threat from one of the heads of the PLO was reported by the Associated Press, "American interests in the Middle East, and elsewhere in the world, are well known to us, and we will hit them, because we realize the enormity of the animosity that the Americans harbour for the Palestinians . . . we Palestinians will perpetuate the war of attrition against Israel, until our rights are completely regained. I am prepared to extend a hand of friendship and alliance to any power, even the devil, to crush Israel, and undermine American machinations."

This statement was also released through the Associated Press: "Council of Churches urges role for PLO in peace talks. The Palestinian Liberation Organization is the organized voice of the Palestinian people and should be a party to peace negotiations in the Middle East, says the National Council of Churches."

I cannot overstate the importance of seriously devoting ourselves to prayer. Nothing is more needed at this moment. True prayer is not and never has been an excuse for indolence or inaction. Bernard Lichtenberg was a priest in Berlin who began to pray for the Jews after he saw how the Nazis were burning the synagogues and Jewish places of business. An American visitor reports following a crowd of people into the St. Hedwig Church in 1940. It was evening and no service was scheduled. Inside, however, the visitor found the people kneeling in their pews. The sanctuary was dark, except for a single candle. Coming from the front, near the altar, he could hear Lichtenberg's voice imploring God. Occasionally the priest would stop, and, when he did, the parishioners would pray aloud, saying, "Lord, have mercy upon us! O Messiah, hear us!" Then the priest would resume. The entire affair was devoid of any mention of politics or worldly affairs, yet every sentence was weighty with meaning for those troubled times.

The Nazis surely did not regard this as harmless poppycock. Lichtenberg was arrested and placed in a concentration camp. He died on November 3, 1943, while being transported to Dachau.

It is forty years after the Holocaust. It is thirty-three years since the state of Israel was established. To think of a resurgence of anti-Jewishness throughout the world is very painful. The very restoration of Israel is a fulfillment of biblical prophecy (Isa. 11:11). Of Israel, God said, "I will restore the captivity of My people, Israel . . . I will also plant them on their land, and they will not again be rooted out from their land which I have given them, says the Lord your God" (Amos 9:14-15, NAS).

The United States faces a severe test in the 80s. Surely demonic pressure will endeavor to encourage her to betray Israel. This must not happen! Israel is the key to America's survival. For God has said of the nations who will oppose Israel, "Yea, those nations shall be utterly wasted. . . . I will bless them that bless thee, and curse them that curseth thee. . . " (Isa. 60:12; Gen. 12:3).

If America would recognize Jerusalem as the capital of the Jewish state, and stand behind this recognition, other nations would soon follow suit and embassies would be moved from Tel Aviv to Jerusalem.

As we stand with Israel, I believe we will see God perform a mighty work in our day. God is going to bless America and Israel as well. It is not too late. I believe this is the greatest hour to be alive, and the key is unity, standing tall, proclaiming with a voice of love our commitment to the House of Israel, and to the God of Israel.

"Pray for the peace of Jerusalem: they shall prosper that love thee" (Ps. 122:6).

Mike Evans is president of "Lovers of Israel," a new dynamic evangelical intercessory organization, committed to encouraging our nation to stand with Israel. For further information and a subscription to the newsletter write to:

Michael Evans
Lovers of Israel
P.O. Box 61999
Dallas, Texas 75261

Appendixes

Appendix 1

Embassy of Israel
Washington, D.C.

August 27, 1980

BASIC LAW: JERUSALEM

1. From time to time, forces hostile to Israel bring up the "Jerusalem question" in international forum, in an attempt to undermine the city's status as the Capital of Israel and as the living heart of the Jewish people as a whole. The latest furor over Jerusalem was raised, at the U.N. and elsewhere, on the initiative of the Arab states, aided by some of the countries of Europe and the "Third World"; it was not Israel that initiated this move. It is those countries, and not Israel, that are responsible both for the timing and for the strident tone of this most recent assault on the integrity of Jerusalem.

2. Originally established by King David as the capital of the United Jewish Kingdom 3,000 years ago, Jerusalem has known repeated cycles of glory, conquest, destruction and exile, followed each time by return, rebuilding and Jewish renaissance.

3. Upon the creation of the State of Israel in 1948, Transjordan (now Jordan) unleashed its army in a ferocious attack upon Jerusalem. Despite U.N. condemnations and calls for at least a local cease-fire to protect Jerusalem's holy places, the beleaguered and besieged Jewish population, fighting desperately for survival, narrowly escaped annihilation by indiscriminate shelling and round-the-clock armored and infantry attacks—while the world stood by without lifting a finger to help save the city so sacred to all religions. Only the tenacity and heavy sacrifices of Jerusalem's 100,000 Jews ultimately ensured the survival of most of the town, leaving but the walled Old City and some of its surroundings in the attackers' hands. For 19 years, the Jordanian army desecrated the Old City's precious synagogues, vandalized its ancient Jewish quarter and used tombstones from the nearby Jewish cemetery to build latrines. Under the armistice agreement, Jordan undertook to allow access to worship at Judaism's holiest shrine, the Western Wall. Not for one day was that commitment ever honored.

4. Jerusalem became the capital of the modern State of Israel when the Knesset, its democratically elected parliament, convened there on Feb. 15, 1949. On Dec. 13 of that year the then Prime Minister, David Ben-Gurion, declared: "The State of Israel has had in the past, and will have in the future, only one capital, as we believe, till the end of time."

5. On the morning of June 5, 1967, as Israel faced renewed aggression from Egypt and Syria, the late Prime Minister Eshkol sent an urgent and solemn message to King Hussein, calling on Jordan to desist from joining the battle and thereby avoid any action against it by the Israel Defense Forces. Alas, the king chose to spurn that appeal. Having joined in a military pact with Egypt, he went to war against Israel. Jordanian artillery and armor opened up a violent artillery barrage against the Israeli sector of Jerusalem and along the whole border with Israel. In the battles that followed, whilst Israel was fighting for its very existence, the Jordanian aggressors were defeated and withdrew across the Jordan River.

6. The Arab and Islamic campaign against Israel on the subject of Jerusalem began back in 1974, at the Conference of Islamic States, and was given renewed impetus, on the initiative of the Arab Rejectionist States, after the signing of the Camp David Agreements in September, 1978.

7. The subject of Jerusalem came up for discussion at Camp David. When it transpired that agreement could not be reached between the parties, each side presented its position on the subject in a separate letter appended to the Agreements. It was understood by both sides, together with the United States, that priority be given, in the peace negotiations, to the subject of autonomy for the inhabitants of Judea-Samaria and the Gaza district.

8. It was Egypt that first deviated from this understanding. As far back as March 21, 1980, in an interview with NBC, President Sadat minimized the sanctity of Jerusalem for the Jews, in comparison with its sanctity for the Moslems, citing the fact that there are 800 million Moslems but only 13 million Jews. (In Moslem religious law and tradition, Jerusalem actually ranks *third* in holiness after Mecca and Medina—a fact dramatized by President Sadat himself when, on his visit to Jerusalem in November, 1977, he attended prayer services at the El-Aqsa

Mosque and, of course, together with the other Moslem worshippers in the mosque, turned his face southward—towards Mecca, which is *the* center of Islam.)

9. A move of particular gravity was made by Egypt on April 1, 1980, when Egypt's People's Assembly (parliament) issued a statement determining that East Jerusalem was sovereign Arab territory, that it was "an integral part of the West Bank, which had been occupied by armed force." All the steps that had been taken in the city by Israel since the Six-Day War were proclaimed "illegal, null and void and non-binding." The Egyptian parliament called for the establishment of Jerusalem as the seat of the Palestinian autonomous authority.

10. No one outside of Israel raised any objections to this flagrant, unprovoked interference in Israel's internal affairs. Those who stood by in silence when the Egyptian parliament declared Jerusalem to be Arab have forfeited the right to express consternation, now, over the declaration by Israel's Knesset that Jerusalem is Jewish and Israeli.

11. The fact is that no country in the world could fail to react in the strongest terms to so prolonged and persistent a series of provocative interventions in its affairs as has taken place in this instance. Israel was finally compelled to rise to the challenge and to act to protect and clarify its rights. This it did in the form of the Knesset's "Basic Law: Jerusalem," which originated as a Private Member's Bill submitted to the House for the first time on May 14, 1980—in the wake of, and as a reaction to, the anti-Jerusalem campaign that had been mounted in the preceding months and some of whose elements have here been detailed.

12. The wide support given this law by the representatives of the various parties in Israel, in the Coalition as well as the Opposition, underlines the unity of view and of purpose prevailing in this country concerning the fact of Jerusalem's being the eternal capital of Israel—and, in the wider sense, of the entire Jewish people. This fact is deeply rooted in the Jewish consciousness and in the history, culture and religion of the people of Israel.

13. The people and the Government of Israel are keenly aware of the religious meaning of Jerusalem to the followers of Christianity and Islam, whose rights, interests and free access will continue to be meticulously guarded by the Government of Israel,

in the future as in the past. But the nature of their attachment to the city is different from that of the Jews. This difference was defined with admirable clarity and precision in an editorial in the *London Daily Telegraph* on June 25, 1967, shortly after the Six-Day War:

> To Christians and Moslems, Jerusalem is a place where supremely important things happened long ago. To them, therefore, it is an object of pilgrimage. To Jews, on the other hand, it is the living center of their faith, or, if they have no faith, of their identity as a people. To them it is a place to be possessed, today and forever.
>
> There is no essential incompatibility between these differing needs. Jewish political possession of Jerusalem and absolute freedom of access to it by Christians and Moslems— these have always been twin declared principles of the State of Israel.

14. Jerusalem's international standing as a holy city derives essentially from its history and character, as a Jewish city—the city in which Judaism, as a religion and a civilization, and the Jewish people, as a nation, came into their own; the city, moreover, in which, for the last 100 years and more, the Jews have constituted a clear majority of the population. It is indeed unfortunate that so many governments still fail to recognize this reality. But that does not make it any less a reality, molded as it has been by thousands of years of history. Certainly, any attempt to strike at this unalterable reality is to deal a blow to the peace process and to Israel itself. Jerusalem is the very symbol of the sovereignty of Israel and a central element in the self-determination of the Jewish people as a nation.

15. From the juridical point of view, there is virtually nothing new in this law. It simply reaffirms the existing situation as established either by previous laws or by accepted norms:

    (a) The first paragraph of the law reaffirms the long established fact that Jerusalem, complete and united, is the capital of Israel.

    (b) The second paragraph states that Jerusalem is the seat of the President of the State, of the Knesset, of the Government and of the Supreme Court—as already laid down in the specific laws relating to these official bodies.

(c) The third paragraph, dealing with the inviolability of the holy places of all religions and free access to them, repeats what is stated in the Protection of the Holy Places Law, 1967, which, as is universally known, has been fully and meticulously observed.

(d) The fourth paragraph deals with the development of the city and the resources to be allocated for this purpose.

16. The real significance of this law lies in the political-declarative realm—in other words, in its serving as a reply to those who would question or undermine Israel's sovereignty over its capital city. It should be understood as a restatement of basic facts concerning Jerusalem and as an official reaffirmation of Israel's rights, in the wake of the Arab-Moslem campaign to negate those facts—and those rights. In the light of the fact that Jerusalem is and has been Israel's capital, one must understand that the recent legislation merely serves to confirm the prevailing situation. For those who question Israel's rights in this regard, the law will serve to clarify Israel's position.

Appendix 2

PROTECTION OF HOLY PLACES LAW, 5727-1967

1. The Holy Places shall be protected from desecration and any other violation and from anything likely to violate the freedom of access of the members of the different religions to the places sacred to them or their feelings with regard to those places.

2. (a) Whosoever desecrates or otherwise violates a Holy Place shall be liable to imprisonment for a term of seven years.

(b) Whosoever does anything to violate the freedom of access of the members of the different religions to the places sacred to them or their feelings with regard to those places shall be liable to imprisonment for a term of five years.

3. This Law shall add to, and not derogate from, any other Law.

4. The Minister of Religious Affairs is charged with the implementation of this Law, and he may, after consultation with, or upon the proposal of, representatives of the religions concerned and with the consent of the Minister of Justice make regulations as to any matter relating to such implementation.

5. This Law shall come into force on the date of its adoption by the Knesset.

(Passed by the Knesset on June 27, 1967)

Appendix 3

The President
Camp David
Thurmont, Maryland   17 September 1978

Dear Mr. President,
   I have the honor to inform you, Mr. President, that on 28 June
1967—Israel's Parliament (The Knesset) promulgated and adopted
a law to the effect: "The Government is empowered by a decree to
apply the law, the jurisdiction and administration of the State to
any part of Eretz Israel (Land of Israel—Palestine), as stated in
that decree."
   On the basis of this Law, the Government of Israel decreed in
July 1967 that Jerusalem is one city indivisible, the capital of the
State of Israel.

                                   Sincerely,
                                   Menachem Begin

Appendix 4

Official Statement of the Egyptian Foreign Ministry on Jerusalem, February 26, 1980

The following statement was issued on the occasion of the presentation of Ambassador Murtada's credentials in Jerusalem.

- We do not recognize Jerusalem as the capital of Israel, nor do we recognize the annexation of Arab Jerusalem by Israel.

- We do not recognize any of the steps taken by Israel to alter the status and the character of Jerusalem. All these steps are null and void.

- Arab Jerusalem must be under Arab sovereignty.

- Arab Jerusalem is an integral part of the West Bank.

- The legal and historical Arab rights in the city must be preserved and restored.

- Free access to Jerusalem and the freedom of worship for the members of all faiths and peoples, without discrimination, must be assured.

- The Holy Places of each of the three monotheistic faiths may be under the supervision and management of a representative of the religious community concerned.

- A joint Municipal Council may be established to be composed of Israelis and Arabs, in such manner as not to divide the city.

Appendix 5

Statement of the Egyptian People's Assembly
on Jerusalem, April 1, 1980

The operative part of the statement includes the following nine points:

1. Arab Jerusalem is an integral part of the West Bank, which was occupied by military force.

2. Action must be taken to preserve the historical and legal Arab rights in the city in their entirety.

3. All the steps that have been taken by Israel to alter the identity, the demographic composition and the geographic structure of the city are illegal, null and void and non-binding.

4. We demand the implementation of all resolutions of the UN Security Council with regard to Jerusalem and which consider all the steps by Israel as null and void.

5. All the inhabitants of Arab Jerusalem have the right to participate in the establishment of the Autonomy in the West Bank and Gaza.

6. There must be free access for all to the Holy Places in Jerusalem, without hindrance or discrimination.

7. The call for the non-division of Jerusalem cannot and must not be based on or lead to the perpetuation of the Israeli occupation of Arab Jerusalem. This call must be based on the preservation of the Arab rights in the city and should not contradict them.

8. This Assembly calls on all the Nations to raise their voices in the defense of Jerusalem, and the unshakable rights therein, and for an end of the domination of Arab Jerusalem, and for the abolishment of the Israeli steps that have been taken in it.

9. This Assembly calls for making Jerusalem the seat of authority of the full Palestinian autonomy.

Appendix 6

Resolution of the Egyptian Peoples' Assembly
on Jerusalem, July 1, 1980

On July 1, the Peoples' Assembly adopted a resolution confirming the statement issued by the Assembly's Committee for Arab Affairs and Foreign Relations and specifying the following points:

- Jerusalem is an integral part of the West Bank.
- The historical Arab rights in the Holy City must be respected.
- Jerusalem must be under Arab sovereignty.
- The Palestinians must be given the right to realize their legitimate national rights.
- Jerusalem must be regarded as the capital of the Palestinians.

Appendix 7

THE PALESTINIAN NATIONAL COVENANT
English rendition as published in Basic Political Documents
of the Armed Palestinian Resistance Movement

Leila S. Kadi (ed.), PLO Organization Research Centre
Beirut, December 1969, pp. 137-41

The following is the complete and unabridged text of the Palestinian National Covenant, as published officially, in English, by the PLO.

The Israel Information Centre [P.O.B. 13010, Jerusalem] is taking the unusual step of reproducing and distributing this hostile document [May, 1978] in order to give the interested reader an opportunity to draw his own conclusions concerning its message.

It should be borne in mind that the geographical unit called Palestine includes the entire area of the present-day State of Israel, the Hashemite Kingdom of Jordan and the territory in dispute between them. Thus, the "liberation of Palestine" espoused by the Covenant actually means the eradication of Israel—and, eventually, of Jordan as well—as an independent state.

This, indeed, is the central goal of the organization which has adopted the Covenant as its official Charter—the "Palestine Liberation Organization," known as the PLO.

Articles of the Covenant

Article 1: Palestine is the homeland of the Arab Palestinian people; it is an indivisible part of the Arab homeland, and the Palestinian people are an integral part of the Arab nation.

Article 2: Palestine, with the boundaries it had during the British Mandate, is an indivisible territorial unit.

Article 3: The Palestinian people possess the legal right to their homeland and have the right to determine their destiny after achieving the liberation of their country in accordance with their wishes and entirely of their own accord and will.

Article 4: The Palestinian identity is a genuine, essential and inherent characteristic; it is transmitted from parents to children. The Zionist occupation and the dispersal of the Palestinian Arab people, through the disasters which befell them, do not make them lose their Palestinian identity and their membership of the Palestinian community, nor do they negate them.

Article 5: The Palestinians are those Arab nationals who, until 1947, normally resided in Palestine regardless of whether they were evicted from it or have stayed there. Anyone born, after that date, of a Palestinian father—whether inside Palestine or outside it—is also a Palestinian.

Article 6: The Jews who had normally resided in Palestine until the beginning of the Zionist invasion will be considered Palestinians.

Article 7: That there is a Palestinian community and that it has material, spiritual and historical connections with Palestine are indisputable facts. It is a national duty to bring up individual Palestinians in an Arab revolutionary manner. All means of information and education must be adopted in order to acquaint the Palestinian with his country in the most profound manner, both spiritual and material, that is possible. He must be prepared for the armed struggle and ready to sacrifice his wealth and his life in order to win back his homeland and bring about its liberation.

Article 8: The phase in their history, through which the Palestinian people are now living, is that of national (watani) struggle for the liberation of Palestine. Thus the conflicts among the Palestinian national forces are secondary, and should be ended for the sake of the basic conflict that exists between the forces of Zionism and of imperialism on the one hand, and the Palestinian Arab people on the other. On this basis the Palestinian masses, regardless of whether they are residing in the national homeland or in diaspora (mahajir) constitute—both their organization and the individuals—one national front working for the retrieval of Palestine and its liberation through armed struggle.

Article 9: Armed struggle is the only way to liberate Palestine. Thus it is the overall strategy, not merely a tactical phase. The Palestinian Arab people assert their absolute determination and firm resolution to continue their armed struggle and to work for an armed popular revolution for the liberation of their country and their return to it. They also assert their right to normal life in Palestine and to exercise their right to self-determination and sovereignty over it.

Article 10: Commando action constitutes the nucleus of the Palestinian popular liberation war. This requires its escalation, comprehensiveness and mobilization of all the Palestinian popular and educational efforts and their organization and involvement is the armed Palestinian revolution. It also requires the achieving of unity for the national (watani) struggle among the different groupings of the Palestinian people, and between the Palestinian people and the Arab masses so as to secure the continuation of the revolution, its escalation and victory.

Article 11: The Palestinians will have three mottoes: national (wataniyya) unity, national (qawmiyya) mobilization and liberation.

Article 12: The Palestinian people believe in Arab unity. In order to contribute their share towards the attainment of that objective, however, they must, at the present stage of their struggle, safeguard their Palestinian identity and develop their consciousness of that identity, and oppose any plan that may dissolve or impair it.

Article 13: Arab unity and the liberation of Palestine are two complementary objectives, the attainment of either of which facilitates the attainment of the other. Thus, Arab unity leads to the liberation of Palestine; the liberation of Palestine leads to Arab unity; and work towards the realization of one objective proceeds side by side with work towards the realization of the other.

Article 14: The destiny of the Arab nation, and indeed Arab existence itself, depends upon the destiny of the Palestinian cause. From this interdependence springs the Arab nation's pursuit of and striving for, the liberation of Palestine. The people of Palestine play the role of the vanguard in the realization of this sacred national (qawmi) goal.

Article 15: The liberation of Palestine, from an Arab viewpoint, is a national (qawmi) duty and it attempts to repel the Zionist and imperialist aggression against the Arab homeland, and aims at the elimination of Zionism in Palestine. Absolute responsibility for this falls upon the Arab nation—peoples and governments— with the Arab people of Palestine in the vanguard. Accordingly the Arab nation must mobilize all its military, human and moral and spiritual capabilities to participate actively with the Palestinian people in the liberation of Palestine. It must, particularly in the phase of the armed Palestinian revolution, offer and furnish the Palestinian people with all possible help, and material and human support, and make available to them the means and opportunities that will enable them to continue to carry out their leading role in the armed revolution, until they liberate their homeland.

Article 16: The liberation of Palestine, from a spiritual point of view, will provide the Holy Land with an atmosphere of safety and tranquility, which in turn will safeguard the country's religious sanctuaries and guarantee freedom of worship and of visit to all without discrimination of race, colour, language, or religion. Accordingly, the people of Palestine look to all spiritual forces in the world for support.

Article 17: The liberation of Palestine, from a human point of view, will restore to the Palestinian individual his dignity, pride and freedom. Accordingly the Palestinian Arab people look forward to the support of all those who believe in the dignity of man and his freedom in the world.

Article 18: The liberation of Palestine, from an international point of view, is a defensive action necessitated by the demands of self-defense. Accordingly, the Palestinian people, desirous as they are of the friendship of all people, look to freedom-loving, justice-loving and peace-loving states for support in order to restore their legitimate rights in Palestine, to re-establish peace and security in the country, and to enable its people to exercise national sovereignty and freedom.

Article 19: The partition of Palestine in 1947 and the establishment of the State of Israel are entirely illegal, regardless of the passage of time, because they were contrary to the will of the Palestinian people and to their natural right in their homeland, and inconsistent with the principles embodied in the Charter of the United Nations, particularly the right to self-determination.

Article 20: The Balfour Declaration, the Mandate for Palestine and everything that has been based upon them, are deemed null and void. Claims of historical or religious ties of Jews with Palestine are incompatible with the facts of history and the true conception of what constitutes statehood. Judaism, being a religion, is not an independent nationality. Nor do Jews constitute a single nation with an identity of its own; they are citizens of the states to which they belong.

Article 21: The Arab Palestinian people, expressing themselves by the armed Palestinian revolution, reject all solutions which are substitutes for the total liberation of Palestine and reject all proposals aiming at the liquidation of the Palestinian problem, or its internationalization.

Article 22: Zionism is a political movement organically associated with international imperialism and antagonistic to all action for liberation and to progressive movements in the world. It is racist and fanatic in its nature, aggressive, expansionist and colonial in its aims, and fascist in its methods. Israel is the instrument of the Zionist movement, and a geographical base for world imperialism placed strategically in the midst of the Arab homeland to combat the hopes of the Arab nation for liberation, unity and progress. Israel is a constant source of threat vis-à-vis peace in the Middle East and the whole world. Since the liberation of Palestine will destroy the Zionist and imperialist presence and will contribute to the establishment of peace in the Middle East, the Palestinian people look for the support of all the progressive and peaceful forces and urge them all, irrespective of their affiliations and beliefs, to offer the Palestinian people all aid and support in their just struggle for the liberation of their homeland.

Article 23: The demands of security and peace, as well as the demands of right and justice, require all states to consider Zionism an illegitimate movement, to outlaw its existence, and to ban its operations, in order that friendly relations among peoples may be preserved, and the loyalty of citizens to their respective homelands safeguarded.

Article 24: The Palestinian people believe in the principles of justice, freedom, sovereignty, self-determination, human dignity, and in the right of all peoples to exercise them.

Article 25: For the realization of the goals of this Charter and its principles, the Palestinian Liberation Organization will perform its role in the liberation of Palestine in accordance with the Constitution of this Organization.

Article 26: The Palestine Liberation Organization, representative of the Palestinian revolutionary forces, is responsible for the Palestinian Arab people's movement in its struggle—to retrieve its homeland, liberate and return to it and exercise the right to self-determination in it—in all military, political and financial fields and also for whatever may be required by the Palestinian case on the inter-Arab and international levels.

Article 27: The Palestinian Liberation Organization shall cooperate with all Arab states, each according to its potentialities; and will adopt a neutral policy among them in the light of the requirements of the war of liberation; and on this basis it shall not interfere in the internal affairs of any Arab State.

Article 28: The Palestinian Arab people assert the genuineness and independence of their national (wataniyya) revolution and reject all forms of intervention, trusteeship and subordination.

Article 29: The Palestinian people possess the fundamental and genuine legal right to liberate and retrieve their homeland. The Palestinian people determine their attitude towards all states and forces on the basis of the stands they adopt vis-à-vis the Palestinian case and the extent of the support they offer to the Palestinian revolution to fulfill the aims of the Palestinian people.

Article 30: Fighters and carriers of arms in the war of liberation are the nucleus of the popular army which will be the protective force for the gains of the Palestinian Arab people.

Article 31: The Organization shall have a flag, an oath of allegiance and an anthem. All this shall be decided upon in accordance with a special regulation.

Article 32: Regulations, which shall be known as the Constitution of the Palestine Liberation Organization, shall be annexed to this Charter. It shall lay down the manner in which the Organization, and its organs and institutions, shall be constituted; the respective competence of each; and the requirements of its obligations under the Charter.

Article 33: This Charter shall not be amended save by (vote of) a majority of two-thirds of the total membership of the National Congress of the Palestine Liberation Organization (taken) at a special session convened for that purpose.

Appendix 8

The Balfour Declaration

Foreign Office,
November 2nd, 1917

Dear Lord Rothschild,

I have much pleasure in conveying to you, on behalf of His Majesty's Government, the following declaration of sympathy with Jewish Zionist aspirations which has been submitted to, and approved by, the Cabinet

"His Majesty's Government view with favour the establishment in Palestine of a national home for the Jewish people, and will use their best endeavours to facilitate the achievement of this object, it being clearly understood that nothing shall be done which may prejudice the civil and religious rights of existing non-Jewish communities in Palestine, or the rights and political status enjoyed by Jews in any other country."

I should be grateful if you would bring this declaration to the knowledge of the Zionist Federation.

Lord Balfour
British Foreign Secretary

Appendix 9

Declaration of the Establishment
of the State of Israel*

ERETZ ISRAEL[1] was the birthplace of the Jewish people.
Here their spiritual, religious and political identity was shaped.
Here they first attained to statehood, created cultural values of
national and universal significance and gave to the world the
eternal Book of Books.

After being forcibly exiled from their land, the people kept
faith with it throughout their Dispersion and never ceased to
pray and hope for their return to it and for the restoration in it of
their political freedom.

Impelled by this historic and traditional attachment, Jews
strove in every successive generation to re-establish themselves
in their ancient homeland. In recent decades they returned in
their masses. Pioneers, *ma'pilim*[2] and defenders, they made
deserts bloom, revived the Hebrew language, built villages and
towns, and created a thriving community, controlling its own
economy and culture, loving peace but knowing how to defend
itself, bringing the blessings of progress to all the country's
inhabitants, and aspiring towards independent nationhood.

In the year 5657 (1897), at the summons of the spiritual father
of the Jewish State, Theodor Herzl, the First Zionist Congress
convened and proclaimed the right of the Jewish people to
national rebirth in its own country.

This right was recognized in the Balfour Declaration of the
2nd November, 1917, and re-affirmed in the Mandate of the
League of Nations which, in particular, gave international
sanction to the historic connection between the Jewish people
and Eretz-Israel and to the right of the Jewish people to rebuild
its National Home.

The catastrophe which recently befell the Jewish people—the

---

*Published in the *Official Gazette*, No. 1 of the 5th Iyar, 5708 (14th May, 1948).
[1]*Eretz-Israel* (Hebrew)—the Land of Israel, Palestine.
[2]*Ma'pilim* (Hebrew)—immigrants coming to Eretz-Israel in defiance of restrictive legislation.

massacre of millions of Jews in Europe—was another clear demonstration of the urgency of solving the problem of its homelessness by re-establishing in Eretz-Israel the Jewish State, which would open the gates of the homeland wide to every Jew and confer upon the Jewish people the status of a fully-privileged member of the comity of nations.

Survivors of the Nazi holocaust in Europe, as well as Jews from other parts of the world, continued to migrate to Eretz-Israel, undaunted by difficulties, restrictions and dangers, and never ceased to assert their right to a life of dignity, freedom and honest toil in their national homeland.

In the Second World War, the Jewish community of this country contributed its full share to the struggle of the freedom- and peace-loving nations against the forces of Nazi wickedness and, by the blood of its soldiers and its war effort, gained the right to be reckoned among the peoples who founded the United Nations.

On the 29th November, 1947, the United Nations General Assembly passed a resolution calling for the establishment of a Jewish State in Eretz-Israel; the General Assembly required the inhabitants of Eretz-Israel to take such steps as were necessary on their part for the implementation of that resolution. This recognition by the United Nations of the right of the Jewish people to establish their State is irrevocable.

This right is the natural right of the Jewish people to be masters of their own fate, like all other nations, in their own sovereign State.

ACCORDINGLY WE, MEMBERS OF THE PEOPLE'S COUNCIL, REPRESENTATIVES OF THE JEWISH COMMUNITY OF ERETZ-ISRAEL AND OF THE ZION-IST MOVEMENT, ARE HERE ASSEMBLED ON THE DAY OF THE TERMINATION OF THE BRITISH MAN-DATE OVER ERETZ-ISRAEL AND, BY VIRTUE OF OUR NATURAL AND HISTORIC RIGHT AND ON THE STRENGTH OF THE RESOLUTION OF THE UNITED NATIONS GENERAL ASSEMBLY, HEREBY DECLARE THE ESTABLISHMENT OF A JEWISH STATE IN ERETZ-ISRAEL TO BE KNOWN AS THE STATE OF ISRAEL.

WE DECLARE that, with effect from the moment of the

termination of the Mandate, being tonight, the eve of Sabbath, the 6th Iyar, 5708 (15th May, 1948), until the establishment of the elected, regular authorities of the State in accordance with the Constitution which shall be adopted by the Elected Constituent Assembly not later than the 1st October, 1948, the People's Council shall act as a Provisional Council of State, and its executive organ, the People's Administration, shall be the Provisional Government of the Jewish State, to be called "Israel".

THE STATE OF ISRAEL will be open for Jewish immigration and for the Ingathering of the Exiles; it will foster the development of the country for the benefit of all inhabitants; it will be based on freedom, justice and peace as envisaged by the prophets of Israel; it will ensure complete equality of social and political rights to all its inhabitants irrespective of religion, race or sex; it will guarantee freedom of religion, conscience, language, education and culture; it will safeguard the Holy Places of all religions; and it will be faithful to the principles of the Charter of the United Nations.

THE STATE OF ISRAEL is prepared to cooperate with the agencies and representatives of the United Nations in implementing the resolution of the General Assembly of the 29th November, 1947, and will take steps to bring about the economic union of the whole of Eretz-Israel.

WE APPEAL to the United Nations to assist the Jewish people in the building-up of its State and to receive the State of Israel into the comity of nations.

WE APPEAL—in the very midst of the onslaught launched against us now for months—to the Arab inhabitants of the State of Israel to preserve peace and participate in the upbuilding of the State on the basis of full and equal citizenship and due representation in all its provisional and permanent institutions.

WE EXTEND our hand to all neighbouring states and their peoples in an offer of peace and good neighbourliness, and appeal to them to establish bonds of cooperation and mutual help with the sovereign Jewish people settled in its own land. The State of Israel is prepared to do its share in common effort for the advancement of the entire Middle East.

WE APPEAL to the Jewish people throughout the Diaspora to rally round the Jews of Eretz-Israel in the tasks of immigration and upbuilding and to stand by them in the great struggle for the realization of the age-old dream—the redemption of Israel.

PLACING OUR TRUST IN THE ALMIGHTY, WE AFFIX OUR SIGNATURES TO THIS PROCLAMATION AT THIS SESSION OF THE PROVISIONAL COUNCIL OF STATE, ON THE SOIL OF THE HOMELAND, IN THE CITY OF TEL-AVIV, ON THIS SABBATH EVE, THE 5th DAY OF IYAR, 5708 (14th MAY, 1948).

David Ben-Gurion

Daniel Auster
Mordekhai Bentov
Yitzchak Ben Zvi
Eliyahu Berligne
Fritz Bernstein

Rabbi Wolf Gold
Meir Grabovsky
Yitzchak Gruenbaum
Dr. Abraham Granovsky
Eliyahu Dobkin
Meir Wilner-Kovner
Zerach Wahrhaftig
Herzl Vardi
Rachel Cohen
Rabbi Kalman Kahana
Saadia Kobashi
Rabbi Yitzchak Meir
  Levin
Meir David Loevenstein

Zvi Luria
Golda Myerson
Nachum Nir
Zvi Segal
Rabbi Yehuda Leib Hacohen
  Fishman
David Zvi Pinkas
Aharon Zisling
Moshe Kolodny
Eliezer Kaplan
Abraham Katznelson
Felix Rosenblueth
David Remez
Berl Repetur
Mordekhai Shattner
Ben Zion Sternberg
Bekhor Shitreet
Moshe Shapira

Moshe Shertok